# LEAVES OF GRASS, 1860

IOWA WHITMAN SERIES

*Ed Folsom, series editor*

# LEAVES OF GRASS,
## 1860

### WALT WHITMAN

*The 150th Anniversary Facsimile Edition*

EDITED BY JASON STACY

University of Iowa Press, Iowa City

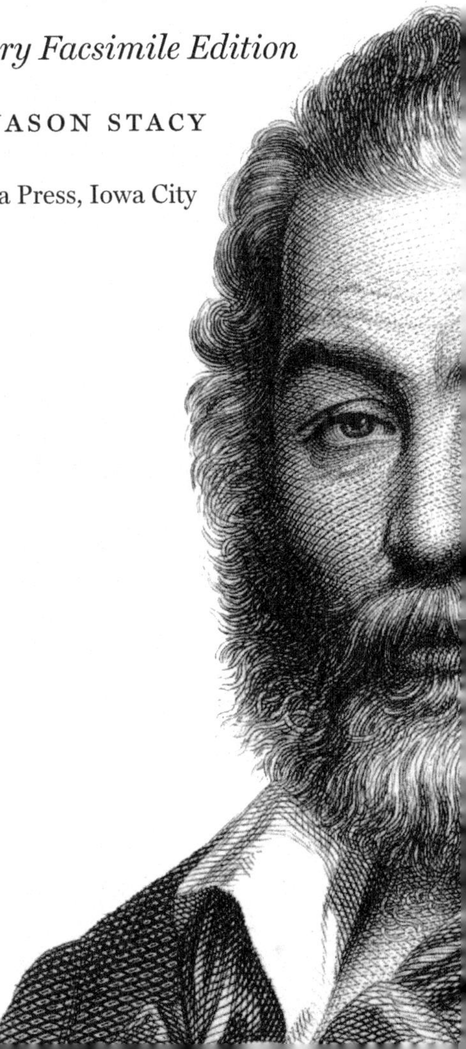

University of Iowa Press, Iowa City 52242

www.uiowapress.org

Copyright © 1860 by Walt Whitman

First University of Iowa Press edition, 2009

Printed in the United States of America

The University of Iowa Press is a member of

Green Press Initiative and is committed to preserving

natural resources.

Printed on acid-free paper


Library of Congress Cataloging-in-Publication Data

Whitman, Walt, 1819–1892.

[Leaves of grass]

Leaves of grass, 1860: the 150th anniversary facsimile edition /

by Walt Whitman; edited by Jason Stacy.—1st University of

Iowa Press ed.

     p.    cm.—(Iowa Whitman series)

Includes bibliographical references.

ISBN-13: 978-1-58729-825-7 (pbk.)

ISBN-10: 1-58729-825-2 (pbk.)

I. Stacy, Jason, 1970–   II. Title.

PS3201 2009

811'.3—dc22 2009009762

# CONTENTS

# ACKNOWLEDGMENTS

The 150th anniversary facsimile of Whitman's
1860 *Leaves of Grass* would not exist without the
help of many people. The Walt Whitman Archive
generously provided the images of Whitman's third
edition. The Office of the Provost, Graduate School,
and College of Arts and Sciences of Southern Illinois
University Edwardsville granted financial support
for the project. Jessica DeSpain, Ed Folsom, and
James Sabathne offered insightful readings of
the introduction and notes. Tom Jordan, Rowena
McClinton, and Eric Ruckh lent their expertise at
important moments. Linda Carlisle, social sciences
librarian at Lovejoy Library, graciously tracked
down a hard-to-find resource. Holly Carver and the
University of Iowa Press cheerfully made a
beautiful book in record time.

And Michelle, Abigail, and Margaret Stacy
continue to help me in ways too numerous to
recount here.

# INTRODUCTION
*Jason Stacy*

When asked by his friend Horace Traubel which version of *Leaves of Grass* he liked best, Walt Whitman said, "They all count, I don't know if I like any one more than the other."[1] To agree with Whitman, we must relinquish the idea that *Leaves* developed progressively, steadily growing and improving from 1855 to 1892, though we are tempted to read an author's corpus in a narrative fashion: Was there a bright burst of talent that peaked early? Did gradual maturation or a sudden break produce the author we know? Does the final version of *Leaves* represent its *denouement*?

The critic Roy Harvey Pearce believed the third edition to be the culmination of what Whitman began in 1855 and only tinkered with after 1860; for Pearce, the third edition was Whitman's "greatest."[2] But Whitman undermines easy narratives like this: "Even while you should think you had unquestionably caught me, behold! / Already you see I have escaped from you."[3] In order to make such judgments, we have to either assert that Whitman did not understand himself as well as we do—a difficult proposition according to the poet who promised to assume what we assume—or we have to take him at his word and find a way to make all versions of *Leaves of Grass* "count."

As a historian, I understand literature as the product of past events, biographical moments, and aesthetic trends produced through the words and actions of the individuals who lived them. This makes it possible to accept Whitman's argument that all versions of *Leaves of Grass* count; each was formed from a particular set of circumstances in the poet's life and times. When I couple this understanding with Whitman's argument that "every atom belonging to me, as good belongs to you," each edition becomes a device by which the poet transformed his contemporary circumstances into universal meaning; each edition, then, is "in and out of the game" and captures historical context while trying to escape it.[4]

In this light, the 1860 edition, Whitman's third, is particularly compelling because it grows out of a highly charged set of political, social, and biographical circumstances. Published as the Union dissolved by a poet intimately concerned with the idea of a United States as "essentially the greatest poem," arranged to be cited chapter and verse in the midst of a culture that embraced both biblical literalism and religious experimentation, fulfilling the poet's notions of a "New Bible," and "a handsome little book . . . like the *Enchiridion*," this edition gave Whitman the opportunity to actualize his idea of himself as the nation's "referee" and "arbiter."[5] Appearing at a time when scripture proved readily available to Americans in inexpensive, portable versions, Whitman intended his third edition to function like the Bible. This *Leaves of Grass* was to inaugurate a new American religion, which cleared away the staid detritus of empty ritual. With a thickness and rough-hewn cover that emulated a simply bound King James Version of the early nineteenth century, the third edition's framework of clusters and verses afforded an experience akin to Bible reading; within this familiar framework, the poet offered a radical revision of American politics and religion as the last best hope to prevent war. Understood in this fashion, the third edition becomes a profoundly rich product of a period when the United States faced its greatest peril. In 1860, Walt Whitman offered up *Leaves of Grass* for national salvation.[6]

## TWO CRISES, A POET AND A NATION: 1855–1860

In the introduction to the first edition of *Leaves of Grass* (1855), Whitman gauged a poet's success by the extent to which the nation "absorbs him as affectionately as he has absorbed it."[7] This democratic standard allowed the poet to forestall any condemnation from highbrow critics and to turn elite criticism into confirmation of the poet's egalitarian *bona fides*. As a newspaper editor, Whitman understood the way in which context shaped printed statements; his writings for the New York and Brooklyn Democratic press in the 1840s utilized the popular editorial tactic of pulling a critic's words into an editorial and holding them up to ridicule.[8] Whitman adapted this tactic to his poetry by printing positive and negative reviews of the first edition in the back of some of the later-bound copies and then including an appendix entitled "Leaves-Droppings" in the second edition, thereby generating controversy and buzz. Critics who claimed, "the author should be kicked from all decent society as below the level of the brute" ironically confirmed Whitman's notion of himself as an artist on the vanguard of an aesthetic and democratic revolution.[9] When Whitman printed Ralph Waldo Emerson's letter of congratulations alongside his own claim that "a few years, and the average annual call for my Poems is ten or twenty thousand copies—more, quite likely," he drew a line of demarcation between experts who aped staid

Old World aesthetics (the first review he included in "Leaves-Droppings" was from the *London Weekly Dispatch*) and fresh artists who captured the democratic essence of the New.[10]

The first two editions of *Leaves of Grass* managed to find an audience of sorts. Three Boston intellectuals—Ralph Waldo Emerson (1803–1882), Henry David Thoreau (1817–1862), and Amos Bronson Alcott (1799–1888)—visited Whitman in 1856 to see the author of what Emerson called "the most extraordinary piece of wit and wisdom that America has yet contributed."[11] Alcott described Whitman as a combination of Silenus, satyr, and Heracles, but portrayed relations between the poet and Thoreau as chilly: "it came to no more than cold compliments between the two." Thoreau later called Whitman "the greatest democrat the world has seen," though it is not clear whether he meant this entirely as a compliment.[12] Whitman likewise expressed some ambivalence toward the Boston Transcendentalists, "the cultivated fellows all carry that air about with them . . . the best of them, Emerson himself . . . compare unfavorably with the urchin on the street."[13] Later in life, Whitman said of Thoreau, "I do not think it was so much a love of woods . . . that made him live in the country, as . . . a morbid dislike of humanity."[14] No wonder Whitman and Thoreau circled each other cautiously; neither was sure whether the other was a compatriot, competitor, or buffoon.

The poet also found a kind of audience in the bohemian scene that rose up around Pfaff's saloon during the late 1850s. There, he "talked, discussed: all sorts of questions" with "a great number of fellows." Christine Stansell describes this bohemian gathering place as one where "cultural outsiders and dissenters . . . made . . .

their work . . . commercially appealing to urban audiences";[15] according to Paul Zweig, the saloon provided Whitman with a friendly audience and access to people who could promote his work.[16] One of Pfaff's denizens, Henry Clapp, editor of the *Saturday Press*, published Whitman's latest poems like "A Child's Reminiscence" and early versions of "Calamus" and "Enfans d'Adam" in 1859.[17] During this same period, Whitman saw "Bardic Symbols," (later "As I Ebb'd with the Ocean of Life") published in the *Atlantic Monthly*.[18] These poems hinted at Whitman's continued effort to add to and revise *Leaves of Grass* so to prove himself the poet whose country had affectionately absorbed him.

But a democratic audience never materialized. Contrary to his confidence that the second edition would elicit high demand among the "freewomen and freemen of The States,"[19] its sales (like those of the first edition) were weak.[20] During this period, Whitman wrote in a notebook, "everything I have done seems to me blank and suspicious. I doubt whether my greatest thoughts . . . are not shallow."[21] By 1857, Fowler and Wells, the anonymous publisher of the second edition, lost interest in publishing the third and expanded edition of *Leaves*.[22] For a time, the poet imagined transforming his image as the democratic bard into a lecturer on the circuit, even going so far as to print an advertisement that offered "Walt Whitman's Lectures," which he promised to give "by degrees through all These States, especially the West and South, and through Kanada."[23] In the *Brooklyn Daily Times*, Whitman celebrated the lecturer who "carefully condenses and popularizes his knowledge on a subject . . ." and "prepare[s] the way . . . for subsequent investigations on [the audience's] part";[24] Whitman's ideal lecturer, like his heroic bard, transformed his audience into active agents in their own enlightenment. Ultimately, however, the poet never pursued this new version of himself; his self-image as the bard of a new democratic sensibility proved too compelling. After the onset of the economic depression of 1857, employment became scarce and Whitman, living at home with his mother and brothers, began a thorough expansion of *Leaves of Grass* in preparation for a third edition.

The nation was suffering a comparable crisis of purpose during the 1850s. The abolitionist movement, begun in earnest in the 1830s with the publication of William Lloyd Garrison's *Liberator*, grew from a relatively small group of boisterous reformers into a major voice of American social discourse. The "Compromise" of 1850, whose measures could only pass Congress in a piecemeal fashion, ostensibly settled the slavery question in the new territories gained after the Mexican-American War (1846–1848) by allowing "popular sovereignty" over the issue and effectively pushing the national debate onto local populations to be fought out amongst themselves. The debate over the Compromise also divided the lionized compromisers of the early nineteenth century: Henry Clay of Kentucky, John C. Calhoun of South Carolina, and Daniel Webster of Massachusetts. Clay and Webster voiced support for the new measures while Calhoun, so morbidly ill that his address to the Senate had to be read by Senator James Murray Mason of Virginia, saw in the Compromise a continued erosion of Southern power and rights: "if something is not done, the South will be forced to choose between abolition and secession."[25]

Northerners also undermined compromise; Daniel Webster faced opposition from his Massachusetts constituents for his support of the strengthened Fugitive

Slave Law, which balanced the interests of the South against the admission of California into the Union as a free state. Webster received such howls of protest from his constituents that he resigned his seat that year and was dead by 1852.[26] The abolitionist minister Theodore Parker summed up Webster's demise: "He made the wings of slavery to gain a lofty eminence. . . . [and] fell until he reached the tomb."[27] Two years later, in 1854, federal troops arrested the runaway slave Anthony Burns in Boston under the new Fugitive Slave Law and, at a trial to decide his fate, Bostonians, led by the abolitionist minister, Thomas Wentworth Higginson, stormed the courthouse and killed a federal marshal. President Pierce eventually called in federal troops to restore order.[28] Whitman, while working on what would become the first edition of *Leaves of Grass*, published a number of poems during the early 1850s that expressed his disdain for the spread of "slave power," by which he meant the domination of Southern officials over federal government policies.[29]

With the publication of Harriet Beecher Stowe's best-selling *Uncle Tom's Cabin* in 1852, antislavery advocates acquired a tract useful for applying names and personalities to the nonfictional accounts in antislavery literature. The book also provided a sentimental feast for the general reader and proved a boon for abolitionist activists both for the publicity it offered and the controversy it stirred. Stowe saw her narrative as a way to instruct readers in proper Bible reading and structured *Uncle Tom's Cabin* like an extended parable[30] where Christlike Tom's sale down the Mississippi River and, ultimately, his martyr's death contrasted with the dehumanizing effects of slavery on slave owners like the demonic Simon Legree and even the sympathetic

Arthur and Emily Shelby, who were forced to divide African American families and trade their humanity for profit. The popularity of the novel provoked a rival industry of "anti-Tom" literature that tapped into popular interest in the issue while offering an alternate and benign version of life on a Southern plantation. The print war between pro- and antislavery partisans in the first half of the 1850s foreshadowed real violence later in the decade.

The Kansas-Nebraska Act (1854) shattered what little calm remained in national politics after the Compromise of 1850; by allowing popular sovereignty in the Kansas and Nebraska Territories, Illinois senator Stephen A. Douglas's legislation voided the Missouri Compromise (1820) and opened to slavery territories formerly deemed permanently closed. Ostensibly written to encourage Southern legislators to support a transcontinental railroad through Chicago (rather than a southern terminus like St. Louis or New Orleans), the Kansas-Nebraska Act effectively made it possible for slavery to extend from the Atlantic seaboard to California and from the Gulf of Mexico to the border of Canada. Within a year of its passage, the Kansas Territory collapsed into civil war between antislavery settlers, mostly from New England, many of whom were supplied with the New England Emigrant Society's famed "Beecher Bibles" (Sharpe's rifles, named after the Society's leader, the minister and brother of Harriet Beecher Stowe, Henry Ward Beecher) and proslavery "Border Ruffians" from Missouri. By May 1856, two rival territorial legislatures governed Kansas, both claiming ultimate authority. Roving militias, determined to mete out the kind of battlefield justice best exemplified by John Brown's murder of five proslavery men at settlements on the Pottawatomie River, set off violence that would serve as a bloody precursor to the Civil War.[31] That same month, the violence spread to the floor of the U.S. Senate where Preston Brooks, representative from South Carolina, bludgeoned Charles Sumner, senator from Massachusetts, in retaliation for an antislavery speech in which Sumner mocked Brooks's uncle, Andrew Butler, senator of South Carolina, both for his assistance in penning the Kansas-Nebraska Act and for his speech impediment.

Popular sovereignty also became the major political issue in the 1856 presidential campaign, where the antislavery Republican Party ran its first candidate for president, John C. Frémont, and in the congressional campaigns of 1858, especially between Abraham Lincoln and Stephen Douglas in Illinois. John Brown further exacerbated sectional tensions when, supported by prominent New England activists and intellectuals like Henry David Thoreau, Ralph Waldo Emerson, and Theodore Parker, he led a small group of supporters in a raid on the federal armory at Harper's Ferry, Virginia, in hopes of sparking a slave uprising. After his capture by U.S. troops and trial for treason, Brown handed his guard a note on the day of his execution that read, "I John Brown am now quite *certain* that the crimes of this *guilty, land*: *will* never be purged *away*; but with Blood."[32] Less than one year later, Abraham Lincoln won a four-way, regionally divided election with only 40 percent of the popular vote, carrying no states south of the Mason-Dixon Line. In December 1860, South Carolina seceded from the United States.

As the nation came apart, an opportunity arose for the third incarnation of *Leaves of Grass*. William Thayer and Charles Eldridge, two former clerks and entrepreneurial publishers in Boston, contacted Whitman with an offer to publish his latest edition, probably after obtaining a copy of the first or second editions of *Leaves of Grass*, or after reading Whitman's poetry in the *Saturday Press* or the *Liberator*, where Whitman's antislavery poems were reprinted.[33] The new publishing house produced progressive political tracts and abolitionist literature; their best-selling book, James Redpath's *The Public Life of Captain John Brown*, compared Brown to American Revolutionary heroes.[34] Once again, Whitman found himself admired by Boston intellectuals and progressive reformers rather than average Americans.[35] However, Thayer and Eldridge's letter to the poet spoke acutely to the poet's interests: "We are young men. We 'celebrate' ourselves by acts. Try us. You can do us good. We can do you good—pecuniarily."[36] With a quote from the first line of the poem that would become "Song of Myself"[37] and the promise of profit, the offer must have sounded like salvation to Whitman, and within the month he arrived in Boston.

The *Leaves of Grass* that Whitman published in 1860 looked substantially different from the previous two editions. The poet transformed his bard-persona from "one of the roughs" to a prophet who made "the most spiritual poems."[38] This is not to say that Whitman softened his message in *Leaves*; in fact, two new "clusters" of poetry, "Calamus" and "Enfans d'Adam," contained sexual imagery that, at least in the case of the latter, shocked nineteenth-century audiences more than any of his other poems. Emerson himself, who visited the poet while he was in Boston reading the proofs for Thayer and Eldridge, tried to persuade Whitman to cut the more erotic poetry: ". . . you are in danger of being tangled up with . . . heresy." When Whitman asked Emerson, though, whether, after a thorough editing of the sexual poems, "there would be as good a book left," Emerson responded, "I did not say as good a book— I said a good book."[39] While Whitman intensified the erotic nature of his poetry, he also repackaged *Leaves of Grass* as a religious tome and, displaying his journalist's sense of popular trends and tastes, transformed his bard from an inspired mechanic to a prophetic sage.

By the 1840s, the King James Version began to lose its place as the de facto English version for Americans. Among the educated elite, the German school of higher criticism made claims of biblical literalism suspect and allowed theologians like the Unitarian Theodore Parker to read the Bible in allegorical, or even radically contemporary ways. Popular publishers offered new versions of scripture, like Harper's *Illustrated Bible* (which Whitman reviewed positively in the mid-1840s[40]) that were mass-produced and relatively inexpensive, and thereby shifted the discourse between readers and the Bible from formally public to functionally private; in this regard, the process of Bible reading took its cue from mass-produced and inexpensive novels, which required individual attention over a sustained period and elicited an intensely intimate relationship between reader and text; reading the Bible in this fashion personalized scripture for a broad swath of the public. The emphasis on individual conversion during the Second Great Awakening fueled this change. In 1816, the American Bible Society began to mass-produce Bibles with missionary zeal; between the 1840s and the 1850s, the Society's output of clothbound Bibles more than doubled; in the following decade, its output nearly doubled again.[41] Paul Gutjahr argues that Americans began to see scripture as highly mutable and adaptable to personal needs and contexts during this period.[42] Examples abound: Joseph Smith's

*The Book of Mormon* (1830) demonstrated the willingness of many Americans to accept a wholesale addition to scripture. William Miller, the self-proclaimed prophet of end-times, blanketed the country with four million pamphlets that contained detailed scriptural charts and explanations of the coming of Armageddon in 1843 (later changed to 1844).[43] With the publication of Pogson Smith's *Zerah: The Believing Jew* (1837), Americans became accustomed to encountering Jesus as a character in works of fiction. By the 1850s, popular authors like Harriet Beecher Stowe and Maria Cummins lent credence to their novels by claiming they functioned like biblical parables rather than merely edifying fictions.[44] Whitman likewise thought creatively about adapting religion to contemporary needs; by 1857, he imagined *"Founding a new American/Religion* (? No Religion)."[45]

The third edition expressed the ambivalence of a New Religion (No Religion). In the frontispiece, Whitman looked a combination of epicure and carefully disheveled minister who, in a fashion similar to images of Theodore Parker and Henry Ward Beecher from the same decade, posed with unkempt hair and eyes staring into the ethereal distance over the viewer's shoulder: Whitman also added 146 new poems to the thirty-two that comprised the second edition, which resulted in the book's thickness rivaling that of the Bible; and he divided it in a manner that allowed *Leaves of Grass* to be demarcated into separate "clusters" as part of a theological whole. He numbered the poems and verses within these clusters in a fashion that mimicked the typography in Bibles and invited citations similar to scripture; "Chants Democratic 7:6," for example, read "In the name of These States, and in your and my name, the Past, / And in the name of These States, and in your and my name, the Present time." By structuring the third edition like scripture, and by presenting himself in a ministerial fashion, Whitman tried to sell the paradoxical idea of a new religion that was no religion; through familiar religious tropes and republican rhetoric, he uncoupled religious and political practices from their traditional moorings and offered a new testimony to the universal Many in One that made the Union a reflection of the cosmos.[46]

## GENESIS AND PROEM

Five years earlier, Whitman began the first edition of *Leaves of Grass* like an editor set free from the constraints of the newspaper; over the course of ten, double-columned pages, he introduced America, Americans, and the poet who saw "the fullest poetical nature" in a prose essay more manifesto than preface.[47] This essay disappeared in the 1856 edition, possibly because the poet found a comment from a review in *Putnam's Monthly* apt:

> The application of these principles, and of many others equally peculiar, which are expounded in a style equally oracular throughout the long preface— is made *passim*, and often with comical success, in the poems themselves, which may briefly be described as a compound of the New England transcendentalist and New York rowdy.[48]

Whitman probably appreciated the reviewer's description of him as part transcendentalist and part rowdy, but perhaps came to see his meandering preface as overkill; was it a primer, qualifier, or explanation? The second edition transformed this prose preface into a new poem ("Poem of Many in One") and, instead of a preface, opened with a simple table of contents that carefully attached the word "poem" to every poem. Still, this must have been ultimately unsatisfying for the poet; he wanted *Leaves of Grass* to declare itself as a unified and self-contained entity, like Martin Tupper's *Proverbial Philosophy* (1837) or Henry Wadsworth Longfellow's *The Song of Hiawatha* (1854), rather than just a collection of poems; a table of contents, even with partially repeating titles, did not necessarily make this clear. Whitman hoped the third edition would be definitive, with "an aspect of completeness" and without a "letter to or from Emerson—no Notices or anything of that sort" that explained in prose what the readers should understand in the poetry.[49] This required a new kind of preface and, in a new poem, "Proto-Leaf" (later titled "Starting from Paumanok"), Whitman introduced *Leaves* anew. "Proto-Leaf" served two purposes: like the book of Genesis, it framed a cosmos and, like the proem of the *Iliad* or the *Odyssey*, suggested major themes without explaining the ultimate meaning of the work itself.

Whitman was as familiar with Homer as he was with the Bible. In an editorial from the early 1840s, he quoted Alexander Pope's translation of the *Odyssey*.[50] Forty years later, while discussing critics of Fanny Wright with Horace Traubel, Whitman called her work, "crude as the Bible and Homer are crude" (which he meant to her merit).[51] Traubel also noted that Whitman always had both a King James Version and Homer on hand in his home in Camden.[52] When a correspondent suggested that Whitman be called a "proet" for his prose-like verse, Whitman commented to Traubel, "yes, and the name belongs, too, to the Bible writers—to the old

Hebrews, all—to the Hindu scripturists—to many of the Greeks and so on. Almost all the earlier fellows, in fact."[53] Toward the end of his life, Whitman placed himself in the company of Homer by connecting his aesthetic sensibility to the ancient poet's, "Of course, Pope had his virtues. . . . But [Pope's translation of the *Iliad*] was not Homer—was certainly not modern—not ours."[54]

The first sentence of the King James Version, "In the beginning God created the heaven and the earth," established the framework by which Americans built a narrative trajectory from the Old through the New Testament; change occurred within the unchanging truth of God the Creator; everything existed under His aegis. Whitman likewise framed a cosmos in "Proto-Leaf": "Free, fresh, savage . . . I strike up for a new world." In this beginning, the poet appealed to original creation and unencumbered living; this justified settlement in a "new world," which, by implication, the poet pioneered for the reader. "Proto-Leaf," like Genesis, established the parameters for the rest of the stories, visions, and exhortations: past and future collapsed in the poet's seminal nature as he guided the reader *back* to a new world.[55] "Proto-Leaf" also served, like the proems of the *Iliad* and the *Odyssey* in their appeal to the muse, to introduce the whole, as in the *Iliad* where Homer set the context for the fight between Agamemnon and Achilles and the disaster it wrought for the Greeks at Troy:

The Wrath of Peleus' Son, the direful Spring
Of all the Grecian Woes, O Goddess, sing!
That Wrath which hurl'd to Pluto's gloomy Reign
The Souls of mighty Chiefs untimely slain;
Whose Limbs unbury'd on the naked Shore

Devouring Dogs and hungry Vultures tore.
Since Great Achilles and Atrides strove,
Such was the Sov'reign Doom, and such the Will
     of Jove.[56]

Whitman's "Proto-Leaf," likewise established topics and themes, but, true to the highly personal nature of *Leaves of Grass*, promised to teach readers to escape ritual and secondhand revelation; these "evangel-poem[s]" led readers to a "new world," without ministry, church, or Bible, where democracy existed in the fabric of things:[57]

Americanos! Masters!
[ ... ]
For you a programme of chants.
[ ... ]
Chants of the Many In One.[58]

I will make the poems of materials, for I think they
     are to be the most spiritual poems,
And I will make the poems of my body and of
     mortality,
For I think I shall then supply myself with the
     poems of my Soul and of immortality.

I will make a song for These States, that no one
     State may under any circumstances be subjected
     to another State,
And I will make a song that there shall be comity
     by day and by night between all The States, and
     between any two of them,
And I will make a song of the organic bargains of
     These States—And a shrill song of curses on
     him who would dissever the Union;
[ ... ]

I will sing the song of companionship,
I will show what alone must compact These,
I believe These are to found their own ideal of
    manly love, indicating it in me;
[ . . . ]
I will write the evangel-poem of comrades and
    of love, [ . . . ]⁵⁹

In this new world, the differences between spirit and
body, between states, and between individuals collapsed
within the bard's benevolent vision. "Proto-Leaf" wor-
shipped the "Many In One" and thus introduced a new
kind of monotheism that pointed ahead to the subject
of the cluster "Chants Democratic," itself, an expanded
version of the 1856 "Poem of the Many In One," and
played upon the nation's motto, "E Pluribus Unum."⁶⁰
When Whitman announced, "the real and permanent
grandeur of These States must be their Religion" he
prepared the reader for a transformation of the nation's
most immediate problem into its greatest strength; se-
cessionists and would-be autocrats proved to be apos-
tates against Whitman's new religion, whose faithful
performed the unifying rituals of the everyday.⁶¹

### THE STRUCTURES OF THEOLOGICAL
### ARGUMENT

"Proto-Leaf" promised a new religion that united spirit
and material, celebrated equality and comity between
the States, cursed those who would destroy the Union,
and hinted at a new kind of comradeship which soothed
the nation's fierce debates. Slavery lay at the center of
these debates and Whitman incorporated the intellec-
tual structures that supported pro- and antislavery ar-
guments into his reorganized and expanded *Leaves of*

*Grass*, but he reworked these structures to foster compromise and mutual empathy.

These intellectual structures generally fell into three broad categories. First, drawing on America's Protestant legacy, partisans on both sides of the slavery debate depended upon a layperson's capacity to glean original and true biblical meaning; this democratized biblical interpretation by replacing the necessity of critical training or guidance to understand scripture with a reliance on sentiment and common sense and allowed dissenters to be charged with coldheartedness, mental deficiency, or sinister designs. Second, both sides of the slavery debate mouthed an American republican ideology that defined the nation's founding as providing the ideals to which the nation aspired; in this way, both sides called their opponents deviants from the nation's pristine origins (and proper future) and framed contemporary social and political debates in historic terms. Third, pro- and antislavery partisans used a nascent scientism to justify moral claims with empirical evidence and appeals to natural law. Thus, these intellectual structures supported solipsistic arguments that allowed pro- and antislavery activists to channel the will of God, the Founders, and Nature.

Democratic exegetics, republican ideology, and popular scientism proved especially useful to theologians engaged in the national debate over slavery. During the first half of the nineteenth century, sermonizing had undergone a transformation from what David Reynolds calls the "doctrinal" to the "imaginative" where popular theologians loosened the traditional homiletic structure of text, doctrine, and proof into a style that allowed sentimental, anecdotal, and even scientific arguments to bolster a sermon.[62] This new style, coupled with the continuing popularity of revivals in the generation before the Civil War, allowed theology to play a public role outside of the church and draw upon secular ideologies to support religious arguments. The democratic nature of this change also required the minister to *persuade* and *move* his listeners, and thereby incorporated many of the rhetorical tactics of secular politicians. Unlike politicians, however, ministers could formulate the arguments for and against slavery that Americans used to express their opinions in universal terms. Religious language, therefore, offered an exceptionally powerful means to shape public opinion by situating contemporary American discourse into transcendent and timeless categories; this perhaps explains why Whitman incorporated theological rhetoric and structure into his third edition.

## DEMOCRATIC EXEGESIS

Traditionally, Protestant ministers served as guides and, through training in proper biblical interpretation, revealed the meaning of scripture for their congregations; theologians thereby unlocked the Bible's general premises and instructed laymen in right reasoning. This made Protestant exegesis particularly compelling; if a listener proved unwilling or unable to accept a minister's claims, it pointed to an essential flaw in the reasoning (or faith) of the dissenter. Thus, the proslavery partisan and minister Frederick Ross (1796–1883) argued there could be no viable biblical argument against slavery because "God says nowhere it is a sin";[63] Leviticus 25:44–46 justified making slaves of the "heathen that are around about you"[64] and Colossians 4:18 showed "that God [h]as . . . sanctioned the relation of master and slave. . . ."[65] According to Ross, proslavery politics represented Christian humility and submission to God's plan against abolitionists who personified the essence of human vanity when they tried to force God's will. On the other hand, antislavery theologians Charles Grandison Finney (1792–1875) and Theodore Parker (1810–1860) defined revelation as an ever-unfolding process where scriptural meaning unveiled itself in the human heart. This appeal to sentiment tapped into the Second Great Awakening's emphasis on revelation-through-emotion; God held people morally responsible "according to their light" and placed His plan in their hands.[66] For Theodore Parker, "The method of . . . Christianity is a very plain one. Obedience, not to that old teacher . . . but to God, who [has written] His law . . . on the tablets of the heart."[67] Proslavery advocates, like modern day Pharisees, closed themselves to God's new revelation.

Contrary to partisan ministers, Whitman used democratized exegetics to repair the nation's fractured discourse and as a model for the religious "I" who found "letters from God dropped in the street."[68] Whitman's first poem after "Proto-Leaf," the self-titled "Walt Whitman" (later to become "Song of Myself"), freed readers from written scripture entirely: seekers found God's Word in the world. Self-titled like the prophetic books of the Bible, "Walt Whitman" began with the famous and still jarring statement:

I celebrate myself,
And what I assume you shall assume,
For every atom belonging to me, as good belongs to
    you.

This beginning established the "smallest known quantity of a chemical compound"[69] as the means by which reader and poet translated individual experience into universal meaning. A dependence upon a shared ability to know "the good of the earth and sun," not "at second or third hand" or "through the eyes of the dead" nor through "spectres in books," but through faith in one's ability to read spiritual meaning in the world, established the new line of demarcation between true believers and those who lacked conviction.[70]

Like a recent convert, Whitman formerly "sweated through fog" and ignorance before revelation came in a new communion between body and soul;[71] this communion revealed eternity in the everyday; simple material objects like the grass became scripture, a "uniform hieroglyphic," ripe with meaning.[72] Whitman's interpretation of the grass revealed new and undeniable ethical imperatives: "Growing among black folks as among white," covering those who "gain the day" and those for whom the "battles are lost,"[73] the grass proved the egalitarian ethos of the cosmos and reflected the famous sentiments of the Gospel of Matthew: "Love your enemies, bless them that curse you . . . for [God] maketh his sun to rise on the evil and on the good." But whereas the Christian imperative to love one's enemy inverted earthly hierarchies by promising the future to the meek, Whitman's exegesis of the grass undercut hierarchy entirely; the grass grew for black and white, winners and losers, and, in its mute regeneration, leveled all. This exegesis-of-the-world invited the reader to draw transcendent truths from everyday experiences and explains the poet's careful tabulations that flow in and out of his purview:

The little one sleeps in its cradle,
I lift the gauze and look a long time, and silently
brush away flies with my hand.[74]

The big doors of the country-barn stand open and
ready,
The dried grass of the harvest-time loads the slow-
drawn wagon,
The clear light plays on the brown gray and green
intertinged,
The armfuls are packed to the sagging mow.[75]

Oxen that rattle the yoke or halt in the shade! what
is that you express in your eyes?
It seems to me more than all the print I have read in
my life.[76]

All truths wait in all things,
They neither hasten their own delivery, nor resist it,
They do not need the obstetric forceps of the
surgeon,
The insignificant is as big to me as any,
What is less or more than a touch?[77]

By collapsing hierarchies and inviting a sentimen-
tal reading of the particular for clues of the universal,
Whitman's scenes worked like spiritual exercises that
proved the world the only authoritative text and the
individual the best theologian.[78] Whitman's atomic
theory of existence saved these radical exegetics from
epistemological relativism; when individuals authored
their own self-titled books of revelation, they upheld
the unity of all things. Divisive disagreements proved to
be only the frothy by-product of the churning cosmos.
Though Whitman offered no model by which this reve-
lation bred practical unity, his thoroughly democratic

exegetics redefined debates from either/or propositions to examples of the Many in One.

## AMERICAN REPUBLICANISM

The generation born in the first decades of the nineteenth century began in earnest to frame the American founding as national myth. With the celebrated visit of the Marquis de Lafayette in 1824–1825 and the deaths of Thomas Jefferson and John Adams in 1826, the American War for Independence faded from living memory and became the preserve of collective self-definition and ownership. Whitman, as a boy, experienced Lafayette's visit to Brooklyn and remembered the kiss he received from the grizzled French revolutionary.[79] An idealization of the Revolution's generation matched the ever-widening discourse about the meanings of 1776 and, by implication, the essence of the United States in the present and future. For this reason, the Fourth of July offered transcendent significance across the social and political spectrum; recently arrived Irish immigrants expressed ethnic pride by marching en masse during Fourth of July parades in New York City; former slave and abolitionist Frederick Douglass used the Fourth of July as an opportunity to expose the hypocrisies of America's idealistic rhetoric; Thoreau took up residence at Walden Pond on the Fourth of July.[80] Indeed, the Fourth of July became so significant that many commentators have falsely claimed that Whitman timed the publication of *Leaves* itself to appear on Independence Day in 1855.[81] Even though the Fourth of July publication of the first edition is mythological, Whitman, himself, inaugurated a new post-Christian calendar for the 1860 edition, dating his book "Year 85 of The States," and thereby positing that the origin of significant historical chronology is, instead of Christ's birth, now set as July 4, 1776. The parenthetical publication date of 1860–61 appeared at the bottom of the title page almost as an afterthought.

Theologians likewise found in American republican rhetoric a convenient way to situate their partisan arguments within the Revolution's legacy. Abolitionist minister Theodore Parker, by placing the Declaration of Independence and the Gospel of Matthew on equal footing, argued that Jefferson's words were "destined to have a great influence on the development of mankind" and the Fourth of July would prove to be the "birthday of whole families of republics that we know not of as yet." According to Charles Grandison Finney, ministers during the American Revolution "discussed in the pulpit . . . [all] the great questions of the revolution," but contemporary ministers were "afraid to stand forth and speak as honest, fearless men." When Finney called for Christian voters to be "united" against proslavery politicians,[82] he commingled revivalist rhetoric with republican practice to fulfill God's plan at the ballot box. Though opposed to Finney and Parker on the issue of slavery, Frederick Ross likewise appealed to the founding generation when he argued that the Declaration of Independence represented nothing more than a "statement of grievances the colonies had borne from the mother-country." Abolitionists, for Ross, committed heresy when they placed a desire for liberty and self-empowerment on par with God's ancient commandments.[83]

As Whitman taught his readers to interpret God's Word in the world and free themselves from secondhand scripture, he likewise revised American republican ideology to liberate citizens from the constitutional debates that threatened to sever the nation. "Chants

Democratic and Native American," the first cluster of
the third edition, began with an "Apostroph" that prom-
ised to prove the Union indissoluble:

> O I believe there is nothing real but America and
>   freedom!
> [ . . . ]
> O a curse on him that would dissever this Union for
>   any reason whatever!
> [ . . . ]
> O Libertad! O compact! O union impossible to
>   dissever![84]

The next poem of the cluster, number "1," first appeared
in prose form in the 1855 preface where Whitman pro-
claimed himself the national "referee." In the 1856
edition, this prose became poetry ("Poem of Many in
One") and Whitman rewrote Christian chronology by
celebrating "the haughty defiance of Year 1" (1776) and
proclaiming himself the prophet of America's "organic
compacts." In 1860, Whitman defined these organic
compacts as the next stage of the republic's progress.
Embedded in natural rather than statutory law, organic
compacts allowed the poet to react ambivalently to the
constitutional crisis of 1860 because ". . . [t]he Ameri-
can compact is altogether with individuals. . . . To hold
men together by paper and seal, or by compulsion, is no
account."[85] Here, the poet clarified his use of "Native
American" in the title of this cluster: whereas the term
carried connotations of anti-immigration politics
through the 1840s and 1850s, especially in light of the
American Party's bid for the presidency in 1856,[86] Whit-
man redefined it in 1860 to establish the nation's native-
ness in the intimate connections between individuals.
In this way, the poet embraced the Declaration's defi-

nition of government as "instituted among men," but accentuated personal relationships over legal ones and transformed "Native American" into a unifying and absorptive phrase by wresting it away from those who used the designation to divide the populace.

Whitman's chants of organic democracy revealed an eternal nation beneath the fractured and failing Union.[87] The second poem of the cluster, called "Broad-Axe Poem" in the 1856 edition, recounted the seminal nature and sweeping culmination of the axe's transformation from a weapon of the Old World to the nation-building tool of the New. "Chants Democratic" 3, later "A Song for Occupations," sounded in the 1855 edition like an attempt to save laborers from industrial alienation, but within this cluster celebrated the republic at work following the chant of the nation-building axe. Robin Hoople sees a cohesive narrative arc in the sequence of these poems where Whitman "propose[d] 'Organic compacts' [as] natural metaphors for emotional and political ties that transcend[ed] imperfect human laws."[88] Justice in the organic republic came "not . . . by legislators," but by the "Soul" with which "natural lawyers and perfect judges" intuited natural laws.[89]

The poet's celebration of natural over legal compacts proved a more radical proposal than his democratic exegesis. Since the 1780s, written constitutions at the state and national levels represented for Americans an improvement on the British model of government, which was built "organically" from ancient documents and self-justifying, long-held traditions. Both sides of the slavery debate upheld traditional American political discourse in their appeals to the Constitution and Declaration of Independence; Whitman, on the other hand, diminished paper agreements in pursuit of national reconciliation. The Constitution, like the second-hand revelations in scripture, proved an impediment to understanding the essential unity of things; in fact, the Constitution exacerbated divisions between Americans by falsely turning legal disagreement into national existential crisis. For the poet, resolution came through the revelation that paper compacts, formerly the foundation of republican practice, turned out to be the cursory by-products of eternal, organic singularity; arguments over the Constitution and the meaning of the Declaration of Independence were, therefore, of "no account." Whitman thereby sought to short-circuit the threat of secession by diminishing the documents over whose meaning both sides fought.

If the Union proved organic rather than merely legal, and fused by natural affection rather than human law, then the United States could weather all constitutional crises and prove as indissoluble as the bonds of affection which people felt naturally for each other. In his First Inaugural Address (1861), Abraham Lincoln likewise appealed to these affectionate bonds, but only after he presented an extended discourse on the constitutional illegality of secession and his legal authority to maintain the Union by force if necessary; for Lincoln, the Constitution was fundamentally a unifying document. Whitman, on the other hand, questioned the unifying potency of "paper and seal" and "compulsion"; for the bard, only the affectionate bonds between people made the Union "impossible to dissever."

## POPULAR SCIENTISM

In light of the evolutionary theories of the geologist Charles Lyell (1797–1875) and the biologist Charles Darwin (1809–1882), the second quarter of the nineteenth century proved the final era when theology and science could still confidently make claims to support one another. Popular works like Robert Chambers' *Vestiges of the Natural History of Creation* (1844) connected scientific discovery with the progressive nature of God's creation, "from the mandibles of insects to the hand of man, all is seen to be in the most harmonious relation . . . thus proving that *design* presided in the creation of the whole. . . ."[90] Whitman echoed these sentiments when he reviewed William Paley's *Natural Theology* (1802) after Harper's published a new edition in 1847 and wrote with approval that Paley proved a "devout" physiologist (though the implication that a scientist could be otherwise hinted at the growing cultural anxiety over the incompatibility of empirical science and contemporary theology); in a review of J. K. Wellman's *Illustrated Botany* (1846), Whitman noted that, through flora, observers could "be impressed . . . with the wisdom and vastness of God!"[91]

Proslavery theologians like Frederick Ross, drawing from the works of scientists like the geologist Arnold Henry Guyot (1807–1884) and the zoologist Louis Agassiz (1807–1873), whose notions of natural hierarchies upheld the idea of a mindful Creator and provided the "rationale for classification,"[92] mixed religious belief and scientific theory to support the continued existence of slavery: "solid, unindented Southern Africa makes an inferior man [because it is] south of the Equator [and] Europe, indented by the sea on every side, with its varied scenery, and climate . . . makes the varied intellect . . . of the master-man of the world":[93]

Ham will be lower than Shem, because he was sent to Central Africa. Man south of the Equator—in

Asia, Australia, Oceanica, America, especially Africa—is inferior to his Northern brother. The *blessing* was upon Shem in his magnificent Asia. The *greater blessing* was upon Japheth in his man-developing Europe. *Both blessings* will be combined, in America, *north of the Zone*, in commingled light and life.[94]

On the other hand, abolitionist theologians like Charles Grandison Finney preached a progressive natural history that framed creation as dynamic and marching toward God's thousand-year reign of peace in anticipation of the Second Coming, and Theodore Parker used scientism to argue that slavery threw humans from an anthropological Eden where "natural man" formerly looked "each man in the eye, and [said] to the invader 'I am also a man. . . .'"[95]

Whitman incorporated popular scientism into his American bible and, in the clusters "Enfans d'Adam" and "Calamus," drew upon the theories of phrenology—an early form of psychology based on indentations and bumps in the skull and popularized by the German physician Johann Gaspar Spurzheim (1776–1832)—to support his argument that nature had written union into existence itself via organic compacts.[96] In doing so, he situated the third *Leaves of Grass* in the heart of an American discourse that upheld political, social, and moral claims with appeals to natural law. Whitman probably learned Spurzheim's theories second-hand through Orson S. Fowler's (1809–1887) periodical, *American Phrenological Journal*, and in Fowler's books, *Hereditary Descent* and *Love and Parentage*, both of which he owned.[97] Fowler and Wells published Whitman's second edition of *Leaves of Grass*, perhaps because of Whitman's affinity for phrenological concepts and his incorporation of them into his verse. Like Whitman, the Fowlers used their books to elicit self-discovery; the *Illustrated Self-Instructor in Phrenology and Physiology* described the self-knowledge born of phrenology in terms that echoed Whitman's own words:

> [S]ince nothing in nature stands alone, but each is reciprocally related to all, and all, collectively, form one magnificent whole—since all stars and worlds mutually act and react upon each other to cause day and night, summer and winter, sun and rain, blossom and fruit; since every genus, species, and individual throughout nature is second or sixteenth cousin to every other; and since man is the epitome of universal nature . . . to understand *him* thoroughly is to know *all* things.[98]

Two phrenological concepts proved especially important to Whitman: "amativeness" (the attraction between men and women) and "adhesiveness" (or attraction between men); both allowed the poet to apply pseudoscientific theory to his idea of organic republics. In "Enfans d'Adam" and "Calamus," Whitman claimed to rediscover unadulterated, original, and natural forms of love while implicitly upholding contemporary notions of gender and sexuality; the poet thereby offered a more perfect Union that, in effect, preserved the status quo.

According to the Fowlers, amativeness, or the love between men and women, established "conjugal love" and was "adapted to perpetuate the race." In men, amativeness inculcated "dignity, power, and persuasiveness" as well as "noble . . . feeling[s] and bearing." In women, it "develope[d] all of the feminine charms and graces." In healthy individuals, amativeness "induced marriage" and achieved its fullest potential in "matrimonial partners"; people with improperly calibrated amativeness manifested a "grossness and vulgarity in expression" and a "licentiousness in all forms." Perversions of amativeness proved socially consequential, inducing individuals to treat the opposite sex as "merely . . . a minister to passion; now caressing, and now abusing them; and renders the love-feeling every way gross, animal, and depraved."[99] Here the Fowlers utilized scientific theory to rationalize contemporary anxieties and offered a natural justification for common mores: people with healthy amativeness expressed their love for the opposite sex in monogamous, loving, and procreative relationships; in men these relationships brought out masculine "power," in women, feminine "charms." Amativeness, in turn, lent Whitman the scientific language to support his theories of organic political health within the seemingly diseased Union.[100] Though contemporary censors found in "Enfans d'Adam" Whitman's most obscene poetry, the cluster did not glorify heterosexual sex for its own sake but tied amativeness to the propagation of the republic:

> Sex contains all,
> Bodies, Souls, meanings, proofs, purities, delicacies,
>     results, promulgations,
> Songs, commands, health, pride, the maternal
>     mystery, the semitic milk,
> All hopes, benefactions, bestowals,
> All the passions, loves, beauties, delights of the
>     earth,

All the governments, judges, gods, followed persons
    of the earth,
These are contained in sex, as parts of itself, and
    justifications of itself.
[ . . . ]
The drops I distil upon you shall grow fierce and
    athletic girls, new artists, musicians, and singers,
The babes I beget upon you are to beget babes in
    their turn,
I shall demand perfect men and women out of my
    love-spendings. . . .[101]

Sex ascended from "bodies" through "passions" to "governments" and thereby served communal ends; amativeness made noble lovers, strong babies, perfect men and women and, ultimately, robust republics. In this light, Whitman's reform-through-amativeness proved, in effect, a confirmation of contemporary sexual mores rather than a radical revision of them.[102] Americans needed only their natural affection for each other to preserve and perpetuate the republic.

"Adhesiveness," or love between men, also served communal ends, but instead of propagating a healthy next generation, this phrenological trait shaped "friendship; social feeling . . . [and] love of society" by eliciting "co-partnership . . . community . . . and . . . social relations." Significantly, the Fowlers' *Illustrated Self-Instructor in Phrenology and Physiology* (1857) said nothing of the traits adhesiveness produced in women, who were implicitly incapable of this kind of male comradeship. In this regard, adhesiveness also proved a "natural" human trait that reflected contemporary social norms, in this case the world of public masculinity: politics, sporting matches, entertainment, and saloons. A man of strong adhesiveness proved a "warm, cordial, ardent friend," who "sacrifice[d] much on the altar of friendship," but also "offer[ed] up friendship on the altar of the stronger passions" and proved "jealous of regards bestowed upon others."[103] This mirrored the parameters of male-centered culture in antebellum America: mutual respect on egalitarian terms built a republic of free men, but jealousy and the desire for distinction engendered civil strife.

Whitman praised adhesiveness numerous times in the third edition and based the cluster "Calamus" on this phrenological trait.[104] The "Calamus" poems are popularly understood as a celebration of homosexual love, but the term is anachronistic in this context; "homosexual" was not coined until the 1880s and, as a sexual identity, became widely recognized only in the early twentieth century. In the sex-segregated world of antebellum America, where identity adhered only loosely to varieties of sexual preference, male physical affection was a common and accepted public occurrence and proved less socially problematic than open physical affection between men and women, which was supposed to remain private and unspoken.[105] This explains why there was outrage over the "Enfans d'Adam" cluster but very little negative public reaction to the "Calamus" poems. Whitman used the physical affection men showed for each other and applied the phrenological ideas that upheld this affection to offer masculine "comradeship" as the indispensable relationship in the organic republic.[106]

Whitman took public signs of masculine affection—holding hands, walking arm-in-arm, professions of love—as proof that an invisible republic waited to manifest itself. Throughout "Calamus," Whitman and friends "saunter . . . the streets" with arms around each other's shoulders; they kiss each other and physically separate with only the greatest reluctance.[107] This casual affection promised a future "City of Friends" that proved "invincible to the attacks of the whole of the rest of the earth":

> There shall from me be a new friendship—It shall
>     be called after my name,
> [ . . . ]
> It shall twist and intertwist them through and
>     around each other—Compact shall they be,
>     showing new signs,
> Affection shall solve every one of the problems of
>     freedom,
> Those who love each other shall be invincible,
> They shall finally make America completely
>     victorious, in my name.

A new fraternity would arise that transcended states without undermining differences, thereby preserving ideals of American federalism and Whitman's celebration of the Many in One:

> One from Massachusetts shall be comrade to a
>     Missourian,
> One from Maine or Vermont, and a Carolinian
>     and an Oregonese, shall be friends triune, more
>     precious to each other than all the riches of the
>     earth.

This national phalanx of brothers, through their adhesive inclinations for one another, would, he hoped, prevent fratricidal war:

No danger shall balk Columbia's lovers,
If need be, a thousand shall sternly immolate
    themselves for one,
The Kanuck shall be willing to lay down his life for
    the Kansian, and the Kansian for the Kanuck, on
    due need.[108]

Whereas amative love made future citizens, adhesive love maintained unity and egalitarian affection; it was the higher, more "robust" quality of love and "led the rest."

In "Calamus," Whitman equated his personal desires with public displays of friendship and justified both with a phrenological category that defined fraternal love as scientific fact.[109] This makes it difficult to characterize the cluster as solely a collection of cryptic paeans to homosexual love, especially since "homosexual love" did not even exist as a discursive possibility in the mid-nineteenth century. Instead, Whitman saw signs of his desires in the world around him and, true to his exegesis of the Word in the world, interpreted these signs as messages of universal meaning. The Fowlers' version of phrenology confirmed Whitman's interpretation and lent a scientific stamp to the poet's love for men and his celebration of the organic republic. Instead of interpreting passion solely in private terms, then, Whitman offered amativeness and adhesiveness as the natural means by which diverse individuals knit themselves into national unity. In the midst of constitutional crisis, conventional affection would preserve the Union.

### THE SPACES IN BETWEEN

Ironically, even as it became the increasing focus of national attention, American slavery was less central to the 1860 edition of *Leaves of Grass* than it had been in Whitman's first edition five years earlier.[110] Thayer and Eldridge were primarily publishers of abolitionist texts, and they no doubt admired Whitman's apparently liberal stance on the peculiar institution, perhaps after seeing his most radical antislavery poems reprinted in the *Liberator*. But the 1860 edition dealt with slavery in a surprisingly muted way. It is not that Whitman ignored slavery; much of his poetry called for overturning this hierarchy as well: "Let the slaves be masters! Let the masters, become slaves," "I say man shall not hold property in man. . . ." And he often empathized intimately with slaves, "I am the hounded slave . . . . I wince at the bite of the dogs."[111] Throughout the first two editions, slaves appeared in contexts that presented little question as to Whitman's opinion: when he portrayed a slave auction, he described the impossibility of setting a price on a human being; when a slave watched the sale of his wife, Whitman spoke as the enraged slave himself; during a scene that echoed Anthony Burns's forced return to Virginia in 1854, Whitman saw the ghostly return of George III in the "parade" of federal marshals and their captive.[112] However, Whitman presented slavery in ways that made it difficult to determine what he proposed to do, specifically, about it. Like the resolution to the sectional crisis, the end of slavery, for Whitman, seemed a gradual and natural outgrowth of his broader revelations about the nobility of the self and the unity of creation: slavery would eventually die out along with other outmoded forms of hierarchy simply by natural progressive evolution.

Unlike the first two editions, the 1860 edition problematically opened spaces for the slaveholding South in

Whitman's idealized republic, as in this example from "Chants Democratic":

> In Tennessee and Kentucky, slaves busy in the coalings, at the forge, by the furnace-blaze, or at the corn-shucking; . . .[113]

Though structurally similar to many of Whitman's pictorial tabulations of the nation, this addition to the 1860 *Leaves* portrayed, for the first time, slaves-as-slaves in the economy that maintained their bondage. Compared to a similar scene from the first edition (repeated in the second and third), "The woollypates hoe in the sugarfield, the overseer views them from his saddle,"[114] Whitman's new scene of slaves-as-slaves was strangely neutral. Though "woollypates" sounds more distinctly racist, Whitman in the earlier scene portrayed the oppression slaves endured by placing the overseer "in his saddle." On the other hand, when presenting enslaved blacksmiths and farm workers in the 1860 edition, Whitman offered no recognition of their oppression. In the first and second editions, the poet regarded slavery as an aberration on American soil; African Americans populated the first two editions, but when identified as slaves, they acted against the institution, as runaways, as victims, as noble in spite of their status. Whitman broadened his slave imagery in the 1860 edition: whereas he identified free workers by their occupations (carpenters, pilots, printers, machinists), he identified blacksmiths and farm workers in the passage above by their status as slaves.

Another passage in "Chants Democratic" also expressed the subtle shift in Whitman's portrayal of slaves:

> In Virginia, the planter's son returning after a long
> absence, joyfully welcomed and kissed by the
> aged mulatto nurse; . . .[115]

Here, the planter's son received a loving welcome from
his mulatto nurse who might, by implication, also be
the boy's aunt (the "aged" nurse is a "mulatto," so she
is presumably the daughter of the planter's father and
thus the planter's half-sister). Whitman probably in-
tended this disturbing moral complexity: the love for a
returning son resonates, but the nurse's status and her
unspoken mixed parentage lend it a troubling tinge.
Whitman had imbued maternal love with moral com-
plexity before:

> The lunatic is carried at last to the asylum a
> confirmed case,
> He will never sleep any more as he did in the cot in
> his mother's bedroom; . . .[116]

But in this second example, the passage elicited a senti-
mental and perhaps resigned wistfulness. On the other
hand, the example of the mulatto nurse and the "son" that
she loved demands a much more ambivalent reaction:
Was this expression of love debased by circumstance?
Did love transcend oppression? Or perhaps even dull
it? Further moral complications arose when Whitman
situated these examples within his older celebrations
of African American dignity and antipathy toward the
institution of slavery. By complicating slavery's moral
status, Whitman opened up troubling spaces between
his empathy for African Americans, his enmity toward
slavery, and his few romanticized scenes of the antebel-
lum South.[117] Perhaps in an attempt to make his book

universally American on the eve of the Civil War, Whitman meant to offer a nuanced place for slavery. Perhaps he believed that when readers followed him to a "new world," slavery and the debates that surrounded it would naturally fall away. Perhaps he thought that with enough words, *Leaves of Grass* could unite the nation, even if it meant muting his distaste for the South's slave economy. But words were not enough. In a little over a year, the nation fought the first battles of the Civil War, and events after 1860 forced the nation to face slavery and its legacy more squarely, monumentally, and dreadfully than Whitman did in his poems of the Many in One. In many ways, the new American bible that Whitman had labored so hard to bring to fruition was quickly outmoded once the war began. The book he hoped would preserve Union was one of the many victims of sectional division that turned more violent than anyone at the time could have imagined.

The 1860 edition of *Leaves of Grass* had a promising beginning: it aroused the usual mix of positive and negative reviews, and around two thousand copies were printed and one thousand sold before Thayer and Eldridge went bankrupt in December 1860.[118] Many critics came around to Whitman's image of himself and accepted his persona as "one of the roughs" who made the "most spiritual poems." Moncure D. Conway, in the transcendentalist periodical the *Dial*, claimed "Walt Whitman has set the pulses of America to music" with his "utterances of New York City, of the prairies, of the Ohio and Mississippi." Conway also noted that the frontispiece showed Whitman "Better dressed than we ever expected to see him."[119] A reviewer from the *Lon-*

*don Review*, perhaps unfamiliar with Whitman's image in the first and second editions, captured the essence of the new frontispiece, "his hair has been allowed to grow in an unkempt fashion . . . his eyes look at you sleepily and sensually." The reviewer also gleaned the religious cues of the third edition and placed the poet within the context of other American religious innovators, "such people as the Mormons."[120] The *New York Times* called much of Whitman's writing "completely . . . repulsive" but admitted "it would be unjust to deny . . . evidences of remarkable power which are . . . in this work."[121] The *London Sunday Times* claimed that Whitman proved "destined to hold a prominent position in American literature," and summarized Whitman's topics in terms he would appreciate: "the apotheosis of the flesh, the exaltation of states [of] life, and the promotion of comradeship."[122] William O'Connor, twelve years Whitman's junior and coiner of Whitman's "Good Grey Poet" persona, met the poet at Thayer and Eldridge's offices in Boston and claimed "all the young men & women are in love with him."[123] The Whitman we know—boisterous, barbaric, and benevolent—appeared full-grown in the third edition of *Leaves of Grass*. Though his revelations of the Many in One failed to save his country in crisis, his transcendent longings in familiar American packaging made a book that contemporaries found inspiring, controversial, erotic, and outrageous. On these terms, the book still appeals to us today, and, 150 years after its first publication, still teaches, challenges, and inspires. Whitman's new bible insisted that readers do their own part to bring it alive. That is as true in the twenty-first century as it was in 1860.

**NOTES**

1. Horace Traubel, *With Walt Whitman in Camden*, vols. 1–3 (New York: Rowman and Littlefield, 1961), I, 280. Whitman published editions of *Leaves of Grass* in 1855, 1856, 1860, 1867, 1871–1872, and 1881–1882; he added "annexes" to the book and published an extended version of the 1881–1882 edition in 1891–1892.

2. Walt Whitman, *Leaves of Grass: Facsimile Edition of the 1860 Text*, Roy Harvey Pearce, ed. (Ithaca, New York: Cornell University Press, 1961), xxiii, l.

3. Walt Whitman, *Leaves of Grass* (Boston: Thayer and Eldridge, 1860), 346.

4. *Leaves of Grass* (1860), 23, 27.

5. "greatest poem," *Leaves of Grass* (1855), iii; "New Bible," Walt Whitman, *Notebooks and Unpublished Prose Manuscripts*, Edward F. Grier, ed. 6 vols. (New York: New York University Press, 1984), I: 353, quoted in Michael Robertson, *Worshipping Walt: The Whitman Disciples* (Princeton, New Jersey: Princeton University Press, 2008), 16; "handsome little book," Traubel, *With Walt Whitman in Camden*, II: 175 (*The Enchiridion* or "Manual" is a collection of aphorisms by the Roman Stoic philosopher, Epictetus); "referee" and "arbiter," *Leaves of Grass* (1855), iv.

6. Other scholars have classified the 1860 edition in less pragmatic terms as a kind of democratic utopia. See Rosemary Graham,"Solving 'All the Problems of Freedom': The Case of the 1860 *Leaves of Grass*," *American Transcendental Quarterly* 7 (1993): 5–23.

7. *Leaves of Grass* (1855), xii.

8. When the *Democratic Review* criticized Charles Dickens's fiction during the author's visit to New York City in 1842, Whitman reprinted the editorial's claim that "there are no such characters [as in Dickens's stories] in human nature," and asked, "Is the Review sure that 'no such characters exist in the world, or in nature,' as Dickens' villains?" *New York Aurora*, April 2, 1842, Herbert Bergman, et al., *The Collected Writings of Walt Whitman: The Journalism*, vol. 1 (New York: Peter Lang Publishing, 1998), 92.

9. From the Boston *Intelligencer*, May 3, 1856, reprinted in *Leaves of Grass* (1856), 384.

10. *Leaves of Grass* (1856), 346. See Edward Whitley, "Present-

ing Walt Whitman: 'Leaves-Droppings as Paratext,'" *Walt Whitman Quarterly Review* 19 (Summer 2001): 1–17.

11. Ralph Waldo Emerson, letter to Walt Whitman dated July 21, 1855, published in *Leaves of Grass* (1856), 345.

12. Bronson Alcott, *The Journals of Bronson Alcott*, Odell Shepard, ed. (Boston: Little, Brown and Company, 1938), quoted in Loving, 225–26; Thoreau continued in the same letter to Harrison Blake, November 19, 1856, "I am still somewhat in a quandary about him—feel that he is essentially strange to me. . . .", Henry David Thoreau, *The Writings of Henry David Thoreau*, ed. F. B. Sanborn (New York: Houghton Mifflin, 1894).

13. Traubel, III: 403.

14. Whitman quoted by Anne Gilchrist in *Anne Gilchrist: Her Life and Writings* (London: Unwin, 1897), 237.

15. Christine Stansell, "Whitman at Pfaff's: Commercial Culture, Literary Life and New York Bohemia at Mid-Century," *Walt Whitman Quarterly Review* 10 (Winter 1993): 109.

16. Paul Zweig, *Walt Whitman: The Making of the Poet* (New York: Basic Books, 1984), 263. Also see David Haven Blake, *Walt Whitman and the Culture of American Celebrity* (New Haven: Yale University Press, 2006).

17. See Amanda Gailey, "Walt Whitman and the King of Bohemia: The Poet in the Saturday Press," *Walt Whitman Quarterly Review* 25 (Spring 2008): 143–66.

18. Loving, 237–38.

19. *Leaves of Grass* (1856), 357.

20. Whitman later claimed of sales of his first edition, "I doubt if even ten were sold—even one," Traubel, III: 116.

21. Walt Whitman, *Notebooks and Unpublished Prose Manuscripts*, Edward F. Grier, I: 167, quoted in Reynolds, *Walt Whitman's America*, 349.

22. Rollo Silver, "Seven Letters of Walt Whitman," *American Literature*, VII (1935), 76–78; quoted in Fredson Bowers, *Whitman's Manuscripts: Leaves of Grass (1860), A Parallel Text* (Chicago: University of Chicago Press, 1955), xxxvi.

23. Walt Whitman, *Notebooks and Unpublished Prose Manuscripts*, Edward F. Grier, ed., IV:1440, quoted in Reynolds, *Walt Whitman's America*, 367.

24. Whitman's editorials on lecturing found in *Brooklyn Daily Times*, December 12, 1857 and January 19, 1859, in Walt Whitman, *I Sit and Look Out: Editorials From the Brooklyn Daily Times*, Emory Holloway, Vernolian Schwarz, ed. (New York: Columbia University Press, 1932), 51–52.

25. John C. Calhoun, "The Clay Compromise Measures," March 4, 1850, *The World's Famous Orations*, vol. IX, William Jennings Bryan (New York: Funk and Wagnalls, 1906), 118.

26. Theodore Parker, *The Collected Works of Theodore Parker* (London: Trübner & Company, 1863), 98.

27. Parker, *The Collected Works*, 98.

28. A poem Whitman wrote in the early 1850s, eventually titled "A Boston Ballad," loosely recounts the arrest of Burns and appeared in the first edition of *Leaves of Grass* and all subsequent editions.

29. "Blood-Money," *New York Daily Tribune*, Supplement, March 22, 1850; "The House of Friends," *New York Daily Tribune*, June 14, 1850.

30. Paul C. Gutjahr, *An American Bible: A History of the Good Book in the United States, 1777–1880* (Stanford, California: Stanford University Press, 1999), 141.

31. See David Reynolds, *John Brown, Abolitionist: The Man Who Killed Slavery, Sparked the Civil War, and Seeded Civil Rights* (New York: Knopf, 2005).

32. Quoted in Reynolds, *John Brown, Abolitionist*, 395.

33. One scholar has Thayer and Eldridge noticing Whitman's poetry in 1855 but coming to the idea of publishing Whitman in 1860 only after Richard Hinton, one of Thayer and Eldridge's authors, viewed John Brown's corpse and noted to his publishers that Brown looked very similar to Whitman. Albert J. Von Frank, "The Secret World of Radical Publishers: The Case of Thayer and Eldridge of Boston," in James M. O'Toole and David Quigley, eds., *Boston's Histories* (Boston: Northeastern University Press, 2004), 52–70, quoted in Gailey.

34. James Redpath, *The Public Life of Captain John Brown* (Boston: Thayer and Eldridge, 1860), 8.

35. Whitman's politics leaned more toward working-class free-soilism, see "American Workingmen, versus Slavery," and "Verdict

of the Undaunted Democracy of the Empire State on Behalf of the Jeffersonian Ordinance," from September 1, 1847 and November 4, 1847, *Brooklyn Daily Eagle*, in Bergman et al., II: 318, 348.

36. Quoted in *Leaves of Grass*, Pearce, ed., viii.

37. *Leaves of Grass* (1855), 13.

38. "roughs," *Leaves of Grass* (1855), 29; "spiritual poems," *Leaves of Grass* (1860), 9.

39. This is the conversation recalled by Whitman almost twenty-five years later and related by Horace Traubel, III: 439.

40. *Brooklyn Daily Eagle*, October 21, 1846, Bergman, et al., II: 92.

41. The American Bible Society's production of clothbound bibles grew from 7 percent in the 1840s to 16 percent in the 1850s to 27 percent in the 1860s, Gutjahr, 192. Incidentally, Whitman's office at the *New York Aurora*, which he edited in 1842, was relatively close to the American Bible Society headquarters on Nassau Street.

42. Ibid., 143–75.

43. Edwin Burrows, Mike Wallace, *Gotham: A History of New York City to 1898* (Oxford: Oxford University Press, 1999), 628.

44. Gutjahr, 159.

45. Walt Whitman, *Notes and Unpublished Prose Manuscripts*, Edward F. Grier, ed., VI: 2046, quoted in W. C. Harris, "Whitman's *Leaves of Grass* and the Writing of a New American Bible," *Walt Whitman Quarterly Review* 16 (Winter/Spring 1999): 175. Harris also notes the importance of the "de-authorization of the King James Bible" and the desire of Americans to "reconstruct . . . relations on an . . . egalitarian basis" as the cultural trends that inspired Whitman to create a "New American Bible," 173.

46. I am indebted to W. C. Harris's interpretation of Whitman's ambivalent New American Religion (No Religion), "Whitman may adopt an ambivalent stance toward formalization . . . ; still, the new housing of religion . . . cannot escape its own creedal . . . status." "Whitman's *Leaves of Grass* and the Writing of a New American Bible," 175.

47. *Leaves of Grass* (1855), iii.

48. In *Leaves of Grass* (1856), 368. Viewed online at www .whitmanarchive.org (accessed August 14, 2008).

49. From Silver, quoted in Bowers, xxxvi. Whitman worked with Thayer and Eldridge to publish a long advertising pamphlet for the book that contained Emerson's letter, reviews, and other notices of *Leaves* and of Whitman; this pamphlet, called *Leaves of Grass Imprints*, was distributed for free by the publisher. While it was thus separate from the 1860 itself, the pamphlet nonetheless served much the same function as "Leaves-Droppings."

50. *New York Aurora*, April 9, 1842, Bergman, et al., I: 106.

51. Traubel, II: 445.

52. Traubel, VIII: 376.

53. Ibid., 525–26.

54. Ibid.

55. Graham also sees in "Proto-Leaf" the beginning of a "journey," 8.

56. From Alexander Pope's translation (published between 1715 and 1726). Whitman was familiar with this translation.

57. For a discussion of the "liberal, post-Christian" spiritually of the 1860 edition, see Robertson, 14–22.

58. "Proto-Leaf," 9–10. Subsequent citations to the third edition of *Leaves of Grass* will follow Whitman's arrangement: Cluster or Poem Title, Number (if applicable): Verse.

59. "Proto-Leaf," 19–22.

60. "Proto-Leaf," 10. Congress adopted this motto in 1782 for the Great Seal of the United States. Whitman may have adopted this idea from George Washington Cutter's poem "E Pluribus Unum": "By the bayonet trac'd at the midnight war, / On the fields where our glory was won; / Oh! perish the heart or the hand that would mar / Our motto of "MANY IN ONE." George Washington Cutter, *Buena Vista and Other Poems* (New York: Morgan & Overend, 1848), 38.

61. "Proto-Leaf," 28. David Kuebrich's *Minor Prophecy: Walt Whitman's New American Religion* (Bloomington: Indiana University Press, 1989) provides a thorough and compelling argument for Whitman's religiosity starting in his novel, *Franklin Evans* (1843) through the final edition of *Leaves of Grass* (1892).

62. David Reynolds, *Beneath the American Renaissance: The Subversive Imagination in the Age of Emerson and Melville* (Cambridge, Massachusetts: Harvard University Press, 1988), 15–17.

63. Frederick A. Ross, *Slavery Ordained of God* (Philadelphia: J. B. Lippincott Publishing, 1857), 6.

64. Ibid., 62–63.

65. Ibid., 64.

66. Charles Grandison Finney, "Guilt Modified by Ignorance—Anti-Slavery Duties," *The Oberlin Evangelist*, August 18, 1852.

67. Theodore Parker, *A Discourse of Matters Pertaining to Religion* (New York: Little, Brown and Company, 1859), 273. In this quote, Parker refers to Jeremiah 31:33, "After those days, saith the LORD, I will put my law in their inward parts, and write it in their hearts; and will be their God, and they shall be my people."

68. "Walt Whitman," 346.

69. Definition of "Atom" circa 1847 from *Oxford Universal English Dictionary* (Oxford: Oxford University Press, 1937), 117.

70. "Walt Whitman," 7.

71. "Walt Whitman," 21.

72. "Walt Whitman," 25–31.

73. "Walt Whitman," 87, 38.

74. "Walt Whitman," 44.

75. "Walt Whitman," 48.

76. "Walt Whitman," 69.

77. "Walt Whitman," 185.

78. Whitman probably drew from Emerson's *Nature* (1836), which, itself owed a debt to the theories of Emanuel Swedenberg (1688–1772). For a discussion of Swedenberg's influence on Emerson, see Philip Gura, *American Transcendentalism: A History* (New York: Hill and Wang, 2008), 93–94.

79. Walt Whitman, *Specimen Days in America* (London: W. Scott, 1887), 25.

80. Mary Ryan, *Civic Wars: Democracy and Public Life in the American City during the Nineteenth Century* (Berkeley: University of California Press, 1997), 84; Frederick Douglass, "The Meaning of July Fourth for the Negro" Speech at Rochester, New York, July 5, 1852, in *Frederick Douglass: Selected Speeches and Writings*, Philip S. Foner, Yuval Taylor, eds. (Chicago: Lawrence Hill Press, 2000), 188.

81. This persistent legend began with an essay by Ralph Adimari, "*Leaves of Grass*—First Edition," *American Book Collector* 5

(May–June 1934), 150–52, and was repeated by subsequent biographers and critics.

82. Finney, "Guilt Modified by Ignorance—Anti-Slavery Duties."

83. Ross, 104.

84. "Chants Democratic," Apostroph.

85. "Chants Democratic," 1:35 and "Chants Democratic," 1:21.

86. The seminal and perhaps still best history of nineteenth-century nativism is John Higham, *Strangers in the Land: Patterns of American Nativism 1860–1925* (New York: Atheneum, 1955). For an analysis of antebellum American nativism, see Jenny Franchot, *Roads to Rome: the Antebellum Protestant Encounter with Catholicism* (Berkeley: University of California Press, 1994).

87. For a more thorough analysis of the structure of "Chants Democratic," see Robin Hoople, "'Chants Democratic and Native American': A Neglected Sequence in the Growth of *Leaves of Grass," American Literature* 42:2 (May 1970), 181–96.

88. Hoople, 188.

89. "Leaves of Grass," 2:20–21.

90. Robert Chambers, *Vestiges of the Natural History of Creation* (London: George Routledge and Sons, 1887, originally published anonymously in 1844), 239.

91. Walt Whitman, *Brooklyn Daily Eagle*, May 4, 1847, August 20, 1846, in Bergman, et al., II: 263, 26. Also see Reynolds, *Walt Whitman's America*, 240–42.

92. Louis Agassiz, *Study of Natural History* (1847) quoted in "Science and Pseudoscience," Harold Aspiz, in *A Companion to Walt Whitman*, Donald Kummings, ed. (Oxford: Blackwell Publishing, 2006), 219.

93. Ross, 51. By "solid" and "unindented" Ross means landlocked.

94. Ibid., 30.

95. Finney, "Guilt Modified by Ignorance"; Parker, "The Effect of Slavery on the American People."

96. See Aspiz, 227–28. Johann Gaspar Spurzheim, *Phrenology, Or, The Doctrine of the Mind; and of the Relations Between Its Manifestations and the Body* (London: Charles Knight, 1825).

97. Aspiz, 228.

98. O. S. Fowler, L. N. Fowler, *The Illustrated Self-Instructor in Phrenology and Physiology with One Hundred Engravings and a Chart of the Character* (New York: Fowler and Wells Publishers, 1857), 10.

99. Ibid., 51–52.

100. "Chants Democratic," 1:28; "Chants Democratic," 16; "Unnamed Lands," 6.

101. "Enfans d'Adam," 4:2, 8.

102. In the chapter "'In Loftiest Spheres': Whitman's Visionary Feminism," Vivian Pollak argues that Whitman disrupts "his own claims to empower women by . . . reaffirm[ing] . . . the mid-nineteenth century cult of the mother," *Breaking Bounds: Whitman and American Cultural Studies*, Betsy Erkkila, Jay Grossman, eds. (Oxford: Oxford University Press, 1996), 92. In reaction to the birth of Horace Traubel's nephew, Whitman said, "Your sister has done the proudest of proud things: she has been a mother—she is a mother: she submitted her body to its noblest office. I look at . . . the childless woman. . . . They are not quite full—not quite entire . . . the woman who has discredited the animal want, the eager physical hunger, the wish of that which though we will not allow it to be freely spoken of . . . still . . . advances the horizon of discovery," Traubel, III: 452.

103. O. S. Fowler, L. N. Fowler, 56–58.

104. "Proto-Leaf," 36, 64; "Poem of the Open Road," 25; "Calamus," 6; "Thoughts," 7; "So Long!" 12; regarding Calamus and adhesiveness, see David Reynolds, *Walt Whitman's America*, 391. In Greek mythology two youths, Calamus (Kalamos) and his lover, Karpos, swam the Meander River. When Karpos drowned, Kalamos, in his grief, drowned himself and was transformed into a reed, which sounded his lamentations when the wind blew through it.

105. Jonathan Ned Katz, *Love Stories: Sex Between Men before Homosexuality* (Chicago: University of Chicago Press, 2001), especially 3–45.

106. See Reynolds, *Walt Whitman's America*, 391–93.

107. "Calamus," 5:9; 10; 7; 19:2; 29; 32, etc.

108. "Calamus," 5:5–8.

109. Michael Sowder provides a useful analysis of the transfor-

mation of Whitman's twelve-poem series "Live Oak With Moss" into the "Calumus" cluster, 127–35. Also see Bowers, lxiv.

110. See Martin Klammer, *Whitman, Slavery, and the Emergence of "Leaves of Grass"* (University Park, Pennsylvania: Pennsylvania State University Press), 141–48.

111. See, for example, "Chants Democratic," 5; "Says," 3; *Leaves of Grass* (1855), 39.

112. *Leaves of Grass* (1855), 81, 74, 89.

113. "Chants Democratic," 4.

114. *Leaves of Grass* (1855), 22.

115. "Chants Democratic," 4.

116. *Leaves of Grass* (1855), 21.

117. Rosemary Graham also notes that in these examples Whitman "compromise[d] the most radical tenants of his democratic philosophy-religion" in the 1860 edition, 16. Also see M. Wynn Thomas, *Transatlantic Connections: Whitman U.S., Whitman, U.K.* (Iowa City: University of Iowa Press, 2005) where he discusses Whitman's "Longings for Home."

118. Eiselein, viewed online at www.whitmanarchive.org (accessed September 2008). The 1860 edition had an odd and surprising afterlife. After Thayer and Eldridge went bankrupt, the plates were auctioned and eventually bought by the unscrupulous publisher, Richard Worthington, who reprinted the edition several times and sold thousands of pirated copies in the 1880s, causing Whitman and his publishers many headaches. The reprinting of the 1860 concerned Whitman and his last publisher, David McKay, especially because pirated copies were sold for less than the 1881 edition. The story of these plates and Worthington's unethical republication of the 1860 edition is most compactly told by Edwin Haviland Miller in a footnote in *The Correspondence*, vol. 3, 196–97.

119. Moncure D. Conway, "[Review of *Leaves of Grass* 1860–61]," the *Dial* (August 1860), 517–19, viewed online at www .whitmanarchive.org (accessed August 28, 2008).

120. [Anonymous], "Verse—and Worse," the *London Review* (October 13, 1860): 353–54, viewed online at www.whitman archive.org (accessed August 28, 2008).

121. [Anonymous], "The New Poets," the *New York Times* (May

19, 1860), [1], viewed online at www.whitmanarchive.org (accessed August 28, 2008).

122. [Anonymous], "Walt Whitman's Works," the *London Sunday Times* (March 3, 1867): 7, viewed online at www.whitman archive.org (accessed August 28, 2008).

123. Quoted in Robertson, 25.

# Leaves of GRASS.

Boston,

Thayer and Eldridge,

Year 85 of The States.

(1860-61)

# *CONTENTS.*

(iii)

iv            CONTENTS.

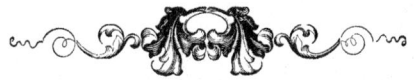

# PROTO-LEAF.

1. FREE, fresh, savage,
   Fluent, luxuriant, self-content, fond of persons and
       places,
   Fond of fish-shape Paumanok, where I was born,
   Fond of the sea — lusty-begotten and various,
   Boy of the Mannahatta, the city of ships, my city,
   Or raised inland, or of the south savannas,
   Or full-breath'd on Californian air, or Texan or
       Cuban air,
   Tallying, vocalizing all — resounding Niagara —
       resounding Missouri,
   Or rude in my home in Kanuck woods,
   Or wandering and hunting, my drink water, my diet
       meat,
   Or withdrawn to muse and meditate in some deep
       recess,
   Far from the clank of crowds, an interval passing,
       rapt and happy,
   Stars, vapor, snow, the hills, rocks, the Fifth Month
       flowers, my amaze, my love,

1*

Aware of the buffalo, the peace-herds, the bull, strong-breasted and hairy,
Aware of the mocking-bird of the wilds at day-break,
Solitary, singing in the west, I strike up for a new world.

2. Victory, union, faith, identity, time, the Soul, your-self, the present and future lands, the indisso-luble compacts, riches, mystery, eternal progress, the kosmos, and the modern reports.

3. This then is life,
Here is what has come to the surface after so many throes and convulsions.

4. How curious! How real!
Underfoot the divine soil — Overhead the sun.

5. See, revolving,
The globe— the ancestor-continents, away, grouped together,
The present and future continents, north and south, with the isthmus between.

6. See, vast, trackless spaces,
As in a dream, they change, they swiftly fill,
Countless masses debouch upon them,
They are now covered with the foremost people, arts, institutions known.

7. See projected, through time,
For me, an audience interminable.

8. With firm and regular step they wend — they never
   stop,
   Successions of men, Americanos, a hundred millions,
   One generation playing its part and passing on,
   And another generation playing its part and passing
   on in its turn,
   With faces turned sideways or backward toward me
   to listen,
   With eyes retrospective toward me.

9. Americanos! Masters!
   Marches humanitarian! Foremost!
   Century marches! Libertad! Masses!
   For you a programme of chants.

10. Chants of the prairies,
    Chants of the long-running Mississippi,
    Chants of Ohio, Indiana, Illinois, Wisconsin, Iowa,
    and Minnesota,
    Inland chants — chants of Kanzas,
    Chants away down to Mexico, and up north to
    Oregon — Kanadian chants,
    Chants of teeming and turbulent cities — chants of
    mechanics,
    Yankee chants — Pennsylvanian chants — chants of
    Kentucky and Tennessee,
    Chants of dim-lit mines — chants of mountain-tops,
    Chants of sailors — chants of the Eastern Sea and the
    Western Sea,
    Chants of the Mannahatta, the place of my dearest
    love, the place surrounded by hurried and
    sparkling currents,
    Health chants — joy chants — robust chants of young
    men,

Chants inclusive — wide reverberating chants,
Chants of the Many In One.

11. In the Year 80 of The States,
My tongue, every atom of my blood, formed from
this soil, this air,
Born here of parents born here,
From parents the same, and their parents' parents
the same,
I, now thirty-six years old, in perfect health,
begin,
Hoping to cease not till death.

12. Creeds and schools in abeyance,
Retiring back a while, sufficed at what they are, but
never forgotten,
With accumulations, now coming forward in front,
Arrived again, I harbor, for good or bad — I permit
to speak,
Nature, without check, with original energy.

13. Take my leaves, America!
Make welcome for them everywhere, for they are
your own offspring;
Surround them, East and West! for they would
surround you,
And you precedents! connect lovingly with them, for
they connect lovingly with you.

14. I conned old times,
I sat studying at the feet of the great masters;
Now, if eligible, O that the great masters might
return and study me!

15. In the name of These States, shall I scorn the
antique?
Why These are the children of the antique, to
justify it.

16. Dead poets, philosophs, priests,
Martyrs, artists, inventors, governments long since,
Language-shapers, on other shores,
Nations once powerful, now reduced, withdrawn, or
desolate,
I dare not proceed till I respectfully credit what you
have left, wafted hither,
I have perused it — I own it is admirable,
I think nothing can ever be greater — Nothing can
ever deserve more than it deserves ;
I regard it all intently a long while,
Then take my place for good with my own day and
race here.

17. Here lands female and male,
Here the heirship and heiress-ship of the world —
Here the flame of materials,
Here Spirituality, the translatress, the openly-avowed,
The ever-tending, the finale of visible forms,
The satisfier, after due long-waiting, now advancing,
Yes, here comes the mistress, the Soul.

18. The Soul!
Forever and forever — Longer than soil is brown and
solid — Longer than water ebbs and flows.

19. I will make the poems of materials, for I think they
are to be the most spiritual poems,

And I will make the poems of my body and of
mortality,
For I think I shall then supply myself with the
poems of my Soul and of immortality.

20. I will make a song for These States, that no one
State may under any circumstances be subjected
to another State,
And I will make a song that there shall be comity by
day and by night between all The States, and
between any two of them,
And I will make a song of the organic bargains of
These States — And a shrill song of curses on
him who would dissever the Union;
And I will make a song for the ears of the President,
full of weapons with menacing points,
And behind the weapons countless dissatisfied faces.

21. I will acknowledge contemporary lands,
I will trail the whole geography of the globe, and
salute courteously every city large and small;
And employments! I will put in my poems, that
with you is heroism, upon land and sea — And I
will report all heroism from an American point
of view;
And sexual organs and acts! do you concentrate in
me — For I am determined to tell you with
courageous clear voice, to prove you illustrious.

22. I will sing the song of companionship,
I will show what alone must compact These,
I believe These are to found their own ideal of manly
love, indicating it in me;

I will therefore let flame from me the burning fires
    that were threatening to consume me,
I will lift what has too long kept down those smoul-
    dering fires,
I will give them complete abandonment,
I will write the evangel-poem of comrades and
    of love,
(For who but I should understand love, with all its
    sorrow and joy?
And who but I should be the poet of comrades?)

23. I am the credulous man of qualities, ages, races,
I advance from the people en-masse in their own
    spirit,
Here is what sings unrestricted faith.

24. Omnes! Omnes!
Let others ignore what they may,
I make the poem of evil also — I commemorate that
    part also,
I am myself just as much evil as good — And I say
    there is in fact no evil,
Or if there is, I say it is just as important to you, to
    the earth, or to me, as anything else.

25. I too, following many, and followed by many, inau-
    gurate a Religion — I too go to the wars,
It may be I am destined to utter the loudest cries
    thereof, the conqueror's shouts,
They may rise from me yet, and soar above every
    thing.

26. Each is not for its own sake,
I say the whole earth, and all the stars in the sky, are
    for Religion's sake.

27. I say no man has ever been half devout enough,
    None has ever adored or worship'd half enough,
    None has begun to think how divine he himself is,
        and how certain the future is.

28. I specifically announce that the real and perma-
        nent grandeur of These States must be their
        Religion,
    Otherwise there is no real and permanent grandeur.

29. What are you doing, young man ?
    Are you so earnest — so given up to literature,
        science, art, amours ?
    These ostensible realities, materials, points ?
    Your ambition or business, whatever it may be ?

30. It is well — Against such I say not a word — I am
        their poet also ;
    But behold ! such swiftly subside — burnt up for
        Religion's sake,
    For not all matter is fuel to heat, impalpable flame,
        the essential life of the earth,
    Any more than such are to Religion.

31. What do you seek, so pensive and silent ?
    What do you need, comrade ?
    Mon cher ! do you think it is love ?

32. Proceed, comrade,
    It is a painful thing to love a man or woman to
        excess — yet it satisfies — it is great,
    But there is something else very great — it makes the
        whole coincide,

It, magnificent, beyond materials, with continuous
hands, sweeps and provides for all.

33. O I see the following poems are indeed to drop in the
earth the germs of a greater Religion.

34. My comrade!
For you, to share with me, two greatnesses — And a
third one, rising inclusive and more resplendent,
The greatness of Love and Democracy — and the
greatness of Religion.

35. Melange mine!
Mysterious ocean where the streams empty,
Prophetic spirit of materials shifting and flickering
around me,
Wondrous interplay between the seen and unseen,
Living beings, identities, now doubtless near us, in
the air, that we know not of,
Extasy everywhere touching and thrilling me,
Contact daily and hourly that will not release me,
These selecting — These, in hints, demanded of me.

36. Not he, adhesive, kissing me so long with his daily
kiss,
Has winded and twisted around me that which holds
me to him,
Any more than I am held to the heavens, to the
spiritual world,
And to the identities of the Gods, my unknown
lovers,
After what they have done to me, suggesting
such themes.

2

37. O such themes! Equalities!
O amazement of things! O divine average!
O warblings under the sun — ushered, as now, or at
noon, or setting!
O strain, musical, flowing through ages — now
reaching hither,
I take to your reckless and composite chords — I
add to them, and cheerfully pass them forward.

38. As I have walked in Alabama my morning walk,
I have seen where the she-bird, the mocking-bird, sat
on her nest in the briers, hatching her brood.

39. I have seen the he-bird also,
I have paused to hear him, near at hand, inflating his
throat, and joyfully singing.

40. And while I paused, it came to me that what he
really sang for was not there only,
Nor for his mate nor himself only, nor all sent back
by the echoes,
But subtle, clandestine, away beyond,
A charge transmitted, and gift occult, for those
being born.

41. Democracy!
Near at hand to you a throat is now inflating itself
and joyfully singing.

42. Ma femme!
For the brood beyond us and of us,
For those who belong here, and those to come,

I, exultant, to be ready for them, will now shake out
carols stronger and haughtier than have ever yet
been heard upon the earth.


43. I will make the songs of passions, to give them
their way,
And your songs, offenders — for I scan you with
kindred eyes, and carry you with me the same
as any.


44. I will make the true poem of riches,
Namely, to earn for the body and the mind, what
adheres, and goes forward, and is not dropt by
death.


45. I will effuse egotism, and show it underlying all —
And I will be the bard of Personality;
And I will show of male and female that either is but
the equal of the other,
And I will show that there is no imperfection in male
or female, or in the earth, or in the present —
and can be none in the future,
And I will show that whatever happens to anybody, it
may be turned to beautiful results — And I will
show that nothing can happen more beautiful
than death;
And I will thread a thread through my poems that no
one thing in the universe is inferior to another
thing,
And that all the things of the universe are perfect
miracles, each as profound as any.

46. I will not make poems with reference to parts,
    But I will make leaves, poems, poemets, songs, says,
    thoughts, with reference to ensemble;
    And I will not sing with reference to a day, but with
    reference to all days,
    And I will not make a poem, nor the least part of
    a poem, but has reference to the Soul,
    Because, having looked at the objects of the universe,
    I find there is no one, nor any particle of one,
    but has reference to the Soul.

47. Was somebody asking to see the Soul?
    See! your own shape and countenance — persons,
    substances, beasts, the trees, the running rivers,
    the rocks and sands.

48. All hold spiritual joys, and afterward loosen them,
    How can the real body ever die, and be buried?

49. Of your real body, and any man's or woman's real
    body, item for item, it will elude the hands of
    the corpse-cleaners, and pass to fitting spheres,
    carrying what has accrued to it from the moment
    of birth to the moment of death.

50. Not the types set up by the printer return their im-
    pression, the meaning, the main concern, any
    more than a man's substance and life, or a
    woman's substance and life, return in the body
    and the Soul, indifferently before death and
    after death.

51. Behold! the body includes and is the meaning, the main concern — and includes and is the Soul ;
Whoever you are! how superb and how divine is your body, or any part of it.

52. Whoever you are! to you endless announcements.

53. Daughter of the lands, did you wait for your poet ?
Did you wait for one with a flowing mouth and indicative hand ?

54. Toward the male of The States, and toward the female of The States,
Toward the President, the Congress, the diverse Governors, the new Judiciary,
Live words — words to the lands.

55. O the lands!
Lands scorning invaders! Interlinked, food-yielding lands!
Land of coal and iron! Land of gold! Lands of cotton, sugar, rice!
Odorous and sunny land! Floridian land!
Land of the spinal river, the Mississippi! Land of the Alleghanies! Ohio's land!
Land of wheat, beef, pork! Land of wool and hemp! Land of the potato, the apple, and the grape!
Land of the pastoral plains, the grass-fields of the world! Land of those sweet-aired interminable plateaus! Land there of the herd, the garden, the healthy house of adobie! Land there of rapt thought, and of the realization of the stars ! Land of simple, holy, untamed lives !

2 *

Lands where the northwest Columbia winds, and
    where the southwest Colorado winds!
Land of the Chesapeake! Land of the Delaware!
Land of Ontario, Erie, Huron, Michigan!
Land of the Old Thirteen! Massachusetts land!
    Land of Vermont and Connecticut!
Land of many oceans! Land of sierras and peaks!
Land of boatmen and sailors! Fishermen's land!
Inextricable lands! the clutched together! the
    passionate lovers!
The side by side! the elder and younger brothers!
    the bony-limbed!
The great women's land! the feminine! the ex-
    perienced sisters and the inexperienced sisters!
Far breath'd land! Arctic braced! Mexican breezed!
    the diverse! the compact!
The Pennsylvanian! the Virginian! the double
    Carolinian!
O all and each well-loved by me! my intrepid nations!
    O I cannot be discharged from you!
O Death! O for all that, I am yet of you, unseen,
    this hour, with irrepressible love,
Walking New England, a friend, a traveller,
Splashing my bare feet in the edge of the summer
    ripples, on Paumanok's sands,
Crossing the prairies — dwelling again in Chicago —
    dwelling in many towns,
Observing shows, births, improvements, structures,
    arts,
Listening to the orators and the oratresses in public
    halls,
Of and through The States, as during life — each
    man and woman my neighbor,

The Louisianian, the Georgian, as near to me, and I
as near to him and her,

The Mississippian and Arkansian — the woman and
man of Utah, Dakotah, Nebraska, yet with me
— and I yet with any of them,

Yet upon the plains west of the spinal river — yet
in my house of adobie,

Yet returning eastward — yet in the Sea-Side State,
or in Maryland,

Yet a child of the North — yet Kanadian, cheerily
braving the winter — the snow and ice welcome
to me,

Yet a true son either of Maine, or of the Granite
State, or of the Narragansett Bay State, or of
the Empire State,

Yet sailing to other shores to annex the same — yet
welcoming every new brother,

Hereby applying these leaves to the new ones, from
the hour they unite with the old ones,

Coming among the new ones myself, to be their
companion — coming personally to you now,

Enjoining you to acts, characters, spectacles, with
me.

56. With me, with firm holding — yet haste, haste on.

57. For your life, adhere to me,

Of all the men of the earth, I only can unloose you
and toughen you,

I may have to be persuaded many times before I
consent to give myself to you — but what of
that ?

Must not Nature be persuaded many times ?

58. No dainty dolce affettuoso I ;
    Bearded, sunburnt, gray-necked, forbidding, I have
        arrived,
    To be wrestled with as I pass, for the solid prizes
        of the universe,
    For such I afford whoever can persevere to win them.

59. On my way a moment I pause,
    Here for you ! And here for America !
    Still the Present I raise aloft — Still the Future of
        The States I harbinge, glad and sublime,
    And for the Past I pronounce what the air holds of
        the red aborigines.

60. The red aborigines !
    Leaving natural breaths, sounds of rain and winds,
        calls as of birds and animals in the woods,
        syllabled to us for names,
    Okonee, Koosa, Ottawa, Monongahela, Sauk, Natchez,
        Chattahoochee, Kaqueta, Oronoco.
    Wabash, Miami, Saginaw, Chippewa, Oshkosh, Walla-
        Walla,
    Leaving such to The States, they melt, they depart,
        charging the water and the land with names.

61. O expanding and swift !   O henceforth,
    Elements, breeds, adjustments, turbulent, quick, and
        audacious,
    A world primal again — Vistas of glory, incessant
        and branching,
    A new race, dominating previous ones, and grander
        far,
    New politics — New literatures and religions — New
        inventions and arts.

62. These! These, my voice announcing — I will sleep
no more, but arise ;

You oceans that have been calm within me! how
I feel you, fathomless, stirring, preparing
unprecedented waves and storms.

63. See! steamers steaming through my poems!

See, in my poems immigrants continually coming
and landing ;

See, in arriere, the wigwam, the trail, the hunter's
hut, the flat-boat, the maize-leaf, the claim, the
rude fence, and the backwoods village ;

See, on the one side the Western Sea, and on the
other side the Eastern Sea, how they advance
and retreat upon my poems, as upon their own
shores ;

See, pastures and forests in my poems — See, animals,
wild and tame — See, beyond the Kanzas, count-
less herds of buffalo, feeding òn short curly
grass ;

See, in my poems, old and new cities, solid, vast,
inland, with paved streets, with iron and stone
edifices, and ceaseless vehicles, and commerce ;

See the populace, millions upon millions, handsome,
tall, muscular, both sexes, clothed in easy and
dignified clothes — teaching, commanding, mar-
rying, generating, equally electing and elective ;

See, the many-cylinder'd steam printing-press — See,
the electric telegraph — See, the strong and
quick locomotive, as it departs, panting, blowing
the steam-whistle ;

See, ploughmen, ploughing farms — See, miners,
digging mines — See, the numberless factories ;

See, mechanics, busy at their benches, with tools —
    See from among them, superior judges, philo-
    sophs, Presidents, emerge, dressed in working
    dresses;
See, lounging through the shops and fields of The
    States, me, well-beloved, close-held by day and
    night,
Hear the loud echo of my songs there! Read the
    hints come at last.


64. O my comrade!
    O you and me at last — and us two only;
    O power, liberty, eternity at last!
    O to be relieved of distinctions! to make as much
        of vices as virtues!
    O to level occupations and the sexes! O to bring
        all to common ground! O adhesiveness!
    O the pensive aching to be together — you know not
        why, and I know not why.


65. O a word to clear one's path ahead endlessly!
    O something extatic and undemonstrable! O music
        wild!
    O now I triumph — and you shall also;
    O hand in hand — O wholesome pleasure — O one
        more desirer and lover,
    O haste, firm holding — haste, haste on, with me.

# WALT WHITMAN.

1. I CELEBRATE myself,
   And what I assume you shall assume,
   For every atom belonging to me, as good belongs
   to you.

2. I loafe and invite my Soul,
   I lean and loafe at my ease, observing a spear of
   summer grass.

3. Houses and rooms are full of perfumes — the shelves
   are crowded with perfumes,
   I breathe the fragrance myself, and know it and
   like it,
   The distillation would intoxicate me also, but I shall
   not let it.

4. The atmosphere is not a perfume — it has no taste of
   the distillation, it is odorless,
   It is for my mouth forever — I am in love with it,
   I will go to the bank by the wood, and become
   undisguised and naked,
   I am mad for it to be in contact with me.

5. The smoke of my own breath,

    Echoes, ripples, buzzed whispers, love-root, silk-
        thread, crotch and vine,

    My respiration and inspiration, the beating of my
        heart, the passing of blood and air through my
        lungs,

    The sniff of green leaves and dry leaves, and of the
        shore, and dark-colored sea-rocks, and of hay in
        the barn,

    The sound of the belched words of my voice, words
        loosed to the eddies of the wind,

    A few light kisses, a few embraces, a reaching around
        of arms,

    The play of shine and shade on the trees as the supple
        boughs wag,

    The delight alone, or in the rush of the streets, or
        along the fields and hill-sides,

    The feeling of health, the full-noon trill, the song of
        me rising from bed and meeting the sun.

6. Have you reckoned a thousand acres much ? Have
        you reckoned the earth much ?

    Have you practised so long to learn to read ?

    Have you felt so proud to get at the meaning of
        poems ?

7. Stop this day and night with me, and you shall pos-
        sess the origin of all poems,

    You shall possess the good of the earth and sun —
        there are millions of suns left,

    You shall no longer take things at second or third
        hand, nor look through the eyes of the dead,
        nor feed on the spectres in books,

You shall not look through my eyes either, nor take
  things from me,
You shall listen to all sides, and filter them from
  yourself.

8. I have heard what the talkers were talking, the talk
  of the beginning and the end,
But I do not talk of the beginning or the end.

9. There was never any more inception than there is
  now,
Nor any more youth or age than there is now,
And will never be any more perfection than there is
  now,
Nor any more heaven or hell than there is now.

10. Urge, and urge, and urge,
Always the procreant urge of the world.

11. Out of the dimness opposite equals advance — always
  substance and increase, always sex,
Always a knit of identity — always distinction —
  always a breed of life.

12. To elaborate is no avail — learned and unlearned
  feel that it is so.

13. Sure as the most certain sure, plumb in the uprights,
  well entretied, braced in the beams,
Stout as a horse, affectionate, haughty, electrical,
I and this mystery here we stand.

14. Clear and sweet is my Soul, and clear and sweet is
  all that is not my Soul.

15. Lack one lacks both, and the unseen is proved by the
    seen,
  Till that becomes unseen, and receives proof in its
    turn.

16. Showing the best, and dividing it from the worst, age
    vexes age,
  Knowing the perfect fitness and equanimity of things,
    while they discuss I am silent, and go bathe
    and admire myself.

17. Welcome is every organ and attribute of me, and of
    any man hearty and clean,
  Not an inch, nor a particle of an inch, is vile, and
    none shall be less familiar than the rest.

18. I am satisfied — I see, dance, laugh, sing;
  As the hugging and loving Bed-fellow sleeps at my
    side through the night, and withdraws at the
    peep of the day,
  And leaves for me baskets covered with white towels,
    swelling the house with their plenty,
  Shall I postpone my acceptation and realization, and
    scream at my eyes,
  That they turn from gazing after and down the road,
  And forthwith cipher and show me to a cent,
  Exactly the contents of one, and exactly the contents
    of two, and which is ahead?

19. Trippers and askers surround me,
  People I meet — the effect upon me of my early life,
    or the ward and city I live in, or the nation,

The latest news, discoveries, inventions, societies,
  authors old and new,
My dinner, dress, associates, looks, work, compliments,
  dues,
The real or fancied indifference of some man or
  woman I love,
The sickness of one of my folks, or of myself, or
  ill-doing, or loss or lack of money, or depressions
  or exaltations,
These come to me days and nights, and go from me
  again,
But they are not the Me myself.

20. Apart from the pulling and hauling stands what I am,
Stands amused, complacent, compassionating, idle,
  unitary,
Looks down, is erect, or bends an arm on an
  impalpable certain rest,
Looking with side-curved head, curious what will
  come next,
Both in and out of the game, and watching and
  wondering at it.

21. Backward I see in my own days where I sweated
  through fog with linguists and contenders,
I have no mockings or arguments — I witness and
  wait.

22. I believe in you, my Soul — the other I am must
  not abase itself to you,
And you must not be abased to the other.

23. Loafe with me on the grass — loose the stop from
  your throat,

Not words, not music or rhyme I want — not custom
   or lecture, not even the best,
Only the lull I like, the hum of your valved voice.


24. I mind how once we lay, such a transparent summer
      morning,
   How you settled your head athwart my hips, and
      gently turned over upon me,
   And parted the shirt from my bosom-bone, and
      plunged your tongue to my bare-stript heart,
   And reached till you felt my beard, and reached till
      you held my feet.


25. Swiftly arose and spread around me the peace and
      joy and knowledge that pass all the art and
      argument of the earth,
   And I know that the hand of God is the promise of
      my own,
   And I know that the spirit of God is the brother of
      my own,
   And that all the men ever born are also my brothers,
      and the women my sisters and lovers,
   And that a kelson of the creation is love,
   And limitless are leaves, stiff or drooping in the
      fields,
   And brown ants in the little wells beneath them,
   And mossy scabs of the worm-fence, and heaped
      stones, elder, mullen, and pokeweed.


26. A child said, *What is the grass?* fetching it to me
      with full hands;
   How could I answer the child?   I do not know what
      it is, any more than he.

27. I guess it must be the flag of my disposition, out of hopeful green stuff woven.

28. Or I guess it is the handkerchief of the Lord,
A scented gift and remembrancer, designedly dropped,
Bearing the owner's name someway in the corners, that we may see and remark, and say *Whose?*

29. Or I guess the grass is itself a child, the produced babe of the vegetation.

30. Or I guess it is a uniform hieroglyphic,
And it means, Sprouting alike in broad zones and narrow zones,
Growing among black folks as among white,
Kanuck, Tuckahoe, Congressman, Cuff, I give them the same, I receive them the same.

31. And now it seems to me the beautiful uncut hair of graves.

32. Tenderly will I use you, curling grass,
It may be you transpire from the breasts of young men,
It may be if I had known them I would have loved them,
It may be you are from old people, and from women, and from offspring taken soon out of their mothers' laps,
And here you are the mothers' laps.

33. This grass is very dark to be from the white heads of old mothers,
Darker than the colorless beards of old men,

Dark to come from under the faint red roofs of mouths.

34. O I perceive after all so many uttering tongues!
And I perceive they do not come from the roofs of mouths for nothing.

35. I wish I could translate the hints about the dead young men and women,
And the hints about old men and mothers, and the offspring taken soon out of their laps.

36. What do you think has become of the young and old men?
And what do you think has become of the women and children?

37. They are alive and well somewhere,
The smallest sprout shows there is really no death,
And if ever there was, it led forward life, and does not wait at the end to arrest it,
And ceased the moment life appeared.

38. All goes onward and outward — nothing collapses,
And to die is different from what any one supposed, and luckier.

39. Has any one supposed it lucky to be born?
I hasten to inform him or her, it is just as lucky to die, and I know it.

40. I pass death with the dying, and birth with the new-washed babe, and am not contained between my hat and boots,

And peruse manifold objects, no two alike, and every
one good,
The earth good, and the stars good, and their
adjuncts all good.

41. I am not an earth, nor an adjunct of an earth,
I am the mate and companion of people, all just as
immortal and fathomless as myself;
They do not know how immortal, but I know.

42. Every kind for itself and its own — for me mine, male
and female,
For me those that have been boys, and that love
women,
For me the man that is proud, and feels how it stings
to be slighted,
For me the sweetheart and the old maid — for me
mothers, and the mothers of mothers,
For me lips that have smiled, eyes that have shed
tears,
For me children, and the begetters of children.

43. Who need be afraid of the merge?
Undrape! you are not guilty to me, nor stale, nor
discarded,
I see through the broadcloth and gingham, whether
or no,
And am around, tenacious, acquisitive, tireless, and
can never be shaken away.

44. The little one sleeps in its cradle,
I lift the gauze and look a long time, and silently
brush away flies with my hand.

45. The youngster and the red-faced girl turn aside up
the bushy hill,
I peeringly view them from the top.

46. The suicide sprawls on the bloody floor of the
bedroom ;
It is so — I witnessed the corpse — there the pistol
had fallen.

47. The blab of the pave, the tires of carts, sluff of boot-
soles, talk of the promenaders,
The heavy omnibus, the driver with his interrogating
thumb, the clank of the shod horses on the
granite floor,
The snow-sleighs, the clinking, shouted jokes, pelts of
snow-balls,
The hurrahs for popular favorites, the fury of roused
mobs,
The flap of the curtained litter, a sick man inside,
borne to the hospital,
The meeting of enemies, the sudden oath, the blows
and fall,
The excited crowd, the policeman with his star,
quickly working his passage to the centre of
the crowd,
The impassive stones that receive and return so many
echoes,
The Souls moving along — (are they invisible, while
the least of the stones is visible ?)
What groans of over-fed or half-starved who fall sun-
struck, or in fits,
What exclamations of women taken suddenly, who
hurry home and give birth to babes,

What living and buried speech is always vibrating
here — what howls restrained by decorum,
Arrests of criminals, slights, adulterous offers made,
acceptances, rejections with convex lips,
I mind them or the show or resonance of them — I
come and I depart.

48. The big doors of the country-barn stand open and
ready,
The dried grass of the harvest-time loads the slow-
drawn wagon,
The clear light plays on the brown gray and green
intertinged,
The armfuls are packed to the sagging mow.

49. I am there — I help — I came stretched atop of the
load,
I felt its soft jolts — one leg reclined on the other ;
I jump from the cross-beams and seize the clover and
timothy,
And roll head over heels, and tangle my hair full of
wisps.

50. Alone, far in the wilds and mountains, I hunt,
Wandering, amazed at my own lightness and glee,
In the late afternoon choosing a safe spot to pass the
night,
Kindling a fire and broiling the fresh-killed game,
Soundly falling asleep on the gathered leaves, with
my dog and gun by my side.

51. The Yankee clipper is under her three sky-sails —
she cuts the sparkle and scud,

My eyes settle the land — I bend at her prow, or shout
joyously from the deck.

52. The boatmen and clam-diggers arose early and
stopped for me,
I tucked my trowser-ends in my boots, and went and
had a good time ;
You should have been with us that day round the
chowder-kettle.

53. I saw the marriage of the trapper in the open air in
the far-west — the bride was a red girl,
Her father and his friends sat near, cross-legged and
dumbly smoking — they had moccasons to their
feet, and large thick blankets hanging from their
shoulders ;
On a bank lounged the trapper — he was dressed
mostly in skins — his luxuriant beard and curls
protected his neck,
One hand rested on his rifle — the other hand held
firmly the wrist of the red girl,
She had long eyelashes — her head was bare — her
coarse straight locks descended upon her volup-
tuous limbs and reached to her feet.

54. The runaway slave came to my house and stopped
outside,
I heard his motions crackling the twigs of the wood-
pile,
Through the swung half-door of the kitchen I saw
him limpsy and weak,
And went where he sat on a log, and led him in and
assured him,

And brought water, and filled a tub for his sweated
body and bruised feet,
And gave him a room that entered from my own, and
gave him some coarse clean clothes,
And remember perfectly well his revolving eyes and
his awkwardness,
And remember putting plasters on the galls of his
neck and ankles;
He staid with me a week before he was recuperated
and passed north,
I had him sit next me at table — my fire-lock leaned
in the corner.

55. Twenty-eight young men bathe by the shore,
Twenty-eight young men, and all so friendly;
Twenty-eight years of womanly life, and all so
lonesome.

56. She owns the fine house by the rise of the bank,
She hides, handsome and richly drest, aft the blinds
of the window.

57. Which of the young men does she like the best?
Ah, the homeliest of them is beautiful to her.

58. Where are you off to, lady? for I see you,
You splash in the water there, yet stay stock still in
your room.

59. Dancing and laughing along the beach came the
twenty-ninth bather,
The rest did not see her, but she saw them and loved
them.

60. The beards of the young men glistened with wet, it
     ran from their long hair,
    Little streams passed all over their bodies.

61. An unseen hand also passed over their bodies,
    It descended tremblingly from their temples and
     ribs.

62. The young men float on their backs — their white
     bellies bulge to the sun — they do not ask who
     seizes fast to them,
    They do not know who puffs and declines with
     pendant and bending arch,
    They do not think whom they souse with spray.

63. The butcher-boy puts off his killing-clothes, or sharp-
     ens his knife at the stall in the market,
    I loiter, enjoying his repartee and his shuffle and
     break-down.

64. Blacksmiths with grimed and hairy chests environ the
     anvil,
    Each has his main-sledge — they are all out — there
     is a great heat in the fire.

65. From the cinder-strewed threshold I follow their
     movements,
    The lithe sheer of their waists plays even with their
     massive arms,
    Overhand the hammers roll — overhand so slow —
     overhand so sure,
    They do not hasten — each man hits in his place.

66. The negro holds firmly the reins of his four horses
— the blocks swags underneath on its tied-over
chain,
The negro that drives the huge dray of the stone-yard
— steady and tall he stands, poised on one leg on
the string-piece,
His blue shirt exposes his ample neck and breast, and
loosens over his hip-band,
His glance is calm and commanding — he tosses the
slouch of his hat away from his forehead,
The sun falls on his crispy hair and moustache —
falls on the black of his polished and perfect
limbs.

67. I behold the picturesque giant and love him — and
I do not stop there,
I go with the team also.

68. In me the caresser of life wherever moving — back-
ward as well as forward slueing,
To niches aside and junior bending.

69. Oxen that rattle the yoke or halt in the shade! what
is that you express in your eyes?
It seems to me more than all the print I have read in
my life.

70. My tread scares the wood-drake and wood-duck, on
my distant and day-long ramble,
They rise together — they slowly circle around.

71. I believe in those winged purposes,
And acknowledge red, yellow, white, playing within
me,

4

And consider green and violet, and the tufted crown,
    intentional,
And do not call the tortoise unworthy because she is
    not something else,
And the mocking-bird in the swamp never studied the
    gamut, yet trills pretty well to me,
And the look of the bay mare shames silliness out
    of me.

72. The wild gander leads his flock through the cool
        night,
    *Ya-honk!* he says, and sounds it down to me like an
        invitation ;
    The pert may suppose it meaningless, but I listen
        close,
    I find its purpose and place up there toward the
        wintry sky.

73. The sharp-hoofed moose of the north, the cat on the
        house-sill, the chickadee, the prairie-dog,
    The litter of the grunting sow as they tug at her
        teats,
    The brood of the turkey-hen, and she with her half-
        spread wings,
    I see in them and myself the same old law.

74. The press of my foot to the earth springs a hundred
        affections,
    They scorn the best I can do to relate them.

75. I am enamoured of growing outdoors,
    Of men that live among cattle, or taste of the ocean
        or woods,

Of the builders and steerers of ships, and the wielders
    of axes and mauls, and the drivers of horses,
I can eat and sleep with them week in and week out.

76. What is commonest, cheapest, nearest, easiest, is Me,
    Me going in for my chances, spending for vast
    returns,
    Adorning myself to bestow myself on the first that
    will take me,
    Not asking the sky to come down to my good will,
    Scattering it freely forever.

77. The pure contralto sings in the organ loft,
    The carpenter dresses his plank — the tongue of his
    foreplane whistles its wild ascending lisp,
    The married and unmarried children ride home to
    their Thanksgiving dinner,
    The pilot seizes the king-pin — he heaves down with
    a strong arm,
    The mate stands braced in the whale-boat — lance
    and harpoon are ready,
    The duck-shooter walks by silent and cautious
    stretches,
    The deacons are ordained with crossed hands at the
    altar,
    The spinning-girl retreats and advances to the hum
    of the big wheel,
    The farmer stops by the bars, as he walks on a First
    Day loafe, and looks at the oats and rye,
    The lunatic is carried at last to the asylum, a con-
    firmed case,
    He will never sleep any more as he did in the cot in
    his mother's bedroom ;

The jour printer with gray head and gaunt jaws works at his case,

He turns his quid of tobacco, while his eyes blurr with the manuscript;

The malformed limbs are tied to the anatomist's table,

What is removed drops horribly in a pail;

The quadroon girl is sold at the stand — the drunkard nods by the bar-room stove,

The machinist rolls up his sleeves — the policeman travels his beat — the gate-keeper marks who pass,

The young fellow drives the express-wagon — I love him, though I do not know him,

The half-breed straps on his light boots to compete in the race,

The western turkey-shooting draws old and young — some lean on their rifles, some sit on logs,

Out from the crowd steps the marksman, takes his position, levels his piece;

The groups of newly-come emigrants cover the wharf or levee,

As the woolly-pates hoe in the sugar-field, the overseer views them from his saddle,

The bugle calls in the ball-room, the gentlemen run for their partners, the dancers bow to each other,

The youth lies awake in the cedar-roofed garret, and harks to the musical rain,

The Wolverine sets traps on the creek that helps fill the Huron,

The reformer ascends the platform, he spouts with his mouth and nose,

The company returns from its excursion, the darkey
  brings up the rear and bears the well-riddled
  target,
The squaw, wrapt in her yellow-hemmed cloth, is
  offering moccasons and bead-bags for sale,
The connoisseur peers along the exhibition-gallery
  with half-shut eyes bent side-ways,
As the deck-hands make fast the steamboat, the plank
  is thrown for the shore-going passengers,
The young sister holds out the skein, while the elder
  sister winds it off in a ball, and stops now and
  then for the knots,
The one-year wife is recovering and happy, having
  a week ago borne her first child, ·
The clean-haired Yankee girl works with her sewing-
  machine, or in the factory or mill,
The nine months' gone is in the parturition chamber,
  her faintness and pains are advancing,
The paving-man leans on his two-handed rammer
  — the reporter's lead flies swiftly over the note-
  book — the sign-painter is lettering with red and
  gold,
The canal-boy trots on the tow-path — the bookkeeper
  counts at his desk — the shoemaker waxes his
  thread,
The conductor beats time for the band, and all the
  performers follow him,
The child is baptized — the convert is making his first
  professions,
The regatta is spread on the bay — how the white
  sails sparkle !
The drover, watching his drove, sings out to them that
  would stray,

4*

The pedler sweats with his pack on his back, the
    purchaser higgling about the odd cent,

The camera and plate are prepared, the lady must sit
    for her daguerreotype,

The bride unrumples her white dress, the minute-
    hand of the clock moves slowly,

The opium-eater reclines with rigid head and just-
    opened lips,

The prostitute draggles her shawl, her bonnet bobs on
    her tipsy and pimpled neck,

The crowd laugh at her blackguard oaths, the men
    jeer and wink to each other,

(Miserable! I do not laugh at your oaths, nor jeer
    you;)

The President, holding a cabinet council, is sur-
    rounded by the Great Secretaries,

On the piazza walk five friendly matrons with twined
    arms,

The crew of the fish-smack pack repeated layers of
    halibut in the hold,

The Missourian crosses the plains, toting his wares
    and his cattle,

As the fare-collector goes through the train, he gives
    notice by the jingling of loose change,

The floor-men are laying the floor — the tinners are
    tinning the roof — the masons are calling for
    mortar,

In single file, each shouldering his hod, pass onward
    the laborers,

Seasons pursuing each other, the indescribable crowd
    is gathered — it is the Fourth of Seventh Month
    — What salutes of cannon and small arms!

Seasons pursuing each other, the plougher ploughs,
the mower mows, and the winter-grain falls in
the ground,

Off on the lakes the pike-fisher watches and waits by
the hole in the frozen surface,

The stumps stand thick round the clearing, the
squatter strikes deep with his axe,

Flatboatmen make fast, towards dusk, near the cotton-
wood or pekan-trees,

Coon-seekers go through the regions of the Red river,
or through those drained by the Tennessee, or
through those of the Arkansaw,

Torches shine in the dark that hangs on the Chatta-
hooche or Altamahaw,

Patriarchs sit at supper with sons and grandsons and
great-grandsons around them,

In walls of adobie, in canvas tents, rest hunters and
trappers after their day's sport,

The city sleeps and the country sleeps,

The living sleep for their time, the dead sleep for
their time,

The old husband sleeps by his wife, and the young
husband sleeps by his wife;

And these one and all tend inward to me, and I tend
outward to them,

And such as it is to be of these, more or less, I am.

78. I am of old and young, of the foolish as much as the
wise,

Regardless of others, ever regardful of others,

Maternal as well as paternal, a child as well as a man,

Stuffed with the stuff that is coarse, and stuffed with
the stuff that is fine,

One of the great nation, the nation of many nations,
the smallest the same, and the largest the same,

A southerner soon as a northerner, a planter non-
chalant and hospitable,

A Yankee, bound my own way, ready for trade, my
joints the limberest joints on earth and the
sternest joints on earth,

A Kentuckian, walking the vale of the Elkhorn in
my deer-skin leggings,

A boatman over lakes or bays, or along coasts – – a
Hoosier, Badger, Buckeye,

A Louisianian or Georgian — a Poke-easy from sand-
hills and pines,

At home on Kanadian snow-shoes, or up in the bush,
or with fishermen off Newfoundland,

At home in the fleet of ice-boats, sailing with the rest,
and tacking,

At home on the hills of Vermont, or in the woods
of Maine, or the Texan ranch,

Comrade of Californians — comrade of free north-
westerners, and loving their big proportions,

Comrade of raftsmen and coalmen — comrade of all
who shake hands and welcome to drink and
meat,

A learner with the simplest, a teacher of the thought-
fullest,

A novice beginning, yet experient of myriads of
seasons,

Of every hue, trade, rank, caste and religion,

Not merely of the New World, but of Africa, Europe,
Asia — a wandering savage,

A farmer, mechanic, artist, gentleman, sailor, lover,
quaker,

A prisoner, fancy-man, rowdy, lawyer, physician, priest.

79. I resist anything better than my own diversity,
And breathe the air, and leave plenty after me,
And am not stuck up, and am in my place.

80. The moth and the fish-eggs are in their place,
The suns I see, and the suns I cannot see, are in their place,
The palpable is in its place, and the impalpable is in its place.

81. These are the thoughts of all men in all ages and lands — they are not original with me,
If they are not yours as much as mine, they are nothing, or next to nothing,
If they do not enclose everything, they are next to nothing,
If they are not the riddle and the untying of the riddle, they are nothing,
If they are not just as close as they are distant, they are nothing.

82. This is the grass that grows wherever the land is and the water is,
This is the common air that bathes the globe.

83. This is the breath for America, because it is my breath,
This is for laws, songs, behavior,
This is the tasteless water of Souls — this is the true sustenance.

84. This is for the illiterate, and for the judges of the
    Supreme Court, and for the Federal capitol and
    the State capitols,
    And for the admirable communes of literats, com-
    posers, singers, lecturers, engineers, and savans,
    And for the endless races of work-people, farmers,
    and seamen.

85. This is the trilling of thousands of clear cornets,
    screaming of octave flutes, striking of triangles.

86. I play not here marches for victors only — I play
    great marches for conquered and slain persons.

87. Have you heard that it was good to gain the day ?
    I also say it is good to fall — battles are lost in the
    same spirit in which they are won.

88. I beat triumphal drums for the dead,
    I blow through my embouchures my loudest and
    gayest music to them.

89. Vivas to those who have failed !
    And to those whose war-vessels sank in the sea !
    And those themselves who sank in the sea !
    And to all generals that lost engagements ! and all
    overcome heroes !
    And the numberless unknown heroes, equal to the
    greatest heroes known.

90. This is the meal pleasantly set — this is the meat and
    drink for natural hunger,
    It is for the wicked just the same as the righteous — I
    make appointments with all,

I will not have a single person slighted or left away,
The kept-woman, sponger, thief, are hereby invited,
The heavy-lipped slave is invited — the venerealee is
  invited,
There shall be no difference between them and the
  rest.


91. This is the press of a bashful hand — this is the float
  and odor of hair,
This is the touch of my lips to yours — this is the
  murmur of yearning,
This is the far-off depth and height reflecting my
  own face,
This is the thoughtful merge of myself, and the outlet
  again.


92. Do you guess I have some intricate purpose?
Well, I have — for the Fourth Month showers have,
  and the mica on the side of a rock has.


93. Do you take it I would astonish?
Does the daylight astonish? Does the early redstart,
  twittering through the woods?
Do I astonish more than they?


94. This hour I tell things in confidence,
I might not tell everybody, but I will tell you.


95. Who goes there! hankering, gross, mystical, nude?
How is it I extract strength from the beef I eat?


96. What is a man anyhow? What am I? What are
  you?

97. All I mark as my own, you shall offset it with your
    own,
    Else it were time lost listening to me.

98. I do not snivel that snivel the world over,
    That months are vacuums, and the ground but
    wallow and filth,
    That life is a suck and a sell, and nothing remains at
    the end but threadbare crape, and tears.

99. Whimpering and truckling fold with powders for
    invalids — conformity goes to the fourth-removed,
    I cock my hat as I please, indoors or out.

100. Why should I pray ?   Why should I venerate and be
    ceremonious ?

101. Having pried through the strata, analyzed to a hair,
    counsell'd with doctors, and calculated close,
    I find no sweeter fat than sticks to my own bones.

102. In all people I see myself — none more, and not one a
    barleycorn less,
    And the good or bad I say of myself I say of them.

103. And I know I am solid and sound,
    To me the converging objects of the universe per-
    petually flow,
    All are written to me, and I must get what the
    writing means.

104. I know I am deathless,
    I know this orbit of mine cannot be swept by a
    carpenter's compass,

I know I shall not pass like a child's carlacue cut
    with a burnt stick at night.

105. I know I am august,
    I do not trouble my spirit to vindicate itself or be
        understood,
    I see that the elementary laws never apologize,
    I reckon I behave no prouder than the level I plant
        my house by, after all.

106. I exist as I am — that is enough,
    If no other in the world be aware, I sit content,
    And if each and all be aware, I sit content.

107. One world is aware, and by far the largest to me, and
        that is myself,
    And whether I come to my own to-day, or in ten
        thousand or ten million years,
    I can cheerfully take it now, or with equal cheerful-
        ness I can wait.

108. My foothold is tenoned and mortised in granite,
    I laugh at what you call dissolution,
    And I know the amplitude of time.

109. I am the poet of the body,
    And I am the poet of the Soul.

110. The pleasures of heaven are with me, and the pains
        of hell are with me,
    The first I graft and increase upon myself — the latter
        I translate into a new tongue.

111. I am the poet of the woman the same as the man,
And I say it is as great to be a woman as to be a
man,
And I say there is nothing greater than the mother
of men.

112. I chant the chant of dilation or pride,
We have had ducking and deprecating about enough,
I show that size is only development.

113. Have you outstript the rest? Are you the President?
It is a trifle — they will more than arrive there every
one, and still pass on.

114. I am He that walks with the tender and growing
Night,
I call to the earth and sea, half-held by the Night.

115. Press close, bare-bosomed Night! Press close, mag-
netic, nourishing Night!
Night of south winds! Night of the large few stars!
Still, nodding night! Mad, naked, summer night.

116. Smile, O voluptuous, cool-breathed Earth!
Earth of the slumbering and liquid trees!
Earth of departed sunset! Earth of the mountains,
misty-topt!
Earth of the vitreous pour of the full moon, just
tinged with blue!
Earth of shine and dark, mottling the tide of the
river!
Earth of the limpid gray of clouds, brighter and
clearer for my sake!

Far-swooping elbowed Earth! Rich, apple-blossomed
    Earth!
Smile, for YOUR LOVER comes!

117. Prodigal, you have given me love! Therefore I to
    you give love!
    O unspeakable passionate love!

118. Thruster holding me tight, and that I hold tight!
    We hurt each other as the bridegroom and the bride
        hurt each other.

119. You Sea! I resign myself to you also — I guess
        what you mean,
    I behold from the beach your crooked inviting fingers,
    I believe you refuse to go back without feeling of me;
    We must have a turn together — I undress — hurry
        me out of sight of the land,
    Cushion me soft, rock me in billowy drowse,
    Dash me with amorous wet — I can repay you.

120. Sea of stretched ground-swells!
    Sea breathing broad and convulsive breaths!
    Sea of the brine of life! Sea of unshovelled and
        always-ready graves!
    Howler and scooper of storms! Capricious and dainty
        Sea!
    I am integral with you — I too am of one phase, and
        of all phases.

121. Partaker of influx and efflux — extoller of hate and
        conciliation,
    Extoller of amies, and those that sleep in each others'
        arms.

122. I am he attesting sympathy,
    Shall I make my list of things in the house, and skip
       the house that supports them ?

123. I am the poet of common sense, and of the demon-
       strable, and of immortality,
    And am not the poet of goodness only — I do not
       decline to be the poet of wickedness also.

124. Washes and razors for foofoos — for me freckles and
    a bristling beard.

125. What blurt is this about virtue and about vice ?
    Evil propels me, and reform of evil propels me — I
       stand indifferent,
    My gait is no fault-finder's or rejecter's gait,
    I moisten the roots of all that has grown.

126. Did you fear some scrofula out of the unflagging
       pregnancy ?
    Did you guess the celestial laws are yet to be worked
       over and rectified ?

127. I step up to say that what we do is right, and what
       we affirm is right — and some is only the ore of
       right,
    Witnesses of us — one side a balance, and the antip-
       odal side a balance,
    Soft doctrine as steady help as stable doctrine,
    Thoughts and deeds of the present, our rouse and
       early start.

128. This minute that comes to me over the past decillions,
    There is no better than it and now.

129. What behaved well in the past, or behaves well
to-day, is not such a wonder,
The wonder is, always and always, how can there be
a mean man or an infidel.

130. Endless unfolding of words of ages!
And mine a word of the modern — a word en-masse.

131. A word of the faith that never balks,
One time as good as another time — here or hence-
forward, it is all the same to me.

132. A word of reality — materialism first and last im-
buing.

133. Hurrah for positive Science! long live exact demon-
stration!
Fetch stonecrop, mixt with cedar and branches of
lilac,
This is the lexicographer — this the chemist — this
made a grammar of the old cartouches,
These mariners put the ship through dangerous un-
known seas,
This is the geologist — this works with the scalpel —
and this is a mathematician.

134. Gentlemen! I receive you, and attach and clasp
hands with you,
The facts are useful and real — they are not my
dwelling — I enter by them to an area of the
dwelling.

135. I am less the reminder of property or qualities, and
more the reminder of life,

And go on the square for my own sake and for others'
sakes,

And make short account of neuters and geldings, and
favor men and women fully equipped,

And beat the gong of revolt, and stop with fugitives,
and them that plot and conspire.

136. Walt Whitman, an American, one of the roughs, a
kosmos,

Disorderly, fleshy, sensual, eating, drinking, breeding,

No sentimentalist — no stander above men and wo-
men, or apart from them,

No more modest than immodest.

137. Unscrew the locks from the doors!
Unscrew the doors themselves from their jambs!

138. Whoever degrades another degrades me,
And whatever is done or said returns at last to me,
And whatever I do or say, I also return.

139. Through me the afflatus surging and surging —
through me the current and index.

140. I speak the pass-word primeval — I give the sign of
democracy,

By God! I will accept nothing which all cannot have
their counterpart of on the same terms.

141. Through me many long dumb voices,
Voices of the interminable generations of slaves,
Voices of prostitutes, and of deformed persons,
Voices of the diseased and despairing, and of thieves
and dwarfs,

Voices of cycles of preparation and accretion,
And of the threads that connect the stars — and of
wombs, and of the fatherstuff,
And of the rights of them the others are down upon,
Of the trivial, flat, foolish, despised,
Fog in the air, beetles rolling balls of dung.

142. Through me forbidden voices,
Voices of sexes and lusts — voices veiled, and I
remove the veil,
Voices indecent, by me clarified and transfigured.

143. I do not press my finger across my mouth,
I keep as delicate around the bowels as around the
head and heart,
Copulation is no more rank to me than death is.

144. I believe in the flesh and the appetites,
Seeing, hearing, feeling, are miracles, and each part
and tag of me is a miracle.

145. Divine am I inside and out, and I make holy whatever I touch or am touched from,
The scent of these arm-pits, aroma finer than prayer,
This head more than churches, bibles, and all the
creeds.

146. If I worship any particular thing, it shall be some of
the spread of my own body.

147. Translucent mould of me, it shall be you!
Shaded ledges and rests, it shall be you!
Firm masculine colter, it shall be you.

148. Whatever goes to the tilth of me, it shall be you!
    You my rich blood! Your milky stream, pale strip-
       pings of my life.

149. Breast that presses against other breasts, it shall be
       you!
    My brain, it shall be your occult convolutions.

150. Root of washed sweet-flag! Timorous pond-snipe!
       Nest of guarded duplicate eggs! it shall be
       you!
    Mixed tussled hay of head, beard, brawn, it shall
       be you!
    Trickling sap of maple! Fibre of manly wheat! it
       shall be you!

151. Sun so generous, it shall be you!
    Vapors lighting and shading my face, it shall be
       you!
    You sweaty brooks and dews, it shall be you!
    Winds whose soft-tickling genitals rub against me, it
       shall be you!
    Broad, muscular fields! Branches of live oak! Lov-
       ing lounger in my winding paths! it shall be
       you!
    Hands I have taken — face I have kissed — mortal I
       have ever touched! it shall be you.

152. I dote on myself — there is that lot of me, and all so
       luscious,
    Each moment, and whatever happens, thrills me with
       joy.

153. O I am so wonderful!
   I cannot tell how my ankles bend, nor whence the
      cause of my faintest wish,
   Nor the cause of the friendship I emit, nor the cause
      of the friendship I take again.

154. That I walk up my stoop, I pause to consider if it
      really be,
   That I eat and drink is spectacle enough for the great
      authors and schools,
   A morning-glory at my window satisfies me more than
      the metaphysics of books.

155. To behold the day-break!
   The little light fades the immense and diaphanous
      shadows,
   The air tastes good to my palate.

156. Hefts of the moving world, at innocent gambols,
      silently rising, freshly exuding,
   Scooting obliquely high and low.

157. Something I cannot see puts upward libidinous
      prongs,
   Seas of bright juice suffuse heaven.

158. The earth by the sky staid with — the daily close of
      their junction,
   The heaved challenge from the east that moment over
      my head,
   The mocking taunt, See then whether you shall be
      master!

159. Dazzling and tremendous, how quick the sun-rise
     would kill me,
   If I could not now and always send sun-rise out
     of me.

160. We also ascend, dazzling and tremendous as the sun,
   We found our own, O my Soul, in the calm and cool
     of the day-break.

161. My voice goes after what my eyes cannot reach,
   With the twirl of my tongue I encompass worlds, and
     volumes of worlds.

162. Speech is the twin of my vision — it is unequal to
     measure itself;
   It provokes me forever,
   It says sarcastically, *Walt, you understand enough —*
     *why don't you let it out then?*

163. Come now, I will not be tantalized — you conceive
     too much of articulation.

164. Do you not know how the buds beneath are folded?
   Waiting in gloom, protected by frost,
   The dirt receding before my prophetical screams,
   I underlying causes, to balance them at last,
   My knowledge my live parts — it keeping tally with
     the meaning of things,
   Happiness — which, whoever hears me, let him or her
     set out in search of this day.

165. My final merit I refuse you — I refuse putting from
     me the best I am.

166. Encompass worlds, but never try to encompass me,
   I crowd your sleekest talk by simply looking toward
      you.

167. Writing and talk do not prove me,
   I carry the plenum of proof, and everything else, in
      my face,
   With the hush of my lips I confound the topmost
      skeptic.

168. I think I will do nothing for a long time but listen,
   To accrue what I hear into myself — to let sounds
      contribute toward me.

169. I hear bravuras of birds, bustle of growing wheat,
      gossip of flames, clack of sticks cooking my
      meals.

170. I hear the sound I love, the sound of the human
      voice,
   I hear all sounds running together, combined, fused
      or following,
   Sounds of the city and sounds out of the city —
      sounds of the day and night,
   Talkative young ones to those that like them — the
      recitative of fish-pedlers and fruit-pedlers — the
      loud laugh of work-people at their meals,
   The angry base of disjointed friendship — the faint
      tones of the sick,
   The judge with hands tight to the desk, his shaky lips
      pronouncing a death-sentence,
   The heave'e'yo of stevedores unlading ships by the
      wharves — the refrain of the anchor-lifters,

The ring of alarm-bells — the cry of fire — the whirr
   of swift-streaking engines and hose-carts, with
   premonitory tinkles, and colored lights,
The steam-whistle — the solid roll of the train of
   approaching cars,
The slow-march played at night at the head of the
   association, marching two and two,
(They go to guard some corpse — the flag-tops are
   draped with black muslin.)

171. I hear the violoncello, or man's heart's complaint;
I hear the keyed cornet — it glides quickly in through
   my ears,
It shakes mad-sweet pangs through my belly and
   breast.

172. I hear the chorus — it is a grand-opera,
Ah, this indeed is music! This suits me.

173. A tenor large and fresh as the creation fills me,
The orbic flex of his mouth is pouring and filling
   me full.

174. I hear the trained soprano — she convulses me like
   the climax of my love-grip,
The orchestra wrenches such ardors from me, I did
   not know I possessed them,
It throbs me to gulps of the farthest down horror,
It sails me — I dab with bare feet — they are licked
   by the indolent waves,
I am exposed, cut by bitter and poisoned hail,
Steeped amid honeyed morphine, my windpipe throt-
   tled in fakes of death,

At length let up again to feel the puzzle of puzzles,
And that we call BEING.

175. To be in any form — what is that?
(Round and round we go, all of us, and ever come
back thither,)
If nothing lay more developed, the quahaug in its
callous shell were enough.

176. Mine is no callous shell,
I have instant conductors all over me, whether I pass
or stop,
They seize every object, and lead it harmlessly
through me.

177. I merely stir, press, feel with my fingers, and am
happy,
To touch my person to some one else's is about as
much as I can stand.

178. Is this then a touch? quivering me to a new identity,
Flames and ether making a rush for my veins,
Treacherous tip of me reaching and crowding to
help them,
My flesh and blood playing out lightning to strike
what is hardly different from myself,
On all sides prurient provokers stiffening my limbs,
Straining the udder of my heart for its withheld
drip,
Behaving licentious toward me, taking no denial,
Depriving me of my best, as for a purpose,
Unbuttoning my clothes, holding me by the bare
waist,

6

Deluding my confusion with the calm of the sun-light
    and pasture-fields,
Immodestly sliding the fellow-senses away,
They bribed to swap off with touch, and go and graze
    at the edges of me,
No consideration, no regard for my draining strength
    or my anger,
Fetching the rest of the herd around to enjoy them
    a while,
Then all uniting to stand on a headland and worry
    me.

179. The sentries desert every other part of me,
They have left me helpless to a red marauder,
They all come to the headland, to witness and assist
    against me.

180. I am given up by traitors,
I talk wildly — I have lost my wits — I and nobody
    else am the greatest traitor,
I went myself first to the headland — my own hands
    carried me there.

181. You villain touch! what are you doing? My breath
    is tight in its throat,
Unclench your floodgates! you are too much for me.

182. Blind, loving, wrestling touch! sheathed, hooded,
    sharp-toothed touch!
Did it make you ache so, leaving me?

183. Parting, tracked by arriving — perpetual payment of
    perpetual loan,

Rich showering rain, and recompense richer after-
ward.

184. Sprouts take and accumulate — stand by the curb
prolific and vital,
Landscapes, projected, masculine, full-sized, and
golden.

185. All truths wait in all things,
They neither hasten their own delivery, nor resist it,
They do not need the obstetric forceps of the
surgeon,
The insignificant is as big to me as any,
What is less or more than a touch?

186. Logic and sermons never convince,
The damp of the night drives deeper into my Soul.

187. Only what proves itself to every man and woman
is so,
Only what nobody denies is so.

188. A minute and a drop of me settle my brain,
I believe the soggy clods shall become lovers and
lamps,
And a compend of compends is the meat of a man or
woman,
And a summit and flower there is the feeling they
have for each other,
And they are to branch boundlessly out of that lesson
until it becomes omnific,
And until every one shall delight us, and we them.

189. I believe a leaf of grass is no less than the journey-
work of the stars,
    And the pismire is equally perfect, and a grain of
sand, and the egg of the wren,
    And the tree-toad is a chef-d'œuvre for the highest,
    And the running blackberry would adorn the parlors
of heaven,
    And the narrowest hinge in my hand puts to scorn all
machinery,
    And the cow crunching with depressed head surpasses
any statue,
    And a mouse is miracle enough to stagger sextillions
of infidels,
    And I could come every afternoon of my life to look
at the farmer's girl boiling her iron tea-kettle
and baking short-cake.

190. I find I incorporate gneiss, coal, long-threaded moss,
fruits, grains, esculent roots,
    And am stuccoed with quadrupeds and birds all over,
    And have distanced what is behind me for good
reasons,
    And call anything close again, when I desire it.

191. In vain the speeding or shyness,
    In vain the plutonic rocks send their old heat against
my approach,
    In vain the mastodon retreats beneath its own pow-
dered bones,
    In vain objects stand leagues off, and assume manifold
shapes,
    In vain the ocean settling in hollows, and the great
monsters lying low,

In vain the buzzard houses herself with the sky,
In vain the snake slides through the creepers and
logs,
In vain the elk takes to the inner passes of the
woods,
In vain the razor-billed auk sails far north to
Labrador,
I follow quickly, I ascend to the nest in the fissure
of the cliff.

192. I think I could turn and live with animals, they are
so placid and self-contained,
I stand and look at them sometimes an hour at a
stretch.

193. They do not sweat and whine about their condition,
They do not lie awake in the dark and weep for their
sins,
They do not make me sick discussing their duty to
God,
No one is dissatisfied — not one is demented with the
mania of owning things,
Not one kneels to another, nor to his kind that lived
thousands of years ago,
Not one is respectable or industrious over the whole
earth.

194. So they show their relations to me, and I accept
them,
They bring me tokens of myself — they evince them
plainly in their possession.

195. I do not know where they get those tokens,

6 *

I may have passed that way untold times ago, and
    negligently dropt them,
Myself moving forward then and now forever,
Gathering and showing more always and with
    velocity,
Infinite and omnigenous, and the like of these among
    them,
Not too exclusive toward the reachers of my remem-
    brancers,
Picking out here one that I love, to go with on
    brotherly terms.

196. A gigantic beauty of a stallion, fresh and responsive
    to my caresses,
Head high in the forehead, wide between the ears,
Limbs glossy and supple, tail dusting the ground,
Eyes well apart, full of sparkling wickedness — ears
    finely cut, flexibly moving.

197. His nostrils dilate, as my heels embrace him,
His well-built limbs tremble with pleasure, as we
    speed around and return.

198. I but use you a moment, then I resign you stallion,
Why do I need your paces, when I myself out-gallop
    them?
Even, as I stand or sit, passing faster than you.

199. O swift wind! Space! my Soul! now I know it is
    true, what I guessed at,
What I guessed when I loafed on the grass,
What I guessed while I lay alone in my bed,
And again as I walked the beach under the paling
    stars of the morning.

200. My ties and ballasts leave me — I travel — I sail —
    my elbows rest in the sea-gaps,
I skirt the sierras — my palms cover continents,
I am afoot with my vision.

201. By the city's quadrangular houses — in log huts —
    camping with lumbermen,
Along the ruts of the turnpike — along the dry gulch
    and rivulet bed,
Weeding my onion-patch, or hoeing rows of carrots
    and parsnips — crossing savannas — trailing in
    forests,
Prospecting — gold-digging — girdling the trees of a
    new purchase,
Scorched ankle-deep by the hot sand — hauling my
    boat down the shallow river,
Where the panther walks to and fro on a limb over-
    head — Where the buck turns furiously at the
    hunter,
Where the rattlesnake suns his flabby length on a
    rock — Where the otter is feeding on fish,
Where the alligator in his tough pimples sleeps by the
    bayou,
Where the black bear is searching for roots or honey
    —Where the beaver pats the mud with his
    paddle-tail,
Over the growing sugar — over the cotton plant —
    over the rice in its low moist field,
Over the sharp-peaked farm house, with its scalloped
    scum and slender shoots from the gutters,
Over the western persimmon — over the long-leaved
    corn — over the delicate blue-flowered flax,
Over the white and brown buckwheat, a hummer
    and buzzer there with the rest,

Over the dusky green of the rye as it ripples and
　　shades in the breeze,
Scaling mountains, pulling myself cautiously up,
　　holding on by low scragged limbs,
Walking the path worn in the grass and beat through
　　the leaves of the brush,
Where the quail is whistling betwixt the woods and
　　the wheat-lot,
Where the bat flies in the Seventh Month eve —
　　Where the great gold-bug drops through the
　　dark,
Where the flails keep time on the barn floor,
Where the brook puts out of the roots of the old tree
　　and flows to the meadow,
Where cattle stand and shake away flies with the
　　tremulous shuddering of their hides,
Where the cheese-cloth hangs in the kitchen — Where
　　andirons straddle the hearth-slab — Where cob-
　　webs fall in festoons from the rafters,
Where trip-hammers crash — Where the press is
　　whirling its cylinders,
Wherever the human heart beats with terrible throes
　　out of its ribs,
Where the pear-shaped balloon is floating aloft, float-
　　ing in it myself and looking composedly down,
Where the life-car is drawn on the slip-noose — Where
　　the heat hatches pale-green eggs in the dented
　　sand,
Where the she-whale swims with her calf, and never
　　forsakes it,
Where the steam-ship trails hind-ways its long pen-
　　nant of smoke,
Where the fin of the shark cuts like a black chip out
　　of the water,

Where the half-burned brig is riding on unknown
    currents,

Where shells grow to her slimy deck — Where the
    dead are corrupting below,

Where the striped and starred flag is borne at the
    head of the regiments,

Approaching Manhattan, up by the long-stretching
    island,

Under Niagara, the cataract falling like a veil over
    my countenance,

Upon a door-step — upon the horse-block of hard
    wood outside,

Upon the race-course, or enjoying picnics or jigs, or
    a good game of base-ball,

At he-festivals, with blackguard gibes, ironical license,
    bull-dances, drinking, laughter,

At the cider-mill, tasting the sweet of the brown
    sqush, sucking the juice through a straw,

At apple-peelings, wanting kisses for all the red fruit
    I find,

At musters, beach-parties, friendly bees, huskings,
    house-raisings;

Where the mocking-bird sounds his delicious gur-
    gles, cackles, screams, weeps,

Where the hay-rick stands in the barn-yard — Where
    the dry-stalks are scattered — Where the brood
    cow waits in the hovel,

Where the bull advances to do his masculine work —
    Where the stud to the mare — Where the cock
    is treading the hen,

Where heifers browse — Where geese nip their food
    with short jerks,

Where sun-down shadows lengthen over the limitless
    and lonesome prairie,

Where herds of buffalo make a crawling spread of
the square miles far and near,

Where the humming-bird shimmers — Where the
neck of the long-lived swan is curving and
winding,

Where the laughing-gull scoots by the shore, where
she laughs her near-human laugh,

Where bee-hives range on a gray bench in the garden,
half hid by the high weeds,

Where band-necked partridges roost in a ring on the
ground with their heads out,

Where burial coaches enter the arched gates of a
cemetery,

Where winter wolves bark amid wastes of snow and
icicled trees,

Where the yellow-crowned heron comes to the edge of
the marsh at night and feeds upon small crabs,

Where the splash of swimmers and divers cools the
warm noon,

Where the katy-did works her chromatic reed on the
walnut-tree over the well,

Through patches of citrons and cucumbers with
silver-wired leaves,

Through the salt-lick or orange glade, or under con-
ical firs,

Through the gymnasium — through the curtained
saloon — through the office or public hall,

Pleased with the native, and pleased with the foreign
— pleased with the new and old,

Pleased with women, the homely as well as the
handsome,

Pleased with the quakeress as she puts off her bonnet
and talks melodiously,

Pleased with the tunes of the choir of the white-
washed church,

Pleased with the earnest words of the sweating
Methodist preacher, or any preacher — Impressed
seriously at the camp-meeting,

Looking in at the shop-windows of Broadway the
whole forenoon — flatting the flesh of my nose
on the thick plate-glass,

Wandering the same afternoon with my face turned
up to the clouds,

My right and left arms round the sides of two
friends, and I in the middle;

Coming home with the silent and dark-cheeked
bush-boy — riding behind him at the drape of
the day,

Far from the settlements, studying the print of ani-
mals' feet, or the moccason print,

By the cot in the hospital, reaching lemonade to a
feverish patient,

By the coffined corpse when all is still, examining
with a candle,

Voyaging to every port, to dicker and adventure,

Hurrying with the modern crowd, as eager and fickle
as any,

Hot toward one I hate, ready in my madness to knife
him,

Solitary at midnight in my back yard, my thoughts
gone from me a long while,

Walking the old hills of Judea, with the beautiful
gentle God by my side,

Speeding through space — speeding through heaven
and the stars,

Speeding amid the seven satellites, and the broad
    ring, and the diameter of eighty thousand miles,
Speeding with tailed meteors — throwing fire-balls
    like the rest,
Carrying the crescent child that carries its own full
    mother in its belly,
Storming, enjoying, planning, loving, cautioning,
Backing and filling, appearing and disappearing,
I tread day and night such roads.

202. I visit the orchards of spheres, and look at the product,
    And look at quintillions ripened, and look at quin-
    tillions green.

203. I fly the flight of the fluid and swallowing soul,
    My course runs below the soundings of plummets.

204. I help myself to material and immaterial,
    No guard can shut me off, nor law prevent me.

205. I anchor my ship for a little while only,
    My messengers continually cruise away, or bring their
    returns to me.

206. I go hunting polar furs and the seal — Leaping
    chasms with a pike-pointed staff — Clinging to
    topples of brittle and blue.

207. I ascend to the foretruck,
    I take my place late at night in the crow's-nest,
    We sail the arctic sea — it is plenty light enough,
    Through the clear atmosphere I stretch around on
    the wonderful beauty,

The enormous masses of ice pass me, and I pass them
— the scenery is plain in all directions,
The white-topped mountains show in the distance —
I fling out my fancies toward them,
We are approaching some great battle-field in which
we are soon to be engaged,
We pass the colossal out-posts of the encampment —
we pass with still feet and caution,
Or we are entering by the suburbs some vast and
ruined city,
The blocks and fallen architecture more than all the
living cities of the globe.

208. I am a free companion — I bivouac by invading
watchfires.

209. I turn the bridegroom out of bed, and stay with the
bride myself,
I tighten her all night to my thighs and lips.

210. My voice is the wife's voice, the screech by the rail
of the stairs,
They fetch my man's body up, dripping and drowned.

211. I understand the large hearts of heroes,
The courage of present times and all times,
How the skipper saw the crowded and rudderless
wreck of the steam-ship, and Death chasing it up
and down the storm,
How he knuckled tight, and gave not back one inch,
and was faithful of days and faithful of nights,
And chalked in large letters, on a board, *Be of good
cheer*, *We will not desert you*,

7

How he followed with them, and tacked with them —
and would not give it up,

How he saved the drifting company at last,

How the lank loose-gowned women looked when
boated from the side of their prepared graves,

How the silent old-faced infants, and the lifted sick,
and the sharp-lipped unshaved men,

All this I swallow — it tastes good — I like it well —
it becomes mine,

I am the man — I suffered — I was there.

212. The disdain and calmness of martyrs,

The mother, condemned for a witch, burnt with dry
wood, her children gazing on,

The hounded slave that flags in the race, leans by the
the fence, blowing, covered with sweat,

The twinges that sting like needles his legs and neck
— the murderous buck-shot and the bullets,

All these I feel or am.

213. I am the hounded slave, I wince at the bite of the
dogs,

Hell and despair are upon me, crack and again crack
the marksmen,

I clutch the rails of the fence, my gore dribs, thinned
with the ooze of my skin,

I fall on the weeds and stones,

The riders spur their unwilling horses, haul close,

Taunt my dizzy ears, and beat me violently over the
head with whip-stocks.

214. Agonies are one of my changes of garments,

I do not ask the wounded person how he feels — I
myself become the wounded person,

My hurt turns livid upon me as I lean on a cane and observe.

215. I am the mashed fireman with breastbone broken,
Tumbling walls buried me in their debris,
Heat and smoke I inspired — I heard the yelling shouts of my comrades,
I heard the distant click of their picks and shovels,
They have cleared the beams away — they tenderly lift me forth.

216. I lie in the night air in my red shirt — the pervading hush is for my sake,
Painless after all I lie, exhausted but not so unhappy,
White and beautiful are the faces around me — the heads are bared of their fire-caps,
The kneeling crowd fades with the light of the torches.

217. Distant and dead resuscitate,
They show as the dial or move as the hands of me — I am the clock myself.

218. I am an old artillerist — I tell of my fort's bombardment,
I am there again.

219. Again the reveille of drummers,
Again the attacking cannon, mortars, howitzers,
Again the attacked send cannon responsive.

220. I take part — I see and hear the whole,
The cries, curses, roar — the plaudits for well-aimed shots,

The ambulanza slowly passing, trailing its red drip,
Workmen searching after damages, making indis-
pensable repairs,
The fall of grenades through the rent roof — the
fan-shaped explosion,
The whizz of limbs, heads, stone, wood, iron, high in
the air.

221. Again gurgles the mouth of my dying general — he
furiously waves with his hand,
He gasps through the clot, *Mind not me — mind —
the entrenchments.*

222. I tell not the fall of Alamo,
Not one escaped to tell the fall of Alamo,
The hundred and fifty are dumb yet at Alamo.

223. Hear now the tale of the murder in cold blood of four
hundred and twelve young men.

224. Retreating, they had formed in a hollow square, with
their baggage for breastworks,
Nine hundred lives out of the surrounding enemy's,
nine times their number, was the price they took
in advance,
Their colonel was wounded and their ammunition
gone,
They treated for an honorable capitulation, received
writing and seal, gave up their arms, and
marched back prisoners of war.

225. They were the glory of the race of rangers,
Matchless with horse, rifle, song, supper, courtship,

Large, turbulent, generous, brave, handsome, proud,
  and affectionate,
Bearded, sunburnt, dressed in the free costume of
  hunters,
Not a single one over thirty years of age.

226. The second First Day morning they were brought out
  in squads and massacred — it was beautiful early
  summer,
The work commenced about five o'clock, and was over
  by eight.

227. None obeyed the command to kneel,
Some made a mad and helpless rush — some stood
  stark and straight,
A few fell at once, shot in the temple or heart — the
  living and dead lay together,
The maimed and mangled dug in the dirt — the new-
  comers saw them there,
Some, half-killed, attempted to crawl away,
These were despatched with bayonets, or battered with
  the blunts of muskets,
A youth not seventeen years old seized his assassin till
  two more came to release him,
The three were all torn, and covered with the boy's
  blood.

228. At eleven o'clock began the burning of the bodies:
That is the tale of the murder of the four hundred
  and twelve young men.

229. Did you read in the sea-books of the old-fashioned
  frigate-fight?

7*

Did you learn who won by the light of the moon and
stars ?

230. Our foe was no skulk in his ship, I tell you,
His was the English pluck — and there is no tougher
or truer, and never was, and never will be ;
Along the lowered eve he came, horribly raking us.

231. We closed with him — the yards entangled — the
cannon touched,
My captain lashed fast with his own hands.

232. We had received some eighteen-pound shots under
the water,
On our lower-gun-deck two large pieces had burst at
the first fire, killing all around, and blowing up
overhead.

233. Ten o'clock at night, and the full moon shining, and
the leaks on the gain, and five feet of water
reported,
The master-at-arms loosing the prisoners confined in
the after-hold, to give them a chance for them-
selves.

234. The transit to and from the magazine was now
stopped by the sentinels,
They saw so many strange faces, they did not know
whom to trust.

235. Our frigate was afire,
The other asked if we demanded quarter ?
If our colors were struck, and the fighting done ?

236. I laughed content when I heard the voice of my little
captain,
*We have not struck*, he composedly cried, *We have
just begun our part of the fighting.*

237. Only three guns were in use,
One was directed by the captain himself against the
enemy's main-mast,
Two, well served with grape and canister, silenced his
musketry and cleared his decks.

238. The tops alone seconded the fire of this little battery,
especially the main-top,
They all held out bravely during the whole of the
action.

239. Not a moment's cease,
The leaks gained fast on the pumps — the fire eat
toward the powder-magazine,
One of the pumps was shot away — it was generally
thought we were sinking.

240. Serene stood the little captain,
He was not hurried — his voice was neither high
nor low,
His eyes gave more light to us than our battle-
lanterns.

241. Toward twelve at night, there in the beams of the
moon, they surrendered to us.

242. Stretched and still lay the midnight,
Two great hulls motionless on the breast of the
darkness,

Our vessel riddled and slowly sinking — preparations
to pass to the one we had conquered,
The captain on the quarter-deck coldly giving his
orders through a countenance white as a sheet,
Near by, the corpse of the child that served in the
cabin,
The dead face of an old salt with long white hair and
carefully curled whiskers,
The flames, spite of all that could be done, flickering
aloft and below,
The husky voices of the two or three officers yet fit
for duty,
Formless stacks of bodies, and bodies by themselves
— dabs of flesh upon the masts and spars,
Cut of cordage, dangle of rigging, slight shock of the
soothe of waves,
Black and impassive guns, litter of powder-parcels,
strong scent,
Delicate sniffs of sea-breeze, smells of sedgy grass and
fields by the shore, death-messages given in
charge to survivors,
The hiss of the surgeon's knife, the gnawing teeth of
his saw,
Wheeze, cluck, swash of falling blood, short wild
scream, and long dull tapering groan,
These so — these irretrievable.

243. O Christ! This is mastering me!
Through the conquered doors they crowd. I am
possessed.

244. What the rebel said, gayly adjusting his throat to the
rope-noose,

What the savage at the stump, his eye-sockets empty, his mouth spirting whoops and defiance,
What stills the traveller come to the vault at Mount Vernon,
What sobers the Brooklyn boy as he looks down the shores of the Wallabout and remembers the Prison Ships,
What burnt the gums of the red-coat at Saratoga when he surrendered his brigades,
These become mine and me every one — and they are but little,
I become as much more as I like.

245. I become any presence or truth of humanity here,
See myself in prison shaped like another man,
And feel the dull unintermitted pain.

246. For me the keepers of convicts shoulder their carbines and keep watch,
It is I let out in the morning and barred at night.

247. Not a mutineer walks hand-cuffed to the jail, but I am hand-cuffed to him and walk by his side,
I am less the jolly one there, and more the silent one, with sweat on my twitching lips.

248. Not a youngster is taken for larceny, but I go up too, and am tried and sentenced.

249. Not a cholera patient lies at the last gasp, but I also lie at the last gasp,
My face is ash-colored — my sinews gnarl — away from me people retreat.

250. Askers embody themselves in me, and I am embodied
in them,
I project my hat, sit shame-faced, and beg.

251. Enough — I bring such to a close,
Rise extatic through all, sweep with the true gravita-
tion,
The whirling and whirling elemental within me.

252. Somehow I have been stunned.   Stand back !
Give me a little time beyond my cuffed head, slum-
bers, dreams, gaping,
I discover myself on the verge of a usual mistake.

253. That I could forget the mockers and insults !
That I could forget the trickling tears, and the blows
of the bludgeons and hammers !
That I could look with a separate look on my own
crucifixion and bloody crowning.

254. I remember now,
I resume the overstaid fraction,
The grave of rock multiplies what has been confided
to it, or to any graves,
Corpses rise, gashes heal, fastenings roll from me.

255. I troop forth replenished with supreme power, one of
an average unending procession,
We walk the roads of the six North Eastern States,
and of Virginia, Wisconsin, Manhattan Island,
Philadelphia, New Orleans, Texas, Charleston,
Havana, Mexico,
Inland and by the sea-coast and boundary lines, and
we pass all boundary lines.

256. Our swift ordinances are on their way over the whole earth,

The blossoms we wear in our hats are the growth of two thousand years.

257. Élèves, I salute you!

I see the approach of your numberless gangs — I see you understand yourselves and me,

And know that they who have eyes and can walk are divine, and the blind and lame are equally divine,

And that my steps drag behind yours, yet go before them,

And are aware how I am with you no more than I am with everybody.

258. The friendly and flowing savage, Who is he?

Is he waiting for civilization, or past it and mastering it?

259. Is he some south-westerner, raised out-doors? Is he Kanadian?

Is he from the Mississippi country? Iowa, Oregon, California? the mountains? prairie-life, bush-life? or from the sea?

260. Wherever he goes men and women accept and desire him,

They desire he should like them, touch them, speak to them, stay with them.

261. Behavior lawless as snow-flakes, words simple as grass, uncombed head, laughter, and naïveté,

Slow-stepping feet, common features, common modes and emanations,

They descend in new forms from the tips of his
    fingers,
They are wafted with the odor of his body or breath
    — they fly out of the glance of his eyes.

262. Flaunt of the sunshine, I need not your bask, — lie
    over!
You light surfaces only — I force surfaces and depths
    also.

Earth! you seem to look for something at my hands,
Say, old Top-knot! what do you want?

263. Man or woman! I might tell how I like you, but
    cannot,
And might tell what it is in me, and what it is in
    you, but cannot,
And might tell that pining I have — that pulse of my
    nights and days.

264. Behold! I do not give lectures or a little charity,
What I give, I give out of myself.

265. You there, impotent, loose in the knees,
Open your scarfed chops till I blow grit within you,
Spread your palms, and lift the flaps of your pockets;
I am not to be denied — I compel — I have stores
    plenty and to spare,
And anything I have I bestow.

266. I do not ask who you are — that is not important to
    me,
You can do nothing, and be nothing, but what I will
    infold you.

267. To a drudge of the cotton-fields or cleaner of privies
     I lean,
    On his right cheek I put the family kiss,
    And in my soul I swear, I never will deny him.

268. On women fit for conception I start bigger and nim-
     bler babes,
    This day I am jetting the stuff of far more arrogant
     republics.

269. To any one dying — thither I speed, and twist the
     knob of the door,
    Turn the bed-clothes toward the foot of the bed,
    Let the physician and the priest go home.

270. I seize the descending man, and raise him with resist-
     less will.

271. O despairer, here is my neck,
    By God! you shall not go down! Hang your whole
     weight upon me.

272. I dilate you with tremendous breath — I buoy you up,
    Every room of the house do I fill with an armed force,
    Lovers of me, bafflers of graves.

273. Sleep! I and they keep guard all night,
    Not doubt — not decease shall dare to lay finger upon
     you,
    I have embraced you, and henceforth possess you to
     myself,
    And when you rise in the morning you will find what
     I tell you is so.

8

274. I am he bringing help for the sick as they pant on
        their backs,
    And for strong upright men I bring yet more needed
        help.

275. I heard what was said of the universe,
    Heard it and heard it of several thousand years ;
    It is middling well as far as it goes, — But is that all ?

276. Magnifying and applying come I,
    Outbidding at the start the old cautious hucksters,
    The most they offer for mankind and eternity less
        than a spirt of my own seminal wet,
    Taking myself the exact dimensions of Jehovah,
    Lithographing Kronos, Zeus his son, and Hercules
        his grandson,
    Buying drafts of Osiris, Isis, Belus, Brahma, Buddha,
    In my portfolio placing Manito loose, Allah on a leaf,
        the crucifix engraved,
    With Odin, and the hideous-faced Mexitli, and every
        idol and image,
    Taking them all for what they are worth, and not a
        cent more,
    Admitting they were alive and did the work of their
        day,
    Admitting they bore mites, as for unfledged birds,
        who have now to rise and fly and sing for them-
        selves,
    Accepting the rough deific sketches to fill out better
        in myself — bestowing them freely on each man
        and woman I see,
    Discovering as much, or more, in a framer framing a
        house,

Putting higher claims for him there with his rolled-
up sleeves, driving the mallet and chisel,

Not objecting to special revelations — considering a
curl of smoke or a hair on the back of my hand
just as curious as any revelation,

Those ahold of fire engines and hook-and-ladder ropes
no less to me than the Gods of the antique wars,

Minding their voices peal through the crash of
destruction,

Their brawny limbs passing safe over charred laths —
their white foreheads whole and unhurt out of
the flames ;

By the mechanic's wife with her babe at her nipple
interceding for every person born,

Three scythes at harvest whizzing in a row from
three lusty angels with shirts bagged out at
their waists,

The snag-toothed hostler with red hair redeeming sins
past and to come,

Selling all he possesses, travelling on foot to fee
lawyers for his brother, and sit by him while he
is tried for forgery ;

What was strewn in the amplest strewing the square
rod about me, and not filling the square rod
then,

The bull and the bug never worshipped half enough,

Dung and dirt more admirable than was dreamed,

The supernatural of no account — myself waiting my
time to be one of the Supremes,

The day getting ready for me when I shall do as
much good as the best, and be as prodigious,

Guessing when I am it will not tickle me much to
receive puffs out of pulpit or print ;

By my life-lumps! becoming already a creator,
Putting myself here and now to the ambushed womb
of the shadows.

277. A call in the midst of the crowd,
My own voice, orotund, sweeping, final.

278. Come my children,
Come my boys and girls, my women, household,
and intimates,
Now the performer launches his nerve — he has
passed his prelude on the reeds within.

279. Easily written, loose-fingered chords! I feel the thrum
of their climax and close.

280. My head slues round on my neck,
Music rolls, but not from the organ,
Folks are around me, but they are no household of
mine.

281. Ever the hard unsunk ground,
Ever the eaters and drinkers — Ever the upward
and downward sun — Ever the air and the cease-
less tides,
Ever myself and my neighbors, refreshing, wicked,
real,
Ever the old inexplicable query — Ever that thorned
thumb — that breath of itches and thirsts,
Ever the vexer's *hoot! hoot!* till we find where the
sly one hides, and bring him forth;
Ever love — Ever the sobbing liquid of life,
Ever the bandage under the chin — Ever the tressels
of death.

282. Here and there, with dimes on the eyes walking,
To feed the greed of the belly, the brains liberally
spooning,
Tickets buying, taking, selling, but in to the feast
never once going,
Many sweating, ploughing, thrashing, and then the
chaff for payment receiving,
A few idly owning, and they the wheat continually
claiming.

283. This is the city, and I am one of the citizens,
Whatever interests the rest interests me — politics,
markets, newspapers, schools,
Benevolent societies, improvements, banks, tariffs,
steamships, factories, stocks, stores, real estate,
and personal estate.

284. They who piddle and patter here in collars and tailed
coats — I am aware who they are — they are not
worms or fleas.

285. I acknowledge the duplicates of myself — the weakest
and shallowest is deathless with me,
What I do and say, the same waits for them,
Every thought that flounders in me, the same floun-
ders in them.

286. I know perfectly well my own egotism,
I know my omnivorous words, and cannot say any
less,
And would fetch you, whoever you are, flush with
myself.

8*

287. My words are words of a questioning, and to indicate
        reality and motive power:
    This printed and bound book — but the printer, and
        the printing-office boy?
    The well-taken photographs — but your wife or friend
        close and solid in your arms?
    The fleet of ships of the line, and all the modern
        improvements — but the craft and pluck of the
        admiral?
    The dishes and fare and furniture — but the host and
        hostess, and the look out of their eyes?
    The sky up there — yet here, or next door, or across
        the way?
    The saints and sages in history — but you yourself?
    Sermons, creeds, theology — but the human brain,
        and what is reason? and what is love? and what
        is life?


288. I do not despise you, priests,
    My faith is the greatest of faiths, and the least of
        faiths,
    Enclosing all worship ancient and modern, and all
        between ancient and modern,
    Believing I shall come again upon the earth after
        five thousand years,
    Waiting responses from oracles, honoring the Gods,
        saluting the sun,
    Making a fetish of the first rock or stump, powwowing
        with sticks in the circle of obis,
    Helping the lama or brahmin as he trims the lamps
        of the idols,
    Dancing yet through the streets in a phallic pro-
        cession — rapt and austere in the woods, a
        gymnosophist,

Drinking mead from the skull-cup — to Shastas and
Vedas admirant — minding the Koran,
Walking the teokallis, spotted with gore from the
stone and knife, beating the serpent-skin drum,
Accepting the Gospels — accepting him that was
crucified, knowing assuredly that he is divine,
To the mass kneeling, or the puritan's prayer rising,
or sitting patiently in a pew,
Ranting and frothing in my insane crisis, or waiting
dead-like till my spirit arouses me,
Looking forth on pavement and land, or outside of
pavement and land,
Belonging to the winders of the circuit of circuits.

289. One of that centripetal and centrifugal gang, I turn
and talk like a man leaving charges before a
journey.

290. Down-hearted doubters, dull and excluded,
Frivolous, sullen, moping, angry, affected, disheart-
ened, atheistical,
I know every one of you — I know the unspoken
interrogatories,
By experience I know them.

291. How the flukes splash!
How they contort, rapid as lightning, with spasms,
and spouts of blood!

292. Be at peace, bloody flukes of doubters and sullen
mopers,
I take my place among you as much as among any,
The past is the push of you, me, all, precisely the
same,

Day and night are for you, me, all,
And what is yet untried and afterward is for you,
    me, all, precisely the same.

293. I do not know what is untried and afterward,
    But I know it is sure, alive, sufficient.

294. Each who passes is considered — Each who stops is
    considered — Not a single one can it fail.

295. It cannot fail the young man who died and was
    buried,
    Nor the young woman who died and was put by his
    side,
    Nor the little child that peeped in at the door, and
    then drew back, and was never seen again,
    Nor the old man who has lived without purpose, and
    feels it with bitterness worse than gall,
    Nor him in the poor-house, tubercled by rum and
    the bad disorder,
    Nor the numberless slaughtered and wrecked — nor
    the brutish koboo called the ordure of humanity,
    Nor the sacs merely floating with open mouths for
    food to slip in,
    Nor anything in the earth, or down in the oldest
    graves of the earth,
    Nor anything in the myriads of spheres — nor one of
    the myriads of myriads that inhabit them,
    Nor the present — nor the least wisp that is known.

296. It is time to explain myself — Let us stand up.

297. What is known I strip away,
    I launch all men and women forward with me into
    THE UNKNOWN.

298. The clock indicates the moment — but what does eternity indicate?

299. We have thus far exhausted trillions of winters and summers,
There are trillions ahead, and trillions ahead of them.

300. Births have brought us richness and variety,
And other births will bring us richness and variety.

301. I do not call one greater and one smaller,
That which fills its period and place is equal to any.

302. Were mankind murderous or jealous upon you, my brother, my sister?
I am sorry for you — they are not murderous or jealous upon me,
All has been gentle with me — I keep no account with lamentation,
(What have I to do with lamentation?)

303. I am an acme of things accomplished, and I an encloser of things to be.

304. My feet strike an apex of the apices of the stairs,
On every step bunches of ages, and larger bunches between the steps,
All below duly travelled, and still I mount and mount.

305. Rise after rise bow the phantoms behind me,
Afar down I see the huge first Nothing — I know I was even there,
I waited unseen and always, and slept through the lethargic mist,

And took my time, and took no hurt from the fetid carbon.

303. Long I was hugged close — long and long.

307. Immense have been the preparations for me,
Faithful and friendly the arms that have helped me.

308. Cycles ferried my cradle, rowing and rowing like cheerful boatmen,
For room to me stars kept aside in their own rings,
They sent influences to look after what was to hold me.

309. Before I was born out of my mother, generations guided me,
My embryo has never been torpid — nothing could overlay it.

310. For it the nebula cohered to an orb,
The long slow strata piled to rest it on,
Vast vegetables gave it sustenance,
Monstrous sauroids transported it in their mouths, and deposited it with care.

311. All forces have been steadily employed to complete and delight me,
Now I stand on this spot with my Soul.

312. O span of youth! Ever-pushed elasticity!
O manhood, balanced, florid, and full.

313. My lovers suffocate me!
Crowding my lips, thick in the pores of my skin,
Jostling me through streets and public halls — coming naked to me at night,

Crying by day *Ahoy!* from the rocks of the river
— swinging and chirping over my head,
Calling my name from flower-beds, vines, tangled
under-brush,
Or while I swim in the bath, or drink from the pump
at the corner — or the curtain is· down at the
opera, or I glimpse at a woman's face in the
railroad car,
Lighting on every moment of my life,
Bussing my body with soft balsamic busses,
Noiselessly passing handfuls out of their hearts, and
giving them to be mine.

314. Old age superbly rising! O welcome, ineffable grace
of dying days!

315. Every condition promulges not only itself — it pro-
mulges what grows after and out of itself,
And the dark hush promulges as much as any.

316. I open my scuttle at night and see the far-sprinkled
systems,
And all I see, multiplied as high as I can cipher, edge
but the rim of the farther systems.

317. Wider and wider they spread, expanding, always
expanding,
Outward, outward, and forever outward.

318. My sun has his sun, and round him obediently
wheels,
He joins with his partners a group of superior circuit,
And greater sets follow, making specks of the greatest
inside them.

319. There is no stoppage, and never can be stoppage,
    If I, you, the worlds, all beneath or upon their sur-
        faces, and all the palpable life, were this moment
        reduced back to a pallid float, it would not avail
        in the long run,
    We should surely bring up again where we now
        stand,
    And as surely go as much farther — and then farther
        and farther.

320. A few quadrillions of eras, a few octillions of cubic
        leagues, do not hazard the span, or make it
        impatient,
    They are but parts — anything is but a part.

321. See ever so far, there is limitless space outside
        of that,
    Count ever so much, there is limitless time around
        that.

322. My rendèzvous is appointed,
    The Lord will be there, and wait till I come on per-
        fect terms.

323. I know I have the best of time and space, and was
        never measured, and never will be measured.

324. I tramp a perpetual journey,
    My signs are a rain-proof coat, good shoes, and a staff
        cut from the woods,
    No friend of mine takes his ease in my chair,
    I have no chair, no church, no philosophy,
    I lead no man to a dinner-table, library, or exchange,

But each man and each woman of you I lead upon
a knoll,
My left hand hooking you round the waist,
My right hand pointing to landscapes of continents,
and a plain public road.

325. Not I — not any one else, can travel that road for
you,
You must travel it for yourself.

326. It is not far — it is within reach,
Perhaps you have been on it since you were born,
and did not know,
Perhaps it is every where on water and on land.

327. Shoulder your duds, and I will mine, and let us
hasten forth,
Wonderful cities and free nations we shall fetch as
we go.

328. If you tire, give me both burdens, and rest the chuff
of your hand on my hip,
And in due time you shall repay the same service
to me,
For after we start we never lie by again.

329. This day before dawn I ascended a hill, and looked
at the crowded heaven,
And I said to my Spirit, *When we become the
enfolders of those orbs, and the pleasure and
knowledge of everything in them, shall we be
filled and satisfied then ?*
And my Spirit said *No, we level that lift, to pass and
continue beyond.*

9

330. You are also asking me questions, and I hear you,
I answer that I cannot answer — you must find out
for yourself.

331. Sit a while, wayfarer,
Here are biscuits to eat, and here is milk to drink,
But as soon as you sleep, and renew yourself in
sweet clothes, I will certainly kiss you with my
good-bye kiss, and open the gate for your egress
hence.

332. Long enough have you dreamed contemptible dreams,
Now I wash the gum from your eyes,
You must habit yourself to the dazzle of the light,
and of every moment of your life.

333. Long have you timidly waded, holding a plank by
the shore,
Now I will you to be a bold swimmer,
To jump off in the midst of the sea, rise again, nod
to me, shout, and laughingly dash with your hair.

334. I am the teacher of athletes,
He that by me spreads a wider breast than my own,
proves the width of my own,
He most honors my style who learns under it to
destroy the teacher.

335. The boy I love, the same becomes a man, not through
derived power, but in his own right,
Wicked, rather than virtuous out of conformity or
fear,
Fond of his sweetheart, relishing well his steak,

Unrequited love, or a slight, cutting him worse than
a wound cuts,
First rate to ride, to fight, to hit the bull's-eye, to
sail a skiff, to sing a song, or play on the banjo,
Preferring scars, and faces pitted with small-pox, over
all latherers, and those that keep out of the sun.

336. I teach straying from me — yet who can stray from
me ?
I follow you, whoever you are, from the present
hour,
My words itch at your ears till you understand
them.

337. I do not say these things for a dollar, or to fill up
the time while I wait for a boat,
It is you talking just as much as myself — I act as
the tongue of you,
Tied in your mouth, in mine it begins to be loosened.

338. I swear I will never again mention love or death
inside a house,
And I swear I will never translate myself at all, only
to him or her who privately stays with me in
the open air.

339. If you would understand me, go to the heights or
water-shore,
The nearest gnat is an explanation, and a drop or
motion of waves a key,
The maul, the oar, the hand-saw, second my words.

340. No shuttered room or school can commune with me,
But roughs and little children better than they.

341. The young mechanic is closest to me — he knows me
     pretty well,
     The woodman, that takes his axe and jug with him,
     shall take me with him all day,
     The farm-boy, ploughing in the field, feels good at the
     sound of my voice,
     In vessels that sail, my words sail — I go with fisher-
     men and seamen, and love them.

342. My face rubs to the hunter's face, when he lies down
     alone in his blanket,
     The driver, thinking of me, does not mind the jolt
     of his wagon,
     The young mother and old mother comprehend me,
     The girl and the wife rest the needle a moment, and
     forget where they are,
     They and all would resume what I have told them.

343. I have said that the Soul is not more than the
     body,
     And I have said that the body is not more than
     the Soul,
     And nothing, not God, is greater to one than one's
     self is,
     And whoever walks a furlong without sympathy,
     walks to his own funeral, dressed in his shroud,
     And I or you, pocketless of a dime, may purchase
     the pick of the earth,
     And to glance with an eye, or show a bean in its
     pod, confounds the learning of all times,
     And there is no trade or employment but the young
     man following it may become a hero,

And there is no object so soft but it makes a hub
    for the wheeled universe,

And any man or woman shall stand cool and
    supercilious before a million universes.

344. And I call to mankind, Be not curious about God,
    For I, who am curious about each, am not curious
        about God,
    No array of terms can say how much I am at peace
        about God, and about death.

345. I hear and behold God in every object, yet under-
    stand God not in the least,
    Nor do I understand who there can be more won-
        derful than myself.

346. Why should I wish to see God better than this day?
    I see something of God each hour of the twenty-four,
        and each moment then,
    In the faces of men and women I see God, and in
        my own face in the glass,
    I find letters from God dropped in the street — and
        every one is signed by God's name,
    And I leave them where they are, for I know that
        others will punctually come forever and ever.

347. And as to you Death, and you bitter hug of mortality,
    it is idle to try to alarm me.

348. To his work without flinching the accoucheur comes,
    I see the elder-hand, pressing, receiving, supporting,
    I recline by the sills of the exquisite flexible doors,
        and mark the outlet, and mark the relief and
        escape.

9 *

349. And as to you corpse, I think you are good manure,
   but that does not offend me,
   I smell the white roses sweet-scented and growing,
   I reach to the leafy lips — I reach to the polished
   breasts of melons.

350. And as to you life, I reckon you are the leavings of
   many deaths,
   No doubt I have died myself ten thousand times
   before.

351. I hear you whispering there, O stars of heaven,
   O suns! O grass of graves! O perpetual transfers and
   promotions!
   If you do not say anything, how can I say anything?

352. Of the turbid pool that lies in the autumn forest,
   Of the moon that descends the steeps of the soughing
   twilight,
   Toss, sparkles of day and dusk! toss on the black
   stems that decay in the muck!
   Toss to the moaning gibberish of the dry limbs.

353. I ascend from the moon, I ascend from the night,
   I perceive of the ghastly glimmer the sunbeams re-
   flected,
   And debouch to the steady and central from the
   offspring great or small.

354. There is that in me — I do not know what it is — but
   I know it is in me.

355. Wrenched and sweaty — calm and cool then my body
   becomes,
   I sleep — I sleep long.

356. I do not know it — it is without name — it is a word unsaid,

It is not in any dictionary, utterance, symbol.

357. Something it swings on more than the earth I swing on,

To it the creation is the friend whose embracing awakes me.

358. Perhaps I might tell more. Outlines! I plead for my brothers and sisters.

359. Do you see, O my brothers and sisters?

It is not chaos or death — it is form, union, plan — it is eternal life — it is HAPPINESS.

360. The past and present wilt — I have filled them, emptied them,

And proceed to fill my next fold of the future.

361. Listener up there! Here you! What have you to confide to me?

Look in my face, while I snuff the sidle of evening,

Talk honestly — no one else hears you, and I stay only a minute longer.

362. Do I contradict myself?

Very well, then, I contradict myself,

I am large — I contain multitudes.

363. I concentrate toward them that are nigh — I wait on the door-slab.

364. Who has done his day's work? Who will soonest be through with his supper?

Who wishes to walk with me?

365. Will you speak before I am gone? Will you prove
     already too late?

366. The spotted hawk swoops by and accuses me — he
     complains of my gab and my loitering.

367. I too am not a bit tamed — I too am untranslatable,
     I sound my barbaric yawp over the roofs of the world.

368. The last scud of day holds back for me,
     It flings my likeness, after the rest, and true as any,
       on the shadowed wilds,
     It coaxes me to the vapor and the dusk.

369. I depart as air — I shake my white locks at the
     run-away sun,
     I effuse my flesh in eddies, and drift it in lacy jags.

370. I bequeathe myself to the dirt, to grow from the
     grass I love,
     If you want me again, look for me under your boot-
     soles.

371. You will hardly know who I am, or what I mean,
     But I shall be good health to you nevertheless,
     And filter and fibre your blood.

372. Failing to fetch me at first, keep encouraged,
     Missing me one place, search another,
     I stop somewhere waiting for you.

# CHANTS

# DEMOCRATIC

AND

## NATIVE AMERICAN.

## Apostroph.

O mater! O fils!

O brood continental!

O flowers of the prairies!

O space boundless! O hum of mighty products!

O you teeming cities! O so invincible, turbulent,
proud!

O race of the future! O women!

O fathers! O you men of passion and the storm!

O native power only! O beauty!

O yourself! O God! O divine average!

O you bearded roughs! O bards! O all those slum-
berers!

O arouse! the dawn-bird's throat sounds shrill! Do
you not hear the cock crowing?

O, as I walk'd the beach, I heard the mournful notes
foreboding a tempest — the low, oft-repeated
shriek of the diver, the long-lived loon;

O I heard, and yet hear, angry thunder; — O you
    sailors! O ships! make quick preparation!
O from his masterful sweep, the warning cry of the
    eagle!
(Give way there, all! It is useless! Give up your
    spoils;)
O sarcasms! Propositions! (O if the whole world
    should prove indeed a sham, a sell!)
O I believe there is nothing real but America and
    freedom!
O to sternly reject all except Democracy!
O imperator! O who dare confront you and me?
O to promulgate our own! O to build for that which
    builds for mankind!
O feuillage! O North! O the slope drained by the
    Mexican sea!
O all, all inseparable — ages, ages, ages!
O a curse on him that would dissever this Union for
    any reason whatever!
O climates, labors! O good and evil! O death!
O you strong with iron and wood! O Personality!
O the village or place which has the greatest man or
    woman! even if it be only a few ragged huts;
O the city where women walk in public processions in
    the streets, the same as the men;
O a wan and terrible emblem, by me adopted!
O shapes arising! shapes of the future centuries!
O muscle and pluck forever for me!
O workmen and workwomen forever for me!
O farmers and sailors! O drivers of horses forever
    for me!
O I will make the new bardic list of trades and tools!
O you coarse and wilful! I love you!

O South! O longings for my dear home! O soft and
sunny airs!

O pensive! O I must return where the palm grows
and the mocking-bird sings, or else I die!

O equality! O organic compacts! I am come to be
your born poet!

O whirl, contest, sounding and resounding! I am
your poet, because I am part of you;

O days by-gone! Enthusiasts! Antecedents!

O vast preparations for These States! O years!

O what is now being sent forward thousands of years
to come!

O mediums! O to teach! to convey the invisible faith!

To promulge real things! to journey through all The
States!

O creation! O to-day! O laws! O unmitigated
adoration!

O for mightier broods of orators, artists, and singers!

O for native songs! carpenter's, boatman's, plough-
man's songs! shoemaker's songs!

O haughtiest growth of time! O free and extatic!

O what I, here, preparing, warble for!

O you hastening light! O the sun of the world will
ascend, dazzling, and take his height — and you
too will ascend;

O so amazing and so broad! up there resplendent,
darting and burning;

O prophetic! O vision staggered with weight of light!
with pouring glories!

O copious! O hitherto unequalled!

O Libertad! O compact! O union impossible to
dissever!

O my Soul! O lips becoming tremulous, powerless!

O centuries, centuries yet ahead!

O voices of greater orators! I pause — I listen for
you!

O you States! Cities! defiant of all outside authority!
I spring at once into your arms! you I most
love!

O you grand Presidentiads! I wait for you!

New history! New heroes! I project you!

Visions of poets! only you really last! O sweep on!
sweep on!

O Death! O you striding there! O I cannot yet!

O heights! O infinitely too swift and dizzy yet!

O purged lumine! you threaten me more than I can
stand!

O present! I return while yet I may to you!

O poets to come, I depend upon you!

**I.**

1. A NATION announcing itself, (many in one,)
   I myself make the only growth by which I can be
   appreciated,
   I reject none, accept all, reproduce all in my own
   forms.

2. A breed whose testimony is behavior,
   What we are WE ARE — nativity is answer enough
   to objections;
   We wield ourselves as a weapon is wielded,

We are powerful and tremendous in ourselves,
We are executive in ourselves — We are sufficient
    in the variety of ourselves,
We are the most beautiful to ourselves, and in our-
    selves,
Nothing is sinful to us outside of ourselves,
Whatever appears, whatever does not appear, we are
    beautiful or sinful in ourselves only.


3. Have you thought there could be but a single
    Supreme ?
There can be any number of Supremes — One does
    not countervail another, any more than one eye-
    sight countervails another, or one life counter-
    vails another.


4. All is eligible to all,
All is for individuals — All is for you,
No condition is prohibited, not God's or any,
If one is lost, you are inevitably lost.


5. All comes by the body — only health puts you rapport
    with the universe.


6. Produce great persons, the rest follows.


7. How dare a sick man, or an obedient man, write
    poems for These States?
Which is the theory or book that, for our purposes, is
    not diseased ?


8. Piety and conformity to them that like !
Peace, obesity, allegiance, to them that like !

10

I am he who tauntingly compels men, women, nations, to leap from their seats and contend for their lives.

9. I am he who goes through the streets with a barbed tongue, questioning every one I meet — questioning you up there now :
Who are you, that wanted only to be told what you knew before ?
Who are you, that wanted only a book to join you in your nonsense ?

10. Are you, or would you be, better than all that has ever been before ?
If you would be better than all that has ever been before, come listen to me, and not otherwise.

11. ˙Fear grace — Fear delicatesse,
Fear the mellow sweet, the sucking of honey-juice,
Beware the advancing mortal ripening of nature,
Beware what precedes the decay of the ruggedness of states and men.

12. Ages, precedents, poems, have long been accumulating undirected materials,
America brings builders, and brings its own styles.

13. Mighty bards have done their work, and passed to other spheres,
One work forever remains, the work of surpassing all they have done.

14. America, curious toward foreign characters, stands by its own at all hazards,

Stands removed, spacious, composite, sound,
Sees itself promulger of men and women, initiates
the true use of precedents,
Does not repel them or the past, or what they have
produced under their forms, or amid other pol-
itics, or amid the idea of castes, or the old
religions,
Takes the lesson with calmness, perceives the corpse
slowly borne from the eating and sleeping rooms
of the house,
Perceives that it waits a little while in the door —
that it was fittest for its days,
That its life has descended to the stalwart and well-
shaped heir who approaches,
And that he shall be fittest for his days.


15. Any period, one nation must lead,
One land must be the promise and reliance of the
future.


16. These States are the amplest poem,
Here is not merely a nation, but a teeming nation of
nations,
Here the doings of men correspond with the broad-
cast doings of the day and night,
Here is what moves in magnificent masses, carelessly
faithful of particulars,
Here are the roughs, beards, friendliness, combative-
ness, the Soul loves,
Here the flowing trains — here the crowds, equality,
diversity, the Soul loves.


17. Race of races, and bards to corroborate !

Of them, standing among them, one lifts to the light
    his west-bred face,

To him the hereditary countenance bequeathed, both
    mother's and father's,

His first parts substances, earth, water, animals, trees,

Built of the common stock, having room for far and
    near,

Used to dispense with other lands, incarnating this
    land,

Attracting it body and Soul to himself, hanging on its
    neck with incomparable love,

Plunging his semitic muscle into its merits and
    demerits,

Making its geography, cities, beginnings, events,
    glories, defections, diversities, vocal in him,

Making its rivers, lakes, bays, embouchure in him,

Mississippi with yearly freshets and changing chutes
    — Missouri, Columbia, Ohio, Niagara, Hudson,
    spending themselves lovingly in him,

If the Atlantic coast stretch, or the Pacific coast
    stretch, he stretching with them north or south,

Spanning between them east and west, and touching
    whatever is between them,

Growths growing from him to offset the growth of
    pine, cedar, hemlock, live-oak, locust, chest-
    nut, cypress, hickory, lime-tree, cotton-wood,
    tulip-tree, cactus, tamarind, orange, magnolia,
    persimmon,

Tangles as tangled in him as any cane-brake or
    swamp,

He likening sides and peaks of mountains, forests
    coated with transparent ice, and icicles hanging
    from the boughs,

Off him pasturage sweet and natural as savanna,
upland, prairie,

Through him flights, songs, screams, answering those
of the wild-pigeon, coot, fish-hawk, qua-bird,
mocking-bird, condor, night-heron, eagle;

His spirit surrounding his country's spirit, unclosed
to good and evil,

Surrounding the essences of real things, old times
and present times,

Surrounding just found shores, islands, tribes of red
aborigines,

Weather-beaten vessels, landings, settlements, the
rapid stature and muscle,

The haughty defiance of the Year 1 — war, peace,
the formation of the Constitution,

The separate States, the simple, elastic scheme, the
immigrants,

The Union, always swarming with blatherers, and
always calm and impregnable,

The unsurveyed interior, log-houses, clearings, wild
animals, hunters, trappers;

Surrounding the multiform agriculture, mines, tem-
perature, the gestation of new States,

Congress convening every Twelfth Month, the mem-
bers duly coming up from the uttermost parts;

Surrounding the noble character of mechanics and
farmers, especially the young men,

Responding their manners, speech, dress, friendships
— the gait they have of persons who never knew
how it felt to stand in the presence of superiors,

The freshness and candor of their physiognomy, the
copiousness and decision of their phrenology,

The picturesque looseness of their carriage, their
deathless attachment to freedom, their fierceness
when wronged,

The fluency of their speech, their delight in music,
their curiosity, good temper, and open-handed-
ness — the whole composite make,

The prevailing ardor and enterprise, the large am-
ativeness,

The perfect equality of the female with the male, the
fluid movement of the population,

The superior marine, free commerce, fisheries,
whaling, gold-digging,

Wharf-hemmed cities, railroad and steamboat lines,
intersecting all points,

Factories, mercantile life, labor-saving machinery, the
north-east, north-west, south-west,

Manhattan firemen, the Yankee swap, southern plan-
tation life,

Slavery, the tremulous spreading of hands to shelter
it — the stern opposition to it, which ceases only
when it ceases.


18. For these and the like, their own voices! For these,
space ahead!

Others take finish, but the Republic is ever con-
structive, and ever keeps vista;

Others adorn the past — but you, O, days of the
present, I adorn you!

O days of the future, I believe in you!

O America, because you build for mankind, I build
for you!

O well-beloved stone-cutters! I lead them who plan
with decision and science,

I lead the present with friendly hand toward the future.

19. Bravas to States whose semitic impulses send whole-some children to the next age !
But damn that which spends itself on flaunters and dalliers, with no thought of the stain, pains, dismay, feebleness, it is bequeathing.

20. By great bards only can series of peoples and States be fused into the compact organism of one nation.

21. To hold men together by paper and seal, or by com-pulsion, is no account,
That only holds men together which is living prin-ciples, as the hold of the limbs of the body, or the fibres of plants.

22. Of all races and eras, These States, with veins full of poetical stuff, most need poets, and are to have the greatest, and use them the greatest,
Their Presidents shall not be their common referee so much as their poets shall.

23. Of mankind, the poet is the equable man,
Not in him, but off from him, things are grotesque, eccentric, fail of their full returns,
Nothing out of its place is good, nothing in its place is bad,
He bestows on every object or quality its fit propor-tions, neither more nor less,
He is the arbiter of the diverse, he is the key,

He is the equalizer of his age and land,

He supplies what wants supplying — he checks what
wants checking,

In peace, out of him speaks the spirit of peace, large,
rich, thrifty, building populous towns, encour-
aging agriculture, arts, commerce, lighting the
study of man, the Soul, health, immortality,
government,

In war, he is the best backer of the war — he fetches
artillery as good as the engineer's — he can make
every word he speaks draw blood ;

The years straying toward infidelity, he withholds by
his steady faith,

He is no arguer, he is judgment,

He judges not as the judge judges, but as the sun
falling round a helpless thing ;

As he sees the farthest he has the most faith,

His thoughts are the hymns of the praise of things, ·

In the dispute on God and eternity he is silent,

He sees eternity less like a play with a prologue and
denouement,

He sees eternity in men and women — he does not
see men and women as dreams or dots.

24. Of the idea of perfect and free individuals, the idea
of These States, the bard walks in advance,
leader of leaders,

The attitude of him cheers up slaves, and horrifies
foreign despots.

25. Without extinction is Liberty ! Without retrograde
is Equality !

They live in the feelings of young men, and the
best women,

Not for nothing have the indomitable heads of the
earth been always ready to fall for Liberty!

26. Are YOU indeed for Liberty?
Are you a man who would assume a place to teach
here, or lead here, or be a poet here?
The place is august — the terms obdurate.

27. Who would assume to teach here, may well prepare
himself, body and mind,
He may well survey, ponder, arm, fortify, harden,
make lithe, himself,
He shall surely be questioned beforehand by me with
many and stern questions.

28. Who are you, indeed, who would talk or sing in
America?
Have you studied out MY LAND, its idioms and
men?
Have you learned the physiology, phrenology, poli-
tics, geography, pride, freedom, friendship, of
my land? its substratums and objects?
Have you considered the organic compact of the first
day of the first year of the independence of The
States, signed by the Commissioners, ratified by
The States, and read by Washington at the head
of the army?
Have you possessed yourself of the Federal Constitu-
tion?
Do you acknowledge Liberty with audible and abso-
lute acknowledgment, and set slavery at nought
for life and death?
Do you see who have left described processes and
poems behind them, and assumed new ones?

Are you faithful to things ? Do you teach whatever
the land and sea, the bodies of men, womanhood,
amativeness, angers, excesses, crimes, teach ?
Have you sped through customs, laws, popularities ?
Can you hold your hand against all seductions, follies,
whirls, fierce contentions ? Are you very strong ?
Are you of the whole people ?
Are you not of some coterie ? some school or religion ?
Are you done with reviews and criticisms of life ? ani-
mating to life itself ?
Have you vivified yourself from the maternity of
These States ?
Have you sucked the nipples of the breasts of the
mother of many children ?
Have you too the old, ever-fresh, forbearance and
impartiality ?
Do you hold the like love for those hardening to
maturity ? for the last-born ? little and big ?
and for the errant ?


29. What is this you bring my America ?
Is it uniform with my country ?
Is it not something that has been better told or done
before ?
Have you not imported this, or the spirit of it, in
some ship ?
Is it a mere tale ? a rhyme ? a prettiness ?
Has it never dangled at the heels of the poets, poli-
ticians, literats, of enemies' lands ?
Does it not assume that what is notoriously gone is
still here ?
Does it answer universal needs ? Will it improve
manners ?

Can your performance face the open fields and the
sea-side?

Will it absorb into me as I absorb food, air, nobility,
meanness — to appear again in my strength, gait,
face?

Have real employments contributed to it? original
makers — not amanuenses?

Does it meet modern discoveries, calibers, facts, face
to face?

Does it respect me? Democracy? the Soul? to-day?

What does it mean to me? to American persons,
progresses, cities? Chicago, Kanada, Arkansas?
the planter, Yankee, Georgian, native, immi-
grant, sailors, squatters, old States, new States?

Does it encompass all The States, and the unexcep-
tional rights of all the men and women of the
earth, the genital impulse of These States?

Does it see behind the apparent custodians, the
real custodians, standing, menacing, silent, the
mechanics, Manhattanese, western men, south-
erners, significant alike in their apathy and in
the promptness of their love?

Does it see what befalls and has always befallen
each temporizer, patcher, outsider, partialist,
alarmist, infidel, who has ever asked anything
of America?

What mocking and scornful negligence?

The track strewed with the dust of skeletons?

By the roadside others disdainfully tossed?


30. Rhymes and rhymers pass away — poems distilled
from other poems pass away,

The swarms of reflectors and the polite pass, and
leave ashes;

Admirers, importers, obedient persons, make the soil
of literature ;
America justifies itself, give it time — no disguise can
deceive it, or conceal from it — it is impassive
enough,
Only toward the likes of itself will it advance to meet
them,
If its poets appear, it will advance to meet them —
there is no fear of mistake,
The proof of a poet shall be sternly deferred, till his
country absorbs him as affectionately as he has
absorbed it.


31. He masters whose spirit masters — he tastes sweetest
who results sweetest in the long run,
The blood of the brawn beloved of time is uncon-
straint,
In the need of poems, philosophy, politics, manners,
engineering, an appropriate native grand-opera,
shipcraft, any craft, he or she is greatest who
contributes the greatest original practical ex-
ample.


32. Already a nonchalant breed, silently emerging, fills
the houses and streets,
People's lips salute only doers, lovers, satisfiers,
positive knowers ;
There will shortly be no more priests — I say their
work is done,
Death is without emergencies here, but life is per-
petual emergencies here,
Are your body, days, manners, superb ? after death
you shall be superb ;

Friendship, self-esteem, justice, health, clear the way
with irresistible power ;
How dare you place anything before a man ?

33. Fall behind me, States !
A man, before all — myself, typical, before all.

34. Give me the pay I have served for !
Give me to speak beautiful words ! take all the
rest ;
I have loved the earth, sun, animals—I have despised
riches,
I have given alms to every one that asked, stood up
for the stupid and crazy, devoted my income
and labor to others,
I have hated tyrants, argued not concerning God,
had patience and indulgence toward the people,
taken off my hat to nothing known or unknown,
I have gone freely with powerful uneducated persons,
and with the young, and with the mothers of
families,
I have read these leaves to myself in the open air —
I have tried them by trees, stars, rivers,
I have dismissed whatever insulted my own Soul or
defiled my body,
I have claimed nothing to myself which I have not
carefully claimed for others on the same terms,
I have studied my land, its idioms and men,
I am willing to wait to be understood by the growth
of the taste of myself,
I reject none, I permit all,
Whom I have staid with once I have found longing
for me ever afterward.

11

34. I swear I begin to see the meaning of these things!
   It is not the earth, it is not America, who is so great,
   It is I who am great, or to be great — it is you, or
       any one,
   It is to walk rapidly through civilizations, govern-
       ments, theories, nature, poems, shows, to indi-
       viduals.

35. Underneath all are individuals,
   I swear nothing is good to me now that ignores
       individuals!
   The American compact is altogether with individuals,
   The only government is that which makes minute of
       individuals,
   The whole theory of the universe is directed to one
       single individual — namely, to You.

36. Underneath all is nativity,
   I swear I will stand by my own nativity — pious or
       impious, so be it;
   I swear I am charmed with nothing except nativity,
   Men, women, cities, nations, are only beautiful from
       nativity.

37. Underneath all is the need of the expression of love
       for men and women,
   I swear I have had enough of mean and impotent
       modes of expressing love for men and women,
   After this day I take my own modes of expressing
       love for men and women.

38. I swear I will have each quality of my race in
       myself,

Talk as you like, he only suits These States whose manners favor the audacity and sublime turbulence of The States.

39. Underneath the lessons of things, spirits, nature, governments, ownerships, I swear I perceive other lessons,
Underneath all to me is myself — to you, yourself, (the same monotonous old song,)
If all had not kernels for you and me, what were it to you and me?

40. O I see now, flashing, that this America is only you and me,
Its power, weapons, testimony, are you and me,
Its roughs, beards, haughtiness, ruggedness, are you and me,
Its ample geography, the sierras, the prairies, Mississippi, Huron, Colorado, Boston, Toronto, Raleigh, Nashville, Havana, are you and me,
Its settlements, wars, the organic compact, peace, Washington, the Federal Constitution, are you and me,
Its young men's manners, speech, dress, friendships, are you and me,
Its crimes, lies, thefts, defections, slavery, are you and me,
Its Congress is you and me — the officers, capitols, armies, ships, are you and me,
Its endless gestations of new States are you and me,
Its inventions, science, schools, are you and me,
Its deserts, forests, clearings, log-houses, hunters, are you and me,

Natural and artificial are you and me,

Freedom, language, poems, employments, are you
and me,

Failures, successes, births, deaths, are you and me,

Past, present, future, are only you and me.

41. I swear I dare not shirk any part of myself,

Not any part of America, good or bad,

Not my body — not friendship, hospitality, pro-
creation,

Not my Soul, nor the last explanation of prudence,

Not the similitude that interlocks me with all iden-
tities that exist, or ever have existed,

Not faith, sin, defiance, nor any disposition or duty
of myself,

Not the promulgation of Liberty — not to cheer up
slaves and horrify despots,

Not to build for that which builds for mankind,

Not to balance ranks, complexions, creeds, and the
sexes,

Not to justify science, nor the march of equality,

Nor to feed the arrogant blood of the brawn beloved
of time.

42. I swear I am for those that have never been
mastered !

For men and women whose tempers have never been
mastered,

For those whom laws, theories, conventions, can never
master.

43. I swear I am for those who walk abreast with the
whole earth !

Who inaugurate one to inaugurate all.

44. I swear I will not be outfaced by irrational things!
   I will penetrate what it is in them that is sarcastic
      upon me!
   I will make cities and civilizations defer to me!
   (This is what I have learnt from America — it is the
      amount — and it I teach again.)

45. I will confront these shows of the day and night!
   I will know if I am to be less than they!
   I will see if I am not as majestic as they!
   I will see if I am not as subtle and real as they!
   I will see if I am to be less generous than they!

46. I will see if I have no meaning, while the houses and
      ships have meaning!
   I will see if the fishes and birds are to be enough
      for themselves, and I am not to be enough for
      myself.

47. I match my spirit against yours, you orbs, growths,
      mountains, brutes,
   Copious as you are, I absorb you all in myself, and
      become the master myself.

48. The Many In One — what is it finally except myself?
   These States — what are they except myself?

49. I have learned why the earth is gross, tantalizing,
      wicked — it is for my sake,
   I take you to be mine, you beautiful, terrible, rude
      forms.

11*

# CHANTS DEMOCRATIC.

—

2.

1. BROAD-AXE, shapely, naked, wan!
   Head from the mother's bowels drawn!
   Wooded flesh and metal bone! limb only one and
       lip only one!
   Gray-blue leaf by red-heat grown! helve produced
       from a little seed sown!
   Resting the grass amid and upon,
   To be leaned, and to lean on.

2. Strong shapes, and attributes of strong shapes —
       masculine trades, sights and sounds,
   Long varied train of an emblem, dabs of music,
   Fingers of the organist skipping staccato over the
       keys of the great organ.

3. Welcome are all earth's lands, each for its kind,
   Welcome are lands of pine and oak,
   Welcome are lands of the lemon and fig,
   Welcome are lands of gold,
   Welcome are lands of wheat and maize — welcome
       those of the grape,
   Welcome are lands of sugar and rice,
   Welcome the cotton-lands — welcome those of the
       white potato and sweet potato,
   Welcome are mountains, flats, sands, forests, prairies,

Welcome the rich borders of rivers, table-lands,
 openings,
Welcome the measureless grazing lands — welcome
 the teeming soil of orchards, flax, honey, hemp,
Welcome just as much the other more hard-faced
 lands,
Lands rich as lands of gold, or wheat and fruit lands,
Lands of mines, lands of the manly and rugged ores,
Lands of coal, copper, lead, tin, zinc,
LANDS OF IRON ! lands of the make of the axe !


4. The log at the wood-pile, the axe supported by it,
 The sylvan hut, the vine over the doorway, the space
 cleared for a garden,
 The irregular tapping of rain down on the leaves,
 after the storm is lulled,
 The wailing and moaning at intervals, the thought of
 the sea,
 The thought of ships struck in the storm, and put on
 their beam-ends, and the cutting away of masts ;
 The sentiment of the huge timbers of old-fashioned
 houses and barns ;
 The remembered print or narrative, the voyage at a
 venture of men, families, goods,
 The disembarkation, the founding of a new city,
 The voyage of those who sought a New England and
 found it — the outset anywhere,
 The settlements of the Arkansas, Colorado, Ottawa,
 Willamette,
 The slow progress, the scant fare, the axe, rifle,
 saddle-bags ;
 The beauty of all adventurous and daring persons,
 The beauty of wood-boys and wood-men, with their
 clear untrimmed faces,

The beauty of independence, departure, actions that
 rely on themselves,
The American contempt for statutes and ceremonies,
 the boundless impatience of restraint,
The loose drift of character, the inkling through
 random types, the solidification ;
The butcher in the slaughter-house, the hands aboard
 schooners and sloops, the raftsman, the pioneer,
Lumbermen in their winter camp, daybreak in the
 woods, stripes of snow on the limbs of trees, the
 occasional snapping,
The glad clear sound of one's own voice, the merry
 song, the natural life of the woods, the strong
 day's work,
The blazing fire at night, the sweet taste of supper,
 the talk, the bed of hemlock boughs, and the
 bear-skin ;
The house-builder at work in cities or anywhere,
The preparatory jointing, squaring, sawing, mor-
 tising,
The hoist-up of beams, the push of them in their
 places, laying them regular,
Setting the studs by their tenons in the mortises,
 according as they were prepared,
The blows of mallets and hammers, the attitudes of
 the men, their curved limbs,
Bending, standing, astride the beams, driving in pins,
 holding on by posts and braces,
The hooked arm over the plate, the other arm
 wielding the axe,
The floor-men forcing the planks close, to be nailed,
Their postures bringing their weapons downward on
 the bearers,

The echoes resounding through the vacant building ;

The huge store-house carried up in the city, well under way,

The six framing-men, two in the middle and two at each end, carefully bearing on their shoulders a heavy stick for a cross-beam,

The crowded line of masons with trowels in their right hands, rapidly laying the long side-wall, two hundred feet from front to rear,

The flexible rise and fall of backs, the continual click of the trowels striking the bricks,

The bricks, one after another, each laid so workman-like in its place, and set with a knock of the trowel-handle,

The piles of materials, the mortar on the mortar-boards, and the steady replenishing by the hod-men ;

Spar-makers in the spar-yard, the swarming row of well-grown apprentices,

The swing of their axes on the square-hewed log, shaping it toward the shape of a mast,

The brisk short crackle of the steel driven slantingly into the pine,

The butter-colored chips flying off in great flakes and slivers,

The limber motion of brawny young arms and hips in easy costumes ;

The constructor of wharves, bridges, piers, bulk-heads, floats, stays against the sea ;

The city fireman — the fire that suddenly bursts forth in the close-packed square,

The arriving engines, the hoarse shouts, the nimble stepping and daring,

The strong command through the fire-trumpets, the
    falling in line, the rise and fall of the arms
    forcing the water,

The slender, spasmic blue-white jets — the bringing
    to bear of the hooks and ladders, and their
    execution,

The crash and cut away of connecting wood-work, or
    through floors, if the fire smoulders under them,

The crowd with their lit faces, watching — the glare
    and dense shadows ;

The forger at his forge-furnace, and the user of iron
    after him,

The maker of the axe large and small, and the
    welder and temperer,

The chooser breathing his breath on the cold steel,
    and trying the edge with his thumb,

The one who clean-shapes the handle and sets it
    firmly in the socket,

The shadowy processions of the portraits of the past
    users also,

The primal patient mechanics, the architects and
    engineers,

The far-off Assyrian edifice and Mizra edifice,

The Roman lictors preceding the consuls,

The antique European warrior with his axe in
    combat,

The uplifted arm, the clatter of blows on the
    helmeted head,

The death-howl, the limpsey tumbling body, the rush
    of friend and foe thither,

The siege of revolted lieges determined for liberty,

The summons to surrender, the battering at castle
    gates, the truce and parley,

The sack of an old city in its time,
The bursting in of mercenaries and bigots tumul-
tuously and disorderly,
Roar, flames, blood, drunkenness, madness,
Goods freely rifled from houses and temples, screams
of women in the gripe of brigands,
Craft and thievery of camp-followers, men running,
old persons despairing,
The hell of war, the cruelties of creeds,
The list of all executive deeds and words, just or
unjust,
The power of personality, just or unjust.

5. Muscle and pluck forever !
What invigorates life, invigorates death,
And the dead advance as much as the living advance,
And the future is no more uncertain than the present,
And the roughness of the earth and of man encloses
as much as the delicatesse of the earth and of
man,
And nothing endures but personal qualities.

6. What do you think endures ?
Do you think the greatest city endures ?
Or a teeming manufacturing state ? or a prepared
constitution ? or the best built steamships ?
Or hotels of granite and iron ? or any chef-d'œuvres
of engineering, forts, armaments ?

7. Away ! These are not to be cherished for themselves,
They fill their hour, the dancers dance, the musicians
play for them,
The show passes, all does well enough of course,
All does very well till one flash of defiance.

8. The greatest city is that which has the greatest man
   or woman,
   If it be a few ragged huts, it is still the greatest city
   in the whole world.

9. The place where the greatest city stands is not the
   place of stretched wharves, docks, manufactures,
   deposits of produce,
   Nor the place of ceaseless salutes of new comers, or
   the anchor-lifters of the departing,
   Nor the place of the tallest and costliest buildings,
   or shops selling goods from the rest of the earth,
   Nor the place of the best libraries and schools — nor
   the place where money is plentiest,
   Nor the place of the most numerous population.

10. Where the city stands with the brawniest breed of
    orators and bards,
    Where the city stands that is beloved by these, and
    loves them in return, and understands them,
    Where these may be seen going every day in the
    streets, with their arms familiar to the shoulders
    of their friends,
    Where no monuments exist to heroes, but in the
    common words and deeds,
    Where thrift is in its place, and prudence is in its
    place,
    Where behavior is the finest of the fine arts,
    Where the men and women think lightly of the
    laws,
    Where the slave ceases, and the master of slaves
    ceases,
    Where the populace rise at once against the never-
    ending audacity of elected persons,

Where fierce men and women pour forth, as the sea
    to the whistle of death pours its sweeping and
    unript waves,
Where outside authority enters always after the
    precedence of inside authority,
Where the citizen is always the head and ideal — and
    President, Mayor, Governor, and what not, are
    agents for pay,
Where children are taught from the jump that they
    are to be laws to themselves, and to depend on
    themselves,
Where equanimity is illustrated in affairs,
Where speculations on the Soul are encouraged,
Where women walk in public processions in the
    streets, the same as the men,
Where they enter the public assembly and take
    places the same as the men, and are appealed
    to by the orators, the same as the men,
Where the city of the faithfulest friends stands,
Where the city of the cleanliness of the sexes stands,
Where the city of the healthiest fathers stands,
Where the city of the best-bodied mothers stands,
There the greatest city stands.


11. How beggarly appear poems, arguments, orations,
    before an electric deed !
    How the floridness of the materials of cities shrivels
    before a man's or woman's look !


12. All waits, or goes by default, till a strong being
    appears ;
    A strong being is the proof of the race, and of the
    ability of the universe,

12

When he or she appears, materials are overawed,
The dispute on the Soul stops,
The old customs and phrases are confronted, turned
back, or laid away.

13. What is your money-making now? What can it do
now?
What is your respectability now?
What are your theology, tuition, society, traditions,
statute-books now?
Where are your jibes of being now?
Where are your cavils about the Soul now?

14. Was that your best? Were those your vast and
solid?
Riches, opinions, politics, institutions, to part obe-
diently from the path of one man or woman!
The centuries, and all authority, to be trod under
the foot-soles of one man or woman!

15. — A sterile landscape covers the ore — there is as
good as the best, for all the forbidding appear-
ance,
There is the mine, there are the miners,
The forge-furnace is there, the melt is accomplished,
the hammers-men are at hand with their tongs
and hammers,
What always served and always serves, is at hand.

16. Than this nothing has better served — it has served
all,
Served the fluent-tongued and subtle-sensed Greek,
and long ere the Greek,

Served in building the buildings that last longer
than any,

Served the Hebrew, the Persian, the most ancient
Hindostanee,

Served the mound-raiser on the Mississippi — served
those whose relics remain in Central America,

Served Albic temples in woods or on plains, with
unhewn pillars, and the druids, and the bloody
body laid in the hollow of the great stone,

Served the artificial clefts, vast, high, silent, on the
snow-covered hills of Scandinavia,

Served those who, time out of mind, made on the
granite walls rough sketches of the sun, moon,
stars, ships, ocean-waves,

Served the paths of the irruptions of the Goths —
served the pastoral tribes and nomads,

Served the incalculably distant Kelt — served the
hardy pirates of the Baltic,

Served before any of those, the venerable and harm-
less men of Ethiopia,

Served the making of helms for the galleys of
pleasure, and the making of those for war,

Served all great works on land, and all great works
on the sea,

For the mediæval ages, and before the mediæval
ages,

Served not the living only, then as now, but served
the dead.


17. I see the European headsman,

He stands masked, clothed in red, with huge legs,
and strong naked arms,

And leans on a ponderous axe.

18. Whom have you slaughtered lately, European headsman ?
Whose is that blood upon you, so wet and sticky ?

19. I see the clear sunsets of the martyrs,
I see from the scaffolds the descending ghosts,
Ghosts of dead lords, uncrowned ladies, impeached ministers, rejected kings,
Rivals, traitors, poisoners, disgraced chieftains, and the rest.

20. I see those who in any land have died for the good cause,
The seed is spare, nevertheless the crop shall never run out,
(Mind you, O foreign kings, O priests, the crop shall never run out.)

21. I see the blood washed entirely away from the axe,
Both blade and helve are clean,
They spirt no more the blood of European nobles —
they clasp no more the necks of queens.

22. I see the headsman withdraw and become useless,
I see the scaffold untrodden and mouldy — I see no longer any axe upon it,
I see the mighty and friendly emblem of the power of my own race, the newest largest race.

23. America ! I do not vaunt my love for you,
I have what I have.

24. The axe leaps !
The solid forest gives fluid utterances,

They tumble forth, they rise and form,
Hut, tent, landing, survey,
Flail, plough, pick, crowbar, spade,
Shingle, rail, prop, wainscot, jamb, lath, panel, gable,
Citadel, ceiling, saloon, academy, organ, exhibition-
house, library,
Cornice, trellis, pilaster, balcony, window, shutter,
turret, porch,
Hoe, rake, pitch-fork, pencil, wagon, staff, saw, jack-
plane, mallet, wedge, rounce,
Chair, tub, hoop, table, wicket, vane, sash, floor,
Work-box, chest, stringed instrument, boat, frame,
and what not,
Capitols of States, and capitol of the nation of States,
Long stately rows in avenues, hospitals for orphans or
for the poor or sick,
Manhattan steamboats and clippers, taking the meas-
ure of all seas.


25. The shapes arise!
Shapes of the using of axes anyhow, and the users,
and all that neighbors them,
Cutters down of wood, and haulers of it to the Pe-
nobscot, or Kennebec,
Dwellers in cabins among the Californian mountains,
or by the little lakes, or on the Columbia,
Dwellers south on the banks of the Gila or Rio
Grande — friendly gatherings, the characters and
fun,
Dwellers up north in Minnesota and by the Yellow-
stone river — dwellers on coasts and off coasts,
Seal-fishers, whalers, arctic seamen breaking passages
through the ice.

12 *

26. The shapes arise!
  Shapes of factories, arsenals, foundries, markets,
  Shapes of the two-threaded tracks of railroads,
  Shapes of the sleepers of bridges, vast frameworks,
      girders, arches,
  Shapes of the fleets of barges, tows, lake craft, river
      craft.


27. The shapes arise!
  Ship-yards and dry-docks along the Eastern and
      Western Seas, and in many a bay and by-place,
  The live-oak kelsons, the pine planks, the spars, the
      hackmatack-roots for knees,
  The ships themselves on their ways, the tiers of
      scaffolds, the workmen busy outside and inside,
  The tools lying around, the great auger and little
      auger, the adze, bolt, line, square, gouge, and
      bead-plane.


28. The shapes arise!
  The shape measured, sawed, jacked, joined, stained,
  The coffin-shape for the dead to lie within in his
      shroud;
  The shape got out in posts, in the bedstead posts, in
      the posts of the bride's bed,
  The shape of the little trough, the shape of the
      rockers beneath, the shape of the babe's cradle,
  The shape of the floor-planks, the floor-planks for
      dancers' feet,
  The shape of the planks of the family home, the
      home of the friendly parents and children,
  The shape of the roof of the home of the happy
      young man and woman, the roof over the well-
      married young man and woman,

The roof over the supper joyously cooked by the chaste wife, and joyously eaten by the chaste husband, content after his day's work.

29. The shapes arise !
The shape of the prisoner's place in the court-room, and of him or her seated in the place,
The shape of the pill-box, the disgraceful ointment-box, the nauseous application, and him or her applying it,
The shape of the liquor-bar leaned against by the young rum-drinker and the old rum-drinker,
The shape of the shamed and angry stairs, trod by sneaking footsteps,
The shape of the sly settee, and the adulterous unwholesome couple,
The shape of the gambling-board with its devilish winnings and losings,
The shape of the slats of the bed of a corrupted body, the bed of the corruption of gluttony or alcoholic drinks,
The shape of the step-ladder for the convicted and sentenced murderer, the murderer with haggard face and pinioned arms,
The sheriff at hand with his deputies, the silent and white-lipped crowd, the sickening dangling of the rope.

30. The shapes arise !
Shapes of doors giving so many exits and entrances,
The door passing the dissevered friend, flushed, and in haste,

The door that admits good news and bad news,

The door whence the son left home, confident and
puffed up,

The door he entered again from a long and scan-
dalous absence, diseased, broken down, without
innocence, without means.

31. Their shapes arise, above all the rest — the shapes of
full-sized men,

Men taciturn yet loving, used to the open air, and the
manners of the open air,

Saying their ardor in native forms, saying the old
response,

Take what I have then, (saying fain,) take the pay
you approached for,

Take the white tears of my blood, if that is what you
are after.

32. Her shape arises,

She, less guarded than ever, yet more guarded than
ever,

The gross and soiled she moves among do not make
her gross and soiled,

She knows the thoughts as she passes — nothing is
concealed from her,

She is none the less considerate or friendly therefore,

She is the best-beloved — it is without exception —
she has no reason to fear, and she does not fear,

Oaths, quarrels, hiccupped songs, proposals, smutty
expressions, are idle to her as she passes,

She is silent — she is possessed of herself — they do
not offend her,

She receives them as the laws of nature receive them
— she is strong,
She too is a law of nature—there is no law stronger
than she is.

33. His shape arises,
Arrogant, masculine, naïve, rowdyish,
Laugher, weeper, worker, idler, citizen, countryman,
Saunterer of woods, stander upon hills, summer
swimmer in rivers or by the sea,
Of pure American breed, of reckless health, his body
perfect, free from taint from top to toe, free
forever from headache and dyspepsia, clean-
breathed,
Ample-limbed, a good feeder, weight a hundred and
eighty pounds, full-blooded, six feet high, forty
inches round the breast and back, ˋ
Countenance sun-burnt, bearded, calm, unrefined,
Reminder of animals, meeter of savage and gentleman
on equal terms,
Attitudes lithe and erect, costume free, neck gray
and open, of slow movement on foot,
Passer of his right arm round the shoulders of his
friends, companion of the street,
Persuader always of people to give him their sweetest
touches, and never their meanest,
A Manhattanese bred, fond of Brooklyn, fond of
Broadway, fond of the life of the wharves and
the great ferries,
Enterer everywhere, welcomed everywhere, easily
understood after all,
Never offering others, always offering himself, corrob-
orating his phrenology,

Voluptuous, inhabitive, combative, conscientious,
    alimentive, intuitive, of copious friendship,
    sublimity, firmness, self-esteem, comparison,
    individuality, form, locality, eventuality,
Avowing by life, manners, works, to contribute illus-
    trations of results of The States,
Teacher of the unquenchable creed, namely, egotism,
Inviter of others continually henceforth to try their
    strength against his.


34. The main shapes arise!
    Shapes of Democracy, final — result of centuries,
    Shapes of those that do not joke with life, but are
        in earnest with life,
    Shapes, ever projecting other shapes,
    Shapes of a hundred Free States, begetting another
        hundred north and south,
    Shapes of turbulent manly cities,
    Shapes of an untamed breed of young men, and
        natural persons,
    Shapes of the women fit for These States,
    Shapes of the composition of all the varieties of the
        earth,
    Shapes of the friends and home-givers of the whole
        earth,
    Shapes bracing the whole earth, and braced with the
        whole earth.

# CHANTS DEMOCRATIC.

—

**3.**

1. COME closer to me,
   Push closer, my lovers, and take the best I possess,
   Yield closer and closer, and give me the best you
       possess.

2. This is unfinished business with me — How is it with
       you?
   I was chilled with the cold types, cylinder, wet paper
       between us.

3. Male and Female!
   I pass so poorly with paper and types, I must pass
       with the contact of bodies and souls.

4. American masses!
   I do not thank you for liking me as I am, and liking
       the touch of me — I know that it is good for you
       to do so.

5. Workmen and Workwomen!
   Were all educations, practical and ornamental, well
       displayed out of me, what would it amount to?
   Were I as the head teacher, charitable proprietor,
       wise statesman, what would it amount to?

  Were I to you as the boss employing and paying
    you, would that satisfy you?

6. The learned, virtuous, benevolent, and the usual
    terms,
  A man like me, and never the usual terms.

7. Neither a servant nor a master am I,
  I take no sooner a large price than a small price —
    I will have my own, whoever enjoys me,
  I will be even with you, and you shall be even
    with me.

8. If you stand at work in a shop, I stand as nigh as
    the nighest in the same shop,
  If you bestow gifts on your brother or dearest friend,
    I demand as good as your brother or dearest
    friend,
  If your lover, husband, wife, is welcome by day or
    night, I must be personally as welcome,
  If you become degraded, criminal, ill, then I become
    so for your sake,
  If you remember your foolish and outlawed deeds, do
    you think I cannot remember my own foolish
    and outlawed deeds? plenty of them;
  If you carouse at the table, I carouse at the opposite
    side of the table,
  If you meet some stranger in the streets, and love
    him or her, do I not often meet strangers in the
    street, and love them?
  If you see a good deal remarkable in me, I see just
    as much, perhaps more, in you.

9. Why, what have you thought of yourself?
  Is it you then that thought yourself less?
  Is it you that thought the President greater than
    you?
  Or the rich better off than you? or the educated
    wiser than you?

10. Because you are greasy or pimpled, or that you was
    once drunk, or a thief, or diseased, or rheumatic,
    or a prostitute, or are so now, or from frivolity or
    impotence, or that you are no scholar, and never
    saw your name in print, do you give in that you
    are any less immortal?

11. Souls of men and women! it is not you I call unseen,
    unheard, untouchable and untouching,
  It is not you I go argue pro and con about, and to
    settle whether you are alive or no,
  I own publicly who you are, if nobody else owns —
    I see and hear you, and what you give and take,
  What is there you cannot give and take?

12. I see not merely that you are polite or white-faced,
    married, single, citizens of old States, citizens of
    new States,
  Eminent in some profession, a lady or gentleman in a
    parlor, or dressed in the jail uniform, or pulpit
    uniform;
  Grown, half-grown, and babe, of this country and
    every country, indoors and outdoors, one just as
    much as the other, I see,
  And all else is behind or through them.

13

13. The wife — and she is not one jot less than the
    husband,
    The daughter — and she is just as good as the son,
    The mother — and she is every bit as much as the
    father.

14. Offspring of those not rich, boys apprenticed to
    trades,
    Young fellows working on farms, and old fellows
    working on farms,
    The näive, the simple and hardy, he going to the
    polls to vote, he who has a good time, and he
    has who a bad time,
    Mechanics, southerners, new arrivals, laborers, sailors,
    man-o'wars-men, merchantmen, coasters,
    All these I see — but nigher and farther the same I
    see,
    None shall escape me, and none shall wish to escape
    me.

15. I bring what you much need, yet always have,
    Not money, amours, dress, eating, but as good ;
    I send no agent or medium, offer no representative
    of value, but offer the value itself.

16. There is something that comes home to one now and
    perpetually,
    It is not what is printed, preached, discussed — it
    eludes discussion and print,
    It is not to be put in a book — it is not in this
    book,
    It is for you, whoever you are — it is no farther from
    you than your hearing and sight are from you,

It is hinted by nearest, commonest, readiest — it is not them, though it is endlessly provoked by them, (what is there ready and near you now?)

17. You may read in many languages, yet read nothing about it,

You may read the President's Message, and read nothing about it there,

Nothing in the reports from the State department or Treasury department, or in the daily papers or the weekly papers,

Or in the census returns, assessors' returns, prices current, or any accounts of stock.

18. The sun and stars that float in the open air — the apple-shaped earth, and we upon it — surely the drift of them is something grand!

I do not know what it is, except that it is grand, and that it is happiness,

And that the enclosing purport of us here is not a speculation, or bon-mot, or reconnoissance,

And that it is not something which by luck may turn out well for us, and without luck must be a failure for us,

And not something which may yet be retracted in a certain contingency.

19. The light and shade, the curious sense of body and identity, the greed that with perfect complaisance devours all things, the endless pride and out-stretching of man, unspeakable joys and sorrows,

The wonder every one sees in every one else he sees, and the wonders that fill each minute of time forever, and each acre of surface and space forever,

Have you reckoned them for a trade, or farm-work?
or for the profits of a store? or to achieve your-
self a position? or to fill a gentleman's leisure,
or a lady's leisure?

20. Have you reckoned the landscape took substance and
form that it might be painted in a picture?
Or men and women that they might be written of,
and songs sung?
Or the attraction of gravity, and the great laws and
harmonious combinations, and the fluids of the
air, as subjects for the savans?
Or the brown land and the blue sea for maps and
charts?
Or the stars to be put in constellations and named
fancy names?
Or that the growth of seeds is for agricultural tables,
or agriculture itself?

21. Old institutions — these arts, libraries, legends, col-
lections, and the practice handed along in manu-
factures — will we rate them so high?
Will we rate our cash and business high? I have
no objection,
I rate them high as the highest — then a child born
of a woman and man I rate beyond all rate.

22. We thought our Union grand, and our Constitution
grand,
I do not say they are not grand and good, for they
are,
I am this day just as much in love with them as
you,

Then I am in love with you, and with all my fellows upon the earth.

23. We consider bibles and religions divine — I do not say they are not divine,
I say they have all grown out of you, and may grow out of you still,
It is not they who give the life — it is you who give the life,
Leaves are not more shed from the trees, or trees from the earth, than they are shed out of you.

24. The sum of all known reverence I add up in you, whoever you are,
The President is there in the White House for you — it is not you who are here for him,
The Secretaries act in their bureaus for you — not you here for them,
The Congress convenes every Twelfth Month for you,
Laws, courts, the forming of States, the charters of cities, the going and coming of commerce and mails, are all for you.

25. All doctrines, all politics and civilization, exurge from you,
All sculpture and monuments, and anything inscribed anywhere, are tallied in you,
The gist of histories and statistics as far back as the records reach, is in you this hour, and myths and tales the same,
If you were not breathing and walking here, where would they all be ?

The most renowned poems would be ashes, orations
and plays would be vacuums.

26. All architecture is what you do to it when you look
upon it,
Did you think it was in the white or gray stone? 
or the lines of the arches and cornices?

27. All music is what awakes from you, when you are
reminded by the instruments,
It is not the violins and the cornets — it is not the
oboe nor the beating drums, nor the score of the
baritone singer singing his sweet romanza — nor
that of the men's chorus, nor that of the women's
chorus,
It is nearer and farther than they.

28. Will the whole come back then?
Can each see signs of the best by a look in the
looking-glass? is there nothing greater or more?
Does all sit there with you, and here with me?

29. The old, forever-new things — you foolish child! the
closest, simplest things, this moment with you,
Your person, and every particle that relates to your
person,
The pulses of your brain, waiting their chance and
encouragement at every deed or sight,
Anything you do in public by day, and anything
you do in secret between-days,
What is called right and what is called wrong —
what you behold or touch, or what causes your
anger or wonder,

The ankle-chain of the slave, the bed of the bed-house, the cards of the gambler, the plates of the forger,

What is seen or learnt in the street, or intuitively learnt,

What is learnt in the public school, spelling, reading, writing, ciphering, the black-board, the teacher's diagrams,

The panes of the windows, all that appears through them, the going forth in the morning, the aimless spending of the day,

(What is it that you made money? What is it that you got what you wanted?)

The usual routine, the work-shop, factory, yard, office, store, desk,

The jaunt of hunting or fishing, and the life of hunting or fishing,

Pasture-life, foddering, milking, herding, and all the personnel and usages,

The plum-orchard, apple-orchard, gardening, seedlings, cuttings, flowers, vines,

Grains, manures, marl, clay, loam, the subsoil plough, the shovel, pick, rake, hoe, irrigation, draining,

The curry-comb, the horse-cloth, the halter, bridle, bits, the very wisps of straw,

The barn and barn-yard, the bins, mangers, mows, racks,

Manufactures, commerce, engineering, the building of cities, every trade carried on there, and the implements of every trade,

The anvil, tongs, hammer, the axe and wedge, the square, mitre, jointer, smoothing-plane,

The plumbob, trowel, level, the wall-scaffold, the work of walls and ceilings, or any mason-work,

The steam-engine, lever, crank, axle, piston, shaft, air-pump, boiler, beam, pulley, hinge, flange, band, bolt, throttle, governors, up and down rods,

The ship's compass, the sailor's tarpaulin, the stays and lanyards, the ground tackle for anchoring or mooring, the life-boat for wrecks,

The sloop's tiller, the pilot's wheel and bell, the yacht or fish-smack — the great gay-pennanted three-hundred-foot steamboat, under full headway, with her proud fat breasts, and her delicate swift-flashing paddles,

The trail, line, hooks, sinkers, and the seine, and hauling the seine,

The arsenal, small-arms, rifles, gunpowder, shot, caps, wadding, ordnance for war, and carriages;

Every-day objects, house-chairs, carpet, bed, counterpane of the bed, him or her sleeping at night, wind blowing, indefinite noises,

The snow-storm or rain-storm, the tow-trowsers, the lodge-hut in the woods, the still-hunt,

City and country, fire-place, candle, gas-light, heater, aqueduct,

The message of the Governor, Mayor, Chief of Police — the dishes of breakfast, dinner, supper,

The bunk-room, the fire-engine, the string-team, the car or truck behind,

The paper I write on or you write on, every word we write, every cross and twirl of the pen, and the curious way we write what we think, yet very faintly,

The directory, the detector, the ledger, the books in ranks on the book-shelves, the clock attached to the wall,

The ring on your finger, the lady's wristlet, the scent-powder, the druggist's vials and jars, the draught of lager-beer,

The etui of surgical instruments, the etui of oculist's or aurist's instruments, or dentist's instruments,

The permutating lock that can be turned and locked as many different ways as there are minutes in a year,

Glass-blowing, nail-making, salt-making, tin-roofing, shingle-dressing, candle-making, lock-making and hanging,

Ship-carpentering, dock-building, fish-curing, ferrying, stone-breaking, flagging of side-walks by flaggers,

The pump, the pile-driver, the great derrick, the coal-kiln and brick-kiln,

Coal-mines, all that is down there, the lamps in the darkness, echoes, songs, what meditations, what vast native thoughts looking through smutch'd faces,

Iron-works, forge-fires in the mountains, or by river-banks, men around feeling the melt with huge crowbars — lumps of ore, the due combining of ore, limestone, coal — the blast-furnace and the puddling-furnace, the loup-lump at the bottom of the melt at last — the rolling-mill, the stumpy bars of pig-iron, the strong clean-shaped T rail for railroads,

Oil-works, silk-works, white-lead-works, the sugar-house, steam-saws, the great mills and factories,

Lead-mines, and all that is done in lead-mines, or with the lead afterward,

Copper-mines, the sheets of copper, and what is
formed out of the sheets, and all the work in
forming it,

Stone-cutting, shapely trimmings for façades, or win-
dow or door lintels — the mallet, the tooth-chisel,
the jib to protect the thumb,

Oakum, the oakum-chisel, the caulking-iron — the
kettle of boiling vault-cement, and the fire under
the kettle,

The cotton-bale, the stevedore's hook, the saw and
buck of the sawyer, the screen of the coal-
screener, the mould of the moulder, the work-
ing-knife of the butcher, the ice-saw, and all the
work with ice,

The four-double cylinder press, the hand-press, the
frisket and tympan, the compositor's stick and
rule, type-setting, making up the forms, all the
work of newspaper counters, folders, carriers,
news-men,

The implements for daguerreotyping — the tools of
the rigger, grappler, sail-maker, block-maker,

Goods of gutta-percha, papier-mache, colors, brushes,
brush-making, glazier's implements,

The veneer and glue-pot, the confectioner's orna-
ments, the decanter and glasses, the shears and
flat-iron,

The awl and knee-strap, the pint measure and quart
measure, the counter and stool, the writing-pen
of quill or metal — the making of all sorts of
edged tools,

The ladders and hanging-ropes of the gymnasium,
manly exercises, the game of base-ball, running,
leaping, pitching quoits,

The designs for wall-papers, oil-cloths, carpets, the
fancies for goods for women, the book-binder's
stamps,

The brewery, brewing, the malt, the vats, every
thing that is done by brewers, also by wine-
makers, also vinegar-makers,

Leather-dressing, coach-making, boiler-making, rope-
twisting, distilling, sign-painting, lime-burning,
coopering, cotton-picking — electro-plating, elec-
trotyping, stereotyping,

Stave-machines, planing-machines, reaping-machines,
ploughing-machines, thrashing-machines, steam-
wagons,

The cart of the carman, the omnibus, the ponderous
dray,

The wires of the electric telegraph stretched on land,
or laid at the bottom of the sea, and then the
message in an instant from a thousand miles off,

The snow-plough, and two engines pushing it — the
ride in the express-train of only one car, the
swift go through a howling storm — the locomo-
tive, and all that is done about a locomotive,

The bear-hunt or coon-hunt — the bonfire of shavings
in the open lot in the city, and the crowd of
children watching,

The blows of the fighting-man, the upper-cut, and
one-two-three,

Pyrotechny, letting off colored fire-works at night,
fancy figures and jets,

Shop-windows, coffins in the sexton's ware-room, fruit
on the fruit-stand — beef in the butcher's stall,
the slaughter-house of the butcher, the butcher
in his killing-clothes,

The area of pens of live pork, the killing-hammer, the
    hog-hook, the scalder's tub, gutting, the cutter's
    cleaver, the packer's maul, and the plenteous
    winter-work of pork-packing,

Flour-works, grinding of wheat, rye, maize, rice —
    the barrels and the half and quarter barrels, the
    loaded barges, the high piles on wharves and
    levees,

Bread and cakes in the bakery, the milliner's rib-
    bons, the dress-maker's patterns, the tea-table,
    the home-made sweetmeats;

Cheap literature, maps, charts, lithographs, daily and
    weekly newspapers,

The column of wants in the one-cent paper, the news
    by telegraph, amusements, operas, shows,

The business parts of a city, the trottoirs of a city
    when thousands of well-dressed people walk up
    and down,

The cotton, woollen, linen you wear, the money you
    make and spend,

Your room and bed-room, your piano-forte, the stove
    and cook-pans,

The house you live in, the rent, the other tenants, the
    deposit in the savings-bank, the trade at the
    grocery,

The pay on Seventh Day night, the going home, and
    the purchases;

In them the heft of the heaviest — in them far more
    than you estimated, and far less also,

In them realities for you and me — in them poems for
    you and me,

In them, not yourself — you and your Soul enclose all
    things, regardless of estimation,

In them themes, hints, provokers — if not, the whole
earth has no themes, hints, provokers, and never
had.

30. I do not affirm what you see beyond is futile — I do
not advise you to stop,
I do not say leadings you thought great are not great,
But I say that none lead to greater, sadder, happier,
than those lead to.

31. Will you seek afar off? You surely come back at last,
In things best known to you, finding the best, or as
good as the best,
In folks nearest to you finding also the sweetest,
strongest, lovingest,
Happiness, knowledge, not in another place, but this
place — not for another hour, but this hour,
Man in the first you see or touch — always in your
friend, brother, nighest neighbor — Woman in
your mother, lover, wife,
The popular tastes and occupations taking precedence
in poems or any where,
You workwomen and workmen of These States having
your own divine and strong life,
Looking the President always sternly in the face,
unbending, nonchalant,
Understanding that he is to be kept by you to short
and sharp account of himself,
And all else thus far giving place to men and women
like you.

32. O you robust, sacred!
I cannot tell you how I love you;

14

All I love America for, is contained in men and women like you.

33. When the psalm sings instead of the singer,
When the script preaches instead of the preacher,
When the pulpit descends and goes instead of the carver that carved the supporting-desk,
When I can touch the body of books, by night or by day, and when they touch my body back again,
When the holy vessels, or the bits of the eucharist, or the lath and plast, procreate as effectually as the young silver-smiths or bakers, or the masons in their over-alls,
When a university course convinces like a slumbering woman and child convince,
When the minted gold in the vault smiles like the night-watchman's daughter,
When warrantee deeds loafe in chairs opposite, and are my friendly companions,
I intend to reach them my hand, and make as much of them as I do of men and women like you.

# CHANTS DEMOCRATIC.

———

AMERICA always!

Always me joined with you, whoever you are!

Always our own feuillage!

Always Florida's green peninsula! Always the priceless delta of Louisiana! Always the cotton-fields of Alabama and Texas!

Always California's golden hills and hollows — and the silver mountains of New Mexico! Always soft-breath'd Cuba!

Always the vast slope drained by the Southern Sea — inseparable with the slopes drained by the Eastern and Western Seas,

The area the Eighty-third year of These States — the three and a half millions of square miles,

The eighteen thousand miles of sea-coast and bay-coast on the main — the thirty thousand miles of river navigation,

The seven millions of distinct families, and the same number of dwellings — Always these and more, branching forth into numberless branches;

Always the free range and diversity! Always the continent of Democracy!

Always the prairies, pastures, forests, vast cities, travellers, Kanada, the snows;

Always these compact lands — lands tied at the hips
    with the belt stringing the huge oval lakes;

Always the West, with strong native persons — the
    increasing density there — the habitans, friendly,
    threatening, ironical, scorning invaders;

All sights, South, North, East — all deeds, promis-
    cuously done at all times,

All characters, movements, growths — a few noticed,
    myriads unnoticed,

Through Mannahatta's streets I walking, these things
    gathering;

On interior rivers, by night, in the glare of pine
    knots, steamboats wooding up;

Sunlight by day on the valley of the Susquehanna,
    and on the valleys of the Potomac and Rappa-
    hannock, and the valleys of the Roanoke and
    Delaware;

In their northerly wilds beasts of prey haunting the
    Adirondacks, the hills — or lapping the Saginaw
    waters to drink;

In a lonesome inlet, a sheldrake, lost from the flock,
    sitting on the water, rocking silently;

In farmers' barns, oxen in the stable, their harvest
    labor done — they rest standing — they are too
    tired;

Afar on arctic ice, the she-walrus lying drowsily,
    while her cubs play around;

The hawk sailing where men have not yet sailed —
    the farthest polar sea, ripply, crystalline, open,
    beyond the floes;

White drift spooning ahead, where the ship in the
    tempest dashes;

On solid land, what is done in cities, as the bells all
    strike midnight together;

In primitive woods, the sounds there also sounding —
the howl of the wolf, the scream of the panther,
and the hoarse bellow of the elk;

In winter beneath the hard blue ice of Moosehead
Lake — in summer visible through the clear
waters, the great trout swimming;

In lower latitudes, in warmer air, in the Carolinas,
the large black buzzard floating slowly high
beyond the tree-tops,

Below, the red cedar, festooned with tylandria — the
pines and cypresses, growing out of the white
sand that spreads far and flat;

Rude boats descending the big Pedee — climbing
plants, parasites, with colored flowers and berries,
enveloping huge trees,

The waving drapery on the live oak, trailing long and
low, noiselessly waved by the wind;

The camp of Georgia wagoners, just after dark — the
supper-fires, and the cooking and eating by
whites and negroes,

Thirty or forty great wagons — the mules, cattle,
horses, feeding from troughs,

The shadows, gleams, up under the leaves of the old
sycamore-trees — the flames — also the black
smoke from the pitch-pine, curling and rising;

Southern fishermen fishing — the sounds and inlets
of North Carolina's coast — the shad-fishery
and the herring-fishery — the large sweep-seines
— the windlasses on shore worked by horses —
the clearing, curing, and packing houses;

Deep in the forest, in the piney woods, turpentine
and tar dropping from the incisions in the trees
— There is the turpentine distillery,

14 *

There are the negroes at work, in good health — the ground in all directions is covered with pine straw;

In Tennessee and Kentucky, slaves busy in the coalings, at the forge, by the furnace-blaze, or at the corn-shucking;

In Virginia, the planter's son returning after a long absence, joyfully welcomed and kissed by the aged mulatto nurse;

On rivers, boatmen safely moored at night-fall, in their boats, under the shelter of high banks,

Some of the younger men dance to the sound of the banjo or fiddle — others sit on the gunwale, smoking and talking;

Late in the afternoon, the mocking-bird, the American mimic, singing in the Great Dismal Swamp — there are the greenish waters, the resinous odor, the plenteous moss, the cypress tree, and the juniper tree;

Northward, young men of Mannahatta — the target company from an excursion returning home at evening — the musket-muzzles all bear bunches of flowers presented by women;

Children at play — or on his father's lap a young boy fallen asleep, (how his lips move! how he smiles in his sleep!)

The scout riding on horseback over the plains west of the Mississippi — he ascends a knoll and sweeps his eye around;

California life — the miner, bearded, dressed in his rude costume — the stanch California friendship — the sweet air — the graves one, in passing, meets, solitary, just aside the horse-path;

Down in Texas, the cotton-field, the negro-cabins —
    drivers driving mules or oxen before rude carts
    — cotton-bales piled on banks and wharves ;
Encircling all, vast-darting, up and wide, the Amer-
    ican Soul, with equal hemispheres — one Love,
    one Dilation or Pride ;
In .arriere, the peace-talk with the Iroquois, the
    aborigines — the calumet, the pipe of good-will
    arbitration, and indorsement,
The sachem blowing the smoke first toward the sun
    and then toward the earth,
The drama of the scalp-dance enacted with painted
    faces and guttural exclamations,
The setting out of the war-party — the long and
    stealthy march,
The single file — the swinging hatchets — the surprise
    and slaughter of enemies ;
All the acts, scenes, ways, persons, attitudes of These
    States — reminiscences, all institutions,
All These States, compact — Every square mile of
    These States, without excepting a particle — you
    also — me also,
Me pleased, rambling in lanes and country fields,
    Paumanok's fields,
Me, observing the spiral flight of two little yellow
    butterflies, shuffling between each other, ascend-
    ing high in the air ;
The darting swallow, the destroyer of insects — the
    fall traveller southward, but returning northward
    early in the spring ;
The country boy at the close of the day, driving the
    herd of cows, and shouting to them as they loiter
    to browse by the road-side ;

The city wharf — Boston, Philadelphia, Baltimore,
Charleston, New Orleans, San Francisco,

The departing ships, when the sailors heave at the
capstan ;

Evening — me in my room — the setting sun,

The setting summer sun shining in my open window,
showing me flies, suspended, balancing in the
air in the centre of the room, darting athwart,
up and down, casting swift shadows in specks on
the opposite wall, where the shine is ;

The athletic American matron speaking in public to
crowds of listeners ;

Males, females, immigrants, combinations — the co-
piousness — the individuality and sovereignty
of The States, each for itself — the money-
makers ;

Factories, machinery, the mechanical forces — the
windlass, lever, pulley — All certainties,

The certainty of space, increase, freedom, futurity,

In space, the sporades, the scattered islands, the stars
— on the firm earth, the lands, my lands,

O lands ! all so dear to me — what you are, (what-
ever it is,) I become a part of that, whatever
it is,

Southward there, I screaming, with wings slow flap-
ping, with the myriads of gulls wintering along
the coasts of Florida — or in Louisiana, with
pelicans breeding,

Otherways, there, atwixt the banks of the Arkansaw,
the Rio Grande, the Nueces, the Brazos, the
Tombigbee, the Red River, the Saskatchawan, or
the Osage, I with the spring waters laughing and
skipping and running ;

Northward, on the sands, on some shallow bay of Paumanok, I, with parties of snowy herons wading in the wet to seek worms and aquatic plants;

Retreating, triumphantly twittering, the king-bird, from piercing the crow with its bill, for amusement — And I triumphantly twittering;

The migrating flock of wild geese alighting in autumn to refresh themse'ves — the body of the flock feed — the sentinels outside move around with erect heads watching, and are from time to time relieved by other sentinels — And I feeding and taking turns with the rest;

In Kanadian forests, the moose, large as an ox, cornered by hunters, rising desperately on his hind-feet, and plunging with his fore-feet, the hoofs as sharp as knives — And I, plunging at the hunters, cornered and desperate;

In the Mannahatta, streets, piers, shipping, store-houses, and the countless workmen working in the shops,

And I too of the Mannahatta, singing thereof — and no less in myself than the whole of the Mannahatta in itself,

Singing the song of These, my ever united lands — my body no more inevitably united, part to part, and made one identity, any more than my lands are inevitably united, and made ONE IDENTITY,

Nativities, climates, the grass of the great Pastoral Plains,

Cities, labors, death, animals, products, good and evil — these me,

These afforting, in all their particulars, endless
feuillage to me and to America, how can I do
less than pass the clew of the union of them, to
afford the like to you?

Whoever you are! how can I but offer you divine
leaves, that you also be eligible as I am?

How can I but, as here, chanting, invite you for
yourself to collect bouquets of the incomparable
feuillage of These States?

RESPONDEZ!   Respondez!

Let every one answer!   Let those who sleep be
waked! Let none evade — not you, any more
than others!

(If it really be as is pretended, how much longer must
we go on with our affectations and sneaking?

Let me bring this to a close — I pronounce openly for
a new distribution of roles,)

Let that which stood in front go behind! and let
that which was behind advance to the front and
speak!

Let murderers, thieves, bigots, fools, unclean persons,
offer new propositions!

Let the old propositions be postponed!

Let faces and theories be turned inside out! Let
meanings be freely criminal, as well as results!

Let there be no suggestion above the suggestion of drudgery!

Let none be pointed toward his destination! (Say! do you know your destination?)

Let trillions of men and women be mocked with bodies and mocked with Souls!

Let the love that waits in them, wait! Let it die, or pass still-born to other spheres!

Let the sympathy that waits in every man, wait! or let it also pass, a dwarf, to other spheres!

Let contradictions prevail! Let one thing contradict another! and let one line of my poems contradict another!

Let the people sprawl with yearning aimless hands! Let their tongues be broken! Let their eyes be discouraged! Let none descend into their hearts with the fresh lusciousness of love!

Let the theory of America be management, caste, comparison! (Say! what other theory would you?)

Let them that distrust birth and death lead the rest! (Say! why shall they not lead you?)

Let the crust of hell be neared and trod on! Let the days be darker than the nights! Let slumber bring less slumber than waking-time brings!

Let the world never appear to him or her for whom it was all made!

Let the heart of the young man exile itself from the heart of the old man! and let the heart of the old man be exiled from that of the young man!

Let the sun and moon go! Let scenery take the applause of the audience! Let there be apathy under the stars!

Let freedom prove no man's inalienable right! Every one who can tyrannize, let him tyrannize to his satisfaction!

Let none but infidels be countenanced!

Let the eminence of meanness, treachery, sarcasm, hate, greed, indecency, impotence, lust, be taken for granted above all! Let writers, judges, governments, households, religions, philosophies, take such for granted above all!

Let the worst men beget children out of the worst women!

Let priests still play at immortality!

Let Death be inaugurated!

Let nothing remain upon the earth except the ashes of teachers, artists, moralists, lawyers, and learned and polite persons!

Let him who is without my poems be assassinated!

Let the cow, the horse, the camel, the garden-bee — Let the mud-fish, the lobster, the mussel, eel, the sting-ray, and the grunting pig-fish — Let these, and the like of these, be put on a perfect equality with man and woman!

Let churches accommodate serpents, vermin, and the corpses of those who have died of the most filthy of diseases!

Let marriage slip down among fools, and be for none but fools!

Let men among themselves talk and think obscenely of women! and let women among themselves talk and think obscenely of men!

Let every man doubt every woman! and let every woman trick every man!

Let us all, without missing one, be exposed in public, naked, monthly, at the peril of our lives! Let our bodies be freely handled and examined by whoever chooses!

Let nothing but copies, pictures, statues, reminiscences, elegant works, be permitted to exist upon the earth!

Let the earth desert God, nor let there ever henceforth be mentioned the name of God!

Let there be no God!

Let there be money, business, imports, exports, custom, authority, precedents, pallor, dyspepsia, smut, ignorance, unbelief!

Let judges and criminals be transposed! Let the prison-keepers be put in prison! Let those that were prisoners take the keys! (Say! why might they not just as well be transposed?)

Let the slaves be masters! Let the masters become slaves!

Let the reformers descend from the stands where they are forever bawling! Let an idiot or insane person appear on each of the stands!

Let the Asiatic, the African, the European, the American and the Australian, go armed against the murderous stealthiness of each other! Let them sleep armed! Let none believe in good-will!

Let there be no unfashionable wisdom! Let such be scorned and derided off from the earth!

Let a floating cloud in the sky — Let a wave of the sea — Let one glimpse of your eye-sight upon the landscape or grass — Let growing mint, spinach, onions, tomatoes — Let these be exhibited as shows at a great price for admission!

Let all the men of These States stand aside for a
few smouchers! Let the few seize on what they
choose! Let the rest gawk, giggle, starve, obey!

Let shadows be furnished with genitals! Let sub-
stances be deprived of their genitals!

Let there be wealthy and immense cities — but
through any of them, not a single poet, saviour,
knower, lover!

Let the infidels of These States laugh all faith away!
If one man be found who has faith, let the rest
set upon him! Let them affright faith! Let
them destroy the power of breeding faith!

Let the she-harlots and the he-harlots be prudent!
Let them dance on, while seeming lasts! (O
seeming! seeming! seeming!)

Let the preachers recite creeds! Let them teach only
what they have been taught!

Let the preachers of creeds never dare to go meditate
candidly upon the hills, alone, by day or by
night! (If one ever once dare, he is lost!)

Let insanity have charge of sanity!

Let books take the place of trees, animals, rivers,
clouds!

Let the daubed portraits of heroes supersede heroes!

Let the manhood of man never take steps after itself!
Let it take steps after eunuchs, and after con-
sumptive and genteel persons!

Let the white person tread the black person under his
heel! (Say! which is trodden under heel, after
all?)

Let the reflections of the things of the world be studied
in mirrors! Let the things themselves continue
unstudied!

Let a man seek pleasure everywhere except in himself! Let a woman seek happiness everywhere except in herself! (Say! what real happiness have you had one single time through your whole life?)

Let the limited years of life do nothing for the limitless years of death! (Say! what do you suppose death will do, then?)

1. You just maturing youth! You male or female!
    Remember the organic compact of These States,
    Remember the pledge of the Old Thirteen thenceforward to the rights, life, liberty, equality of man,
    Remember what was promulged by the founders, ratified by The States, signed in black and white by the Commissioners, and read by Washington at the head of the army,
    Remember the purposes of the founders, — Remember Washington;
    Remember the copious humanity streaming from every direction toward America;
    Remember the hospitality that belongs to nations and men; (Cursed be nation, woman, man, without hospitality!)
    Remember, government is to subserve individuals,

Not any, not the President, is to have one jot more
than you or me,

Not any habitan of America is to have one jot less
than you or me.

2. Anticipate when the thirty or fifty millions, are to be-
come the hundred, or two hundred millions, of
equal freemen and freewomen, amicably joined.

3. Recall ages — One age is but a part — ages are but a
part ;

Recall the angers, bickerings, delusions, superstitions,
of the idea of caste,

Recall the bloody cruelties and crimes.

4. Anticipate the best women ;

I say an unnumbered new race of hardy and well-
defined women are to spread through all These
States,

I say a girl fit for These States must be free, capable,
dauntless, just the same as a boy.

5. Anticipate your own life — retract with merciless
power,

Shirk nothing — retract in time — Do you see those
errors, diseases, weaknesses, lies, thefts ?

Do you see that lost character ? — Do you see de-
cay, consumption, rum-drinking, dropsy, fever,
mortal cancer or inflammation ?

Do you see death, and the approach of death ?

6. Think of the Soul ;

I swear to you that body of yours gives proportions to
your Soul somehow to live in other spheres,

I do not know how, but I know it is so.

7. Think of loving and being loved;
  I swear to you, whoever you are, you can interfuse
    yourself with such things that everybody that sees
    you shall look longingly upon you.

8. Think of the past;
  I warn you that in a little while, others will find their
    past in you and your times.

9. The race is never separated — nor man nor woman
    escapes,
  All is inextricable — things, spirits, nature, nations,
    you too — from precedents you come.

10. Recall the ever-welcome defiers, (The mothers precede
    them ;)
  Recall the sages, poets, saviours, inventors, lawgivers,
    of the earth,
  Recall Christ, brother of rejected persons — brother
    of slaves, felons, idiots, and of insane and diseased
    persons.

11. Think of the time when you was not yet born,
  Think of times you stood at the side of the dying,
  Think of the time when your own body will be dying.

12. Think of spiritual results,
  Sure as the earth swims through the heavens, does
    every one of its objects pass into spiritual results.

13. Think of manhood, and you to be a man ;
  Do you count manhood, and the sweet of manhood,
    nothing ?

15*

14. Think of womanhood, and you to be a woman;
    The creation is womanhood,
    Have I not said that womanhood involves all?
    Have I not told how the universe has nothing better
        than the best womanhood?

∼∿ঌ◍ᕎ◍ঌ∿∼

1. WITH antecedents,
    With my fathers and mothers, and the accumulations
        of past ages,
    With all which, had it not been, I would not now be
        here, as I am,
    With Egypt, India, Phenicia, Greece, and Rome,
    With the Celt, the Scandinavian, the Alb, and the
        Saxon,
    With antique maritime ventures — with laws, arti-
        sanship, wars, and journeys,
    With the poet, the skald, the saga, the myth, and the
        oracle,
    With the sale of slaves — with enthusiasts — with
        the troubadour, the crusader, and the monk,
    With those old continents whence we have come to this
        new continent,
    With the fading kingdoms and kings over there,
    With the fading religions and priests,
    With the small shores we look back to, from our own
        large and present shores,

With countless years drawing themselves onward, and
   arrived at these years,
You and Me arrived — America arrived, and making
   this year,
This year! sending itself ahead countless years to
   come.

2. O but it is not the years — it is I — it is You,
   We touch all laws, and tally all antecedents,
   We are the skald, the oracle, the monk, and the
      knight — we easily include them, and more,
   We stand amid time, beginningless and endless — we
      stand amid evil and good,
   All swings around us — there is as much darkness as
      light,
   The very sun swings itself and its system of planets
      around us,
   Its sun, and its again, all swing around us.

3. As for me,
   I have the idea of all, and am all, and believe in all;
   I believe materialism is true, and spiritualism is true —
      I reject no part.

4. Have I forgotten any part?
   Come to me, whoever and whatever, till I give you
      recognition.

5. I respect Assyria, China, Teutonia, and the Hebrews,
   I adopt each theory, myth, god, and demi-god,
   I see that the old accounts, bibles, genealogies, are
      true, without exception,
   I assert that all past days were what they should have
      been,

And that they could no-how have been better than
they were,
And that to-day is what it should be — and that
America is,
And that to-day and America could no-how be better
than they are.

6. In the name of These States, and in your and my
name, the Past,
And in the name of These States, and in your and my
name, the Present time.

7. I know that the past was great, and the future will
be great,
And I know that both curiously conjoint in the pres-
ent time,
(For the sake of him I typify — for the common
average man's sake — your sake, if you are he;)
And that where I am, or you are, this present day,
there is the centre of all days, all races,
And there is the meaning, to us, of all that has ever
come of races and days, or ever will come.

8.

1. Splendor of falling day, floating and filling me,
Hour prophetic — hour resuming the past,
Inflating my throat — you, divine average!
You, Earth and Life, till the last ray gleams, I sing.

2. Open mouth of my Soul, uttering gladness,
   Eyes of my Soul, seeing perfection,
   Natural life of me, faithfully praising things,
   Corroborating forever the triumph of things.

3. Illustrious every one!
   Illustrious what we name space — sphere of unnum-
       bered spirits,
   Illustrious the mystery of motion, in all beings, even
       the tiniest insect,
   Illustrious the attribute of speech — the senses — the
       body,
   Illustrious the passing light! Illustrious the pale
       reflection on the moon in the western sky!
   Illustrious whatever I see, or hear, or touch, to the
       last.

4. Good in all,
   In the satisfaction and aplomb of animals,
   In the annual return of the seasons,
   In the hilarity of youth,
   In the strength and flush of manhood,
   In the grandeur and exquisiteness of old age,
   In the superb vistas of Death.

5. Wonderful to depart!
   Wonderful to be here!
   The heart, to jet the all-alike and innocent blood,
   To breathe the air, how delicious!
   To speak! to walk! to seize something by the hand!
   To prepare for sleep, for bed — to look on my rose-
       colored flesh,
   To be conscious of my body, so amorous, so large,

To be this incredible God I am,
To have gone forth among other Gods — those men
and women I love.


6. Wonderful how I celebrate you and myself!
How my thoughts play subtly at the spectacles
around!
How the clouds pass silently overhead!
How the earth darts on and on! and how the sun,
moon, stars, dart on and on!
How the water sports and sings! (Surely it is
alive!)
How the trees rise and stand up — with strong trunks
— with branches and leaves!
(Surely there is something more in each of the trees —
some living Soul.)


7. O amazement of things! even the least particle!
O spirituality of things!
O strain musical, flowing through ages and continents
— now reaching me and America!
I take your strong chords — I intersperse them, and
cheerfully pass them forward.


8. I too carol the sun, ushered, or at noon, or setting,
I too throb to the brain and beauty of the earth, and
of all the growths of the earth,
I too have felt the resistless call of myself.


9. As I sailed down the Mississippi,
As I wandered over the prairies,
As I have lived — As I have looked through my
windows, my eyes,

As I went forth in the morning — As I beheld the
light breaking in the east,

As I bathed on the beach of the Eastern Sea, and
again on the beach on the Western Sea,

As I roamed the streets of inland Chicago — whatever
streets I have roamed,

Wherever I have been, I have charged myself with
contentment and triumph.

10. I sing the Equalities,

I sing the endless finales of things,

I say Nature continues — Glory continues,

I praise with electric voice,

For I do not see one imperfection in the universe,

And I do not see one cause or result lamentable at
last in the universe.

11. O setting sun! O when the time comes,

I still warble under you, if none else does, unmiti-
gated adoration!

A THOUGHT of what I am here for,

Of these years I sing — how they pass through con-
vulsed pains, as through parturitions;

How America illustrates birth, gigantic youth, the
promise, the sure fulfilment, despite of people
— Illustrates evil as well as good;

Of how many hold despairingly yet to the models
departed, caste, myths, obedience, compulsion,
and to infidelity;

How few see the arrived models, the Athletes, The
States — or see freedom or spirituality — or hold
any faith in results,

(But I see the Athletes — and I see the results
glorious and inevitable — and they again leading
to other results;)

How the great cities appear — How the Democratic
masses, turbulent, wilful, as I love them,

How the whirl, the contest, the wrestle of evil with
good, the sounding and resounding, keep on
and on;

How society waits unformed, and is between things
ended and things begun;

How America is the continent of glories, and of the
triumph of freedom, and of the Democracies, and
of the fruits of society, and of all that is begun;

And how The States are complete in themselves —
And how all triumphs and glories are complete
in themselves, to lead onward,

And how these of mine, and of The States, will in
their turn be convulsed, and serve other par-
turitions and transitions,

And how all people, sights, combinations, the Demo-
cratic masses too, serve — and how every fact
serves,

And how now, or at any time, each serves the
exquisite transition of Death.

HISTORIAN! you who celebrate bygones!

You have explored the outward, the surface of the races — the life that has exhibited itself,

You have treated man as the creature of politics, aggregates, rulers, and priests;

But now I also, arriving, contribute something:

I, an habitué of the Alleghanies, treat man as he is in the influences of Nature, in himself, in his own inalienable rights,

Advancing, to give the spirit and the traits of new Democratic ages, myself, personally,

(Let the future behold them all in me — Me, so puzzling and contradictory — Me, a Manhattanese, the most loving and arrogant of men;)

I do not tell the usual facts, proved by records and documents,

What I tell, (talking to every born American,) requires no further proof than he or she who will hear me, will furnish, by silently meditating alone;

I press the pulse of the life that has hitherto seldom exhibited itself, but has generally sought concealment, (the great pride of man, in himself,)

I illuminate feelings, faults, yearnings, hopes — I have come at last, no more ashamed nor afraid;

Chanter of Personality, outlining a history yet to be,

I project the ideal man, the American of the future.

16

THE thought of fruitage,

Of Death, (the life greater) — of seeds dropping into
the ground — of birth,

Of the steady concentration of America, inland,
upward, to impregnable and swarming places,

Of what Indiana, Kentucky, Ohio and the rest, are
to be,

Of what a few years will show there in Missouri,
Kansas, Iowa, Wisconsin, Minnesota and the
rest,

Of what the feuillage of America is the preparation
for — and of what all the sights, North, South,
East and West, are;

Of the temporary use of materials for identity's
sake,

Of departing — of the growth of a mightier race
than any yet,

Of myself, soon, perhaps, closing up my songs by
these shores,

Of California — of Oregon — and of me journeying
hence to live and sing there;

Of the Western Sea — of the spread inland between
it and the spinal river,

Of the great pastoral area, athletic and feminine,

Of all sloping down there where the fresh free-
giver, the mother, the Mississippi flows — and
Westward still;

Of future men and women there — of happiness in
those high plateaus, ranging three thousand
miles, warm and cold,

Of cities yet unsurveyed and unsuspected, (as I am
also, and as it must be,)

Of the new and good names — of the strong develop-
ments — of the inalienable homesteads,

Of a free original life there — of simple diet, and
clean and sweet blood,

Of litheness, majestic faces, clear eyes, and perfect
physique there,

Of immense spiritual results, future years, inland,
spread there each side of the Anahuacs,

Of these Leaves well-understood there, (being made
for that area,)

Of the native scorn of grossness and gain there,

(O it lurks in me night and day — What is gain,
after all, to savageness and freedom?)

12.

1. To oratists — to male or female,
Vocalism, breath, measure, concentration, determina-
tion, and the divine power to use words.

2. Are you eligible?
Are you full-lung'd and limber-lipp'd from long trial?
from vigorous practice? from physique?

Do you move in these broad lands as broad as they?
Remembering inland America, the high plateaus,
    stretching long?
Remembering Kanada — Remembering what edges
    the vast round˙edge of the Mexican Sea?
Come duly to the divine power to use words?

3. For only at last, after many years — after chastity,
    friendship, procreation, prudence, and nakedness,
After treading ground and breasting river and lake,
After a loosened throat — after absorbing eras, tem-
    peraments, races — after knowledge, freedom,
    crimes,
After complete faith — after clarifyings, elevations,
    and removing obstructions,
After these, and more, it is just possible there comes
    to a man, a woman, the divine power to use
    words.

4. Then toward that man or that woman swiftly hasten
    all — None refuse, all attend,
Armies, ships, antiquities, the dead, libraries, paint-
    ings, machines, cities, hate, despair, amity, pain,
    theft, murder, aspiration, form in close ranks,
They debouch as they are wanted to march obediently
    through the mouth of that man, or that woman.

5. O now I see arise orators fit for inland America,
And I see it is as slow to become an orator as to
    become a man,
And I see that power is folded in a great vocalism.

6. Of a great vocalism, when you hear it, the merciless
    light shall pour, and the storm rage around,

Every flash shall be a revelation, an insult,
The glaring flame turned on depths, on heights, on
    suns, on stars,
On the interior and exterior of man or woman,
On the laws of Nature — on passive materials,
On what you called death — and what to you there-
    fore was death,
As far as there can be death.

## 13.

1. Laws for Creations,
    For strong artists and leaders — for fresh broods of
        teachers, and perfect literats for America,
    For diverse savans, and coming musicians.


2. There shall be no subject but it shall be treated with
        reference to the ensemble of the world, and the
        compact truth of the world — And no coward or
        copyist shall be allowed ;
    There shall be no subject too pronounced — All works
        shall illustrate the divine law of indirections ;
    There they stand — I see them already, each poised
        and in its place,
    Statements, models, censuses, poems, dictionaries,
        biographies, essays, theories — How complete !
        How relative and interfused ! No one super-
        sedes another ;
    They do not seem to me like the old specimens,

They seem to me like Nature at last, (America has
    given birth to them, and I have also ;)
They seem to me at last as perfect as the animals,
    and as the rocks and weeds — fitted to them,
Fitted to the sky, to float with floating clouds — to
    rustle among the trees with rustling leaves,
To stretch with stretched and level waters, where
    ships silently sail in the distance.

3. What do you suppose Creation is ?
   What do you suppose will satisfy the Soul, except to
    walk free and own no superior ?
   What do you suppose I have intimated to you in a
    hundred ways, but that man or woman is as good
    as God ?
   And that there is no God any more divine than
    Yourself ?
   And that that is what the oldest and newest myths
    finally mean ?
   And that you or any one must approach Creations
    through such laws ?

## 14.

1. POETS to come !
   Not to-day is to justify me, and Democracy, and
    what we are for,
   But you, a new brood, native, athletic, continental,
    greater than before known,
   You must justify me.

2. Indeed, if it were not for you, what would I be?
What is the little I have done, except to arouse you?


3. I depend on being realized, long hence, where the broad fat prairies spread, and thence to Oregon and California inclusive,
I expect that the Texan and the Arizonian, ages hence, will understand me,
I expect that the future Carolinian and Georgian will understand me and love me,
I expect that Kanadians, a hundred, and perhaps many hundred years from now, in winter, in the splendor of the snow and woods, or on the icy lakes, will take me with them, and permanently enjoy themselves with me.


4. Of to-day I know I am momentary, untouched — I am the bard of the future,
I but write one or two indicative words for the future,
I but advance a moment, only to wheel and hurry back in the darkness.


5. I am a man who, sauntering along, without fully stopping, turns a casual look upon you, and then averts his face,
Leaving it to you to prove and define it,
Expecting the main things from you.

## 15.

Who has gone farthest? For I swear I will go
farther;

And who has been just? For I would be the most
just person of the earth;

And who most cautious? For I would be more
cautious;

And who has been happiest? O I think it is I! I
think no one was ever happier than I;

And who has lavished all? For I lavish constantly
the best I have;

And who has been firmest? For I would be firmer;

And who proudest? For I think I have reason to be
the proudest son alive — for I am the son of the
brawny and tall-topt city;

And who has been bold and true? For I would be
the boldest and truest being of the universe;

And who benevolent? For I would show more be-
nevolence than all the rest;

And who has projected beautiful words through the
longest time? By God! I will outvie him! I
will say such words, they shall stretch through
longer time!

And who has received the love of the most friends?
For I know what it is to receive the passionate
love of many friends;

And to whom has been given the sweetest from
women, and paid them in kind? For I will
take the like sweets and pay them in kind;

And who possesses a perfect and enamoured body?
  For I do not believe any one possesses a more
  perfect or enamoured body than mine;
And who thinks the amplest thoughts? For I will
  surround those thoughts;
And who has made hymns fit for the earth? For I
  am mad with devouring extacy to make joyous
  hymns for the whole earth!

## 16.

THEY shall arise in the States — mediums shall,
They shall report Nature, laws, physiology, and
  happiness,
They shall illustrate Democracy and the kosmos,
They shall be alimentive, amative, perceptive,
They shall be complete women and men — their pose
  brawny and supple, their drink water, their blood
  clean and clear,
They shall enjoy materialism and the sight of prod-
  ucts — they shall enjoy the sight of the beef,
  lumber, bread-stuffs, of Chicago, the great city,
They shall train themselves to go in public to become
  oratists, (orators and oratresses,)
Strong and sweet shall their tongues be — poems and
  materials of poems shall come from their lives —
  they shall be makers and finders,
Of them, and of their works, shall emerge divine
  conveyers, to convey gospels,

Characters, events, retrospections, shall be conveyed in gospels — Trees, animals, waters, shall be conveyed,

Death, the future, the invisible faith, shall all be conveyed.

### 17.

1. Now we start hence, I with the rest, on our journeys through The States,
   We willing learners of all, teachers of all, and lovers of all.

2. I have watched the seasons dispensing themselves, and passing on,
   And I have said, Why should not a man or woman do as much as the seasons, and effuse as much?

3. We dwell a while in every city and town,
   We pass through Kanada, the north-east, the vast valley of the Mississippi, and the Southern States,
   We confer on equal terms with each of The States,
   We make trial of ourselves, and invite men and women to hear,
   We say to ourselves, Remember, fear not, be candid, promulge the body and the Soul,
   Promulge real things — Never forget the equality of humankind, and never forget immortality;

Dwell a while, and pass on — Be copious, temperate,
    chaste, magnetic,
And what you effuse may then return as the seasons
    return,
And may be just as much as the seasons.

### 18.

ME imperturbe,
Me standing at ease in Nature,
Master of all, or mistress of all — aplomb in the
    midst of irrational things,
Imbued as they — passive, receptive, silent as they,
Finding my occupation, poverty, notoriety, foibles,
    crimes, less important than I thought;
Me private, or public, or menial, or solitary — all
    these subordinate, (I am eternally equal with
    the best — I am not subordinate;)
Me toward the Mexican Sea, or in the Mannahatta,
    or the Tennessee, or far north, or inland,
A river-man, or a man of the woods, or of any farm-
    life of These States, or of the coast, or the lakes,
    or Kanada,
Me, wherever my life is to be lived, O to be self-bal-
    anced for contingencies!
O to confront night, storms, hunger, ridicule, acci-
    dents, rebuffs, as the trees and animals do.

# 19.

I was looking a long while for the history of the
　　past for myself, and for these Chants — and now
　　I have found it,
It is not in those paged fables in the libraries, (them
　　I neither accept nor reject,)
It is no more in the legends than in all else,
It is in the present — it is this earth to-day,
It is in Democracy — in this America — the old world
　　also,
It is the life of one man or one woman to-day, the
　　average man of to-day ;
It is languages, social customs, literatures, arts,
It is the broad show of artificial things, ships, ma-
　　chinery, politics, creeds, modern improvements,
　　and the interchanges of nations,
All for the average man of to-day.

# 20.

1. American mouth-songs!
　　Those of mechanics — each one singing his, as it
　　　　should be, blithe and strong,
　　The carpenter singing his, as he measures his plank
　　　　or beam,

The mason singing his, as he makes ready for work,
or leaves off work,

The boatman singing what belongs to him in his boat
— the deck-hand singing on the steamboat deck,

The shoemaker singing as he sits on his bench — the
hatter singing as he stands,

The wood-cutter's song — the ploughboy's, on his way
in the morning, or at the noon intermission, or at
sundown ;

The delicious singing of the mother — or of the
young wife at work — or of the girl sewing or
washing — Each singing what belongs to her,
and to none else,

The day what belongs to the day — At night, the
party of young fellows, robust, friendly, clean-
blooded, singing with melodious voices, melo-
dious thoughts.

2. Come! some of you! still be flooding The States
with hundreds and thousands of mouth-songs,
fit for The States only.

21.

1. As I walk, solitary, unattended,
Around me I hear that eclat of the world — politics,
produce,
The announcements of recognized things — science,
The approved growth of cities, and the spread of
inventions.

2. I see the ships, (they will last a few years,)
The vast factories with their foremen and workmen,
And hear the indorsement of all, and do not object
    to it.

3. But we too announce solid things,
Science, ships, politics, cities, factories, are not noth-
    ing — they serve,
They stand for realities — all is as it should be.

4. Then my realities,   .
What else is so real as mine?
Libertad, and the divine average — Freedom to every
    slave on the face of the earth,
The rapt promises and lumine of seers — the spir-
    itual world — these centuries-lasting songs,
And our visions, the visions of poets, the most solid
    announcements of any.

5. For we support all,
After the rest is done and gone, we remain,
There is no final reliance but upon us,
Democracy rests finally upon us, (I, my brethren,
    begin it,)
And our visions sweep through eternity.

# Leaves of Grass.

# 1.

1. ELEMENTAL drifts!
    O I wish I could impress others as you and the waves
    have just been impressing me.


2. As I ebbed with an ebb of the ocean of life,
    As I wended the shores I know,
    As I walked where the sea-ripples wash you, Pau-
    manok,
    Where they rustle up, hoarse and sibilant,
    Where the fierce old mother endlessly cries for her
    castaways,
    I, musing, late in the autumn day, gazing off south-
    ward,
    Alone, held by the eternal self of me that threatens
    to get the better of me, and stifle me,
    Was seized by the spirit that trails in the lines
    underfoot,
    In the rim, the sediment, that stands for all the water
    and all the land of the globe.

3. Fascinated, my eyes, reverting from the south,
      dropped, to follow those slender winrows,
   Chaff, straw, splinters of wood, weeds, and the sea-
      gluten,
   Scum, scales from shining rocks, leaves of salt-
      lettuce, left by the tide ;
   Miles walking, the sound of breaking waves the other
      side of me,
   Paumanok, there and then, as I thought the old
      thought of likenesses,
   These you presented to me, you fish-shaped island,
   As I wended the shores I know,
   As I walked with that eternal self of me, seeking
      types.

4. As I wend the shores I know not,
   As I listen to the dirge, the voices of men and women
      wrecked,
   As I inhale the impalpable breezes that set in
      upon me,
   As the ocean so mysterious rolls toward me closer
      and closer,
   At once I find, the least thing that belongs to me, or
      that I see or touch, I know not ;
   I, too, but signify, at the utmost, a little washed-up
      drift,
   A few sands and dead leaves to gather,
   Gather, and merge myself as part of the sands and
      drift.

5. O baffled, balked,
   Bent to the very earth, here preceding what follows,
   Oppressed with myself that I have dared to open my
      mouth,

Aware now, that, amid all the blab whose echoes
  recoil upon me, I have not once had the least
  idea who or what I am,
But that before all my insolent poems the real ME
  still stands untouched, untold, altogether un-
  reached,
Withdrawn far, mocking me with mock-congrat-
  ulatory signs and bows,
With peals of distant ironical laughter at every word
  I have written or shall write,
Striking me with insults till I fall helpless upon the
  sand.

6. O I perceive I have not understood anything — not a
  single object — and that no man ever can.

7. I perceive Nature here, in sight of the sea, is taking
  advantage of me, to dart upon me, and sting me,
Because I was assuming so much,
And because I have dared to open my mouth to sing
  at all.

8. You oceans both! You tangible land! Nature!
Be not too rough with me — I submit — I close with
  you,
These little shreds shall, indeed, stand for all.

9. You friable shore, with trails of debris!
You fish-shaped island! I take what is underfoot;
What is yours is mine, my father.

10. I too Paumanok,
I too have bubbled up, floated the measureless float,
  and been washed on your shores;

17 *

I too am but a trail of drift and debris,
I too leave little wrecks upon you, you fish-shaped
island.

11. I throw myself upon your breast, my father,
I cling to you so that you cannot unloose me,
I hold you so firm, till you answer me something.

12. Kiss me, my father,
Touch me with your lips, as I touch those I love,
Breathe to me, while I hold you close, the secret of
the wondrous murmuring I envy,
For I fear I shall become crazed, if I cannot emulate
it, and utter myself as well as it.

13. Sea-raff! Crook-tongued waves!
O, I will yet sing, some day, what you have said
to me.

14. Ebb, ocean of life, (the flow will return,)
Cease not your moaning, you fierce old mother,
Endlessly cry for your castaways — but fear not,
deny not me,
Rustle not up so hoarse and angry against my feet, as
I touch you, or gather from you.

15. I mean tenderly by you,
I gather for myself, and for this phantom, looking
down where we lead, and following me and
mine.

16. Me and mine!
We, loose winrows, little corpses,
Froth, snowy white, and bubbles,

(See! from my dead lips the ooze exuding at last!
See — the prismatic colors, glistening and rolling!)
Tufts of straw, sands, fragments,
Buoyed hither from many moods, one contradicting
    another,
From the storm, the long calm, the darkness, the
    swell,
Musing, pondering, a breath, a briny tear, a dab of
    liquid or soil,
Up just as much out of fathomless workings fer-
    mented and thrown,
A limp blossom or two, torn, just as much over waves
    floating, drifted at random,
Just as much for us that sobbing dirge of Nature,
Just as much, whence we come, that blare of the
    cloud-trumpets;
We, capricious, brought hither, we know not whence,
    spread out before You, up there, walking or
    sitting,
Whoever you are — we too lie in drifts at your feet.

# 2.

1. GREAT are the myths — I too delight in them,
    Great are Adam and Eve — I too look back and
        accept them,
    Great the risen and fallen nations, and their poets,
        women, sages, inventors, rulers, warriors, and
        priests.

2. Great is Liberty! great is Equality! I am their fol-
lower,
   Helmsmen of nations, choose your craft! where you
sail, I sail,
   Yours is the muscle of life or death — yours is the
perfect science — in you I have absolute faith.

3. Great is To-day, and beautiful,
   It is good to live in this age — there never was any
better.

4. Great are the plunges, throes, triumphs, downfalls of
Democracy,
   Great the reformers, with their lapses and screams,
   Great the daring and venture of sailors, on new ex-
plorations.

5. Great are Yourself and Myself,
   We are just as good and bad as the oldest and young-
est or any,
   What the best and worst did, we could do,
   What they felt, do not we feel it in ourselves?
   What they wished, do we not wish the same?

6. Great is Youth — equally great is Old Age — great
are the Day and Night,
   Great is Wealth — great is Poverty — great is Ex-
pression — great is Silence.

7. Youth, large, lusty, loving — Youth, full of grace,
force, fascination,
   Do you know that Old Age may come after you, with
equal grace, force, fascination?

8. Day, full-blown and splendid — Day of the immense
    sun, action, ambition, laughter,
  The Night follows close, with millions of suns, and
    sleep, and restoring darkness.

9. Wealth with the flush hand, fine clothes, hospitality,
  But then the Soul's wealth, which is candor, knowl-
    edge, pride, enfolding love;
  (Who goes for men and women showing Poverty
    richer than wealth?)

10. Expression of speech! in what is written or said, for-
    get not that Silence is also expressive,
  That anguish as hot as the hottest, and contempt as
    cold as the coldest, may be without words,
  That the true adoration is likewise without words,
    and without kneeling.

11. Great is the greatest Nation — the nation of clusters
    of equal nations.

12. Great is the Earth, and the way it became what it is;
  Do you imagine it is stopped at this? the increase
    abandoned?
  Understand then that it goes as far onward from
    this, as this is from the times when it lay in
    covering waters and gases, before man had ap-
    peared.

13. Great is the quality of Truth in man,
  The quality of truth in man supports itself through
    all changes,

It is inevitably in the man — he and it are in love,
and never leave each other.

14. The truth in man is no dictum, it is vital as eye-
sight,
If there be any Soul, there is truth — if there be man
or woman, there is truth — if there be physical
or moral, there is truth,
If there be equilibrium or volition, there is truth —
if there be things at all upon the earth, there
is truth.

15. O truth of the earth! O truth of things! I am de-
termined to press my way toward you,
Sound your voice! I scale mountains, or dive in the
sea after you.

16. Great is Language — it is the mightiest of the sci-
ences,
It is the fulness, color, form, diversity of the earth,
and of men and women, and of all qualities
and processes,
It is greater than wealth — it is greater than build-
ings, ships, religions, paintings, music.

17. Great is the English speech — what speech is so
great as the English?
Great is the English brood — what brood has so vast
a destiny as the English?
It is the mother of the brood that must rule the earth
with the new rule,
The new rule shall rule as the Soul rules, and as the
love, justice, equality in the Soul, rule.

18 Great is Law — great are the old few landmarks of
the law,
They are the same in all times, and shall not be
disturbed.

19. Great are commerce, newspapers, books, free-trade,
railroads, steamers, international mails, tele-
graphs, exchanges.

20 Great is Justice !
Justice is not settled by legislators and laws — it is in
the Soul,
It cannot be varied by statutes, any more than love,
pride, the attraction of gravity, can,
It is immutable — it does not depend on majorities —
majorities or what not come at last before the
same passionless and exact tribunal.

21. For justice are the grand natural lawyers and perfect
judges — it is in their Souls,
It is well assorted — they have not studied for noth-
ing — the great includes the less,
They rule on the highest grounds — they oversee all
eras, states, administrations.

22. The perfect judge fears nothing — he could go front
to front before God,
Before the perfect judge all shall stand back — life
and death shall stand back — heaven and hell
shall stand back.

23. Great is Goodness !
I do not know what it is, any more than I know what
health is — but I know it is great.

24. Great is Wickedness — I find I often admire it, just as
      much as I admire goodness,
   Do you call that a paradox ? It certainly is a paradox.

25. The eternal equilibrium of things is great, and the
      eternal overthrow of things is great,
   And there is another paradox.

26. Great is Life, real and mystical, wherever and whoever,
   Great is Death — sure as Life holds all parts together,
      Death holds all parts together,
   Death has just as much purport as Life has,
   Do you enjoy what Life confers ? you shall enjoy what
      Death confers,
   I do not understand the realities of Death, but I know
      they are great,
   I do not understand the least reality of Life — how then
      can I understand the realities of Death ?

# 3.

1. A YOUNG man came to me with a message from his
      brother,
   How should the young man know the whether and
      when of his brother ?
   Tell him to send me the signs.

2. And I stood before the young man face to face, and
      took his right hand in my left hand, and his left
      hand in my right hand,

And I answered for his brother, and for men, and I
answered for THE POET, and sent these signs.

3. Him all wait for — him all yield up to — his word is
decisive and final,
Him they accept, in him lave, in him perceive them-
selves, as amid light,
Him they immerse, and he immerses them.

4. Beautiful women, the haughtiest nations, laws, the
landscape, people, animals,
The profound earth and its attributes, and the unquiet
ocean,
All enjoyments and properties, and money, and what-
ever money will buy,
The best farms — others toiling and planting, and he
unavoidably reaps,
The noblest and costliest cities — others grading and
building, and he domiciles there,
Nothing for any one, but what is for him — near and
far are for him,
The ships in the offing — the perpetual shows and
marches on land, are for him, if they are for any
body.

5. He puts things in their attitudes,
He puts to-day out of himself, with plasticity and
love,
He places his own city, times, reminiscences, parents,
brothers and sisters, associations, employment,
politics, so that the rest never shame them after-
ward, nor assume to command them.

18

6. He is the answerer,
    What can be answered he answers — and what cannot
        be answered, he shows how it cannot be answered.

7. A man is a summons and challenge ;
    (It is vain to skulk — Do you hear that mocking and
        laughter ?  Do you hear the ironical echoes ?)

8. Books, friendships, philosophers, priests, action, pleas-
        ure, pride, beat up and down, seeking to give
        satisfaction,
    He indicates the satisfaction, and indicates them that
        beat up and down also.

9. Whichever the sex, whatever the season or place, he
        may go freshly and gently and safely, by day or
        by night,
    He has the pass-key of hearts — to him the response
        of the prying of hands on the knobs.

10. His welcome is universal — the flow of beauty is not
        more welcome or universal than he is,
     The person he favors by day or sleeps with at night is
        blessed.

11. Every existence has its idiom — everything has an
        idiom and tongue,
     He resolves all tongues into his own, and bestows it
        upon men, and any man translates, and any man
        translates himself also,
     One part does not counteract another part — he is the
        joiner — he sees how they join.

12. He says indifferently and alike, *How are you, friend ?*
     to the President at his levee,

And he says, *Good-day, my brother!* to Cudge that
hoes in the sugar-field,
And both understand him, and know that his speech
is right.

13. He walks with perfect ease in the capitol,
He walks among the Congress, and one representative
says to another, *Here is our equal, appearing and
new.*

14. Then the mechanics take him for a mechanic,
And the soldiers suppose him to be a captain, and the
sailors that he has followed the sea,
And the authors take him for an author, and the
artists for an artist,
And the laborers perceive he could labor with them
and love them,
No matter what the work is, that he is the one to fol-
low it, or has followed it,
No matter what the nation, that he might find his
brothers and sisters there.

15. The English believe he comes of their English stock,
A Jew to the Jew he seems — a Russ to the Russ —
usual and near, removed from none.

16. Whoever he looks at in the traveller's coffee-house
claims him,
The Italian or Frenchman is sure, and the German is
sure, and the Spaniard is sure, and the island
Cuban is sure;
The engineer, the deck-hand on the great lakes, or on
the Mississippi, or St. Lawrence, or Sacramento,
or Hudson, or Paumanok Sound, claims him.

17. The gentleman of perfect blood acknowledges his per-
     fect blood,
   The insulter, the prostitute, the angry person, the
     beggar, see themselves in the ways of him — he
     strangely transmutes them,
   They are not vile any more — they hardly know them-
     selves, they are so grown.

18. Do you think it would be good to be the writer of
     melodious verses ?
   Well, it would be good to be the writer of melodious
     verses ;
   But what are verses beyond the flowing character you
     could have ? or beyond beautiful manners and
     behavior ?
   Or beyond one manly or affectionate deed of an ap-
     prentice-boy ? or old woman ? or man that has
     been in prison, or is likely to be in prison ?

# 4.

1. SOMETHING startles me where I thought I was safest,
   I withdraw from the still woods I loved,
   I will not go now on the pastures to walk,
   I will not strip the clothes from my body to meet my
     lover the sea,
   I will not touch my flesh to the earth, as to other
     flesh, to renew me.

2. O Earth!
    O how can the ground of you not sicken?
    How can you be alive, you growths of spring?
    How can you furnish health, you blood of herbs, roots,
        orchards, grain?
    Are they not continually putting distempered corpses
        in you?
    Is not every continent worked over and over with sour
        dead?

3. Where have you disposed of those carcasses of the
        drunkards and gluttons of so many generations?
    Where have you drawn off all the foul liquid and meat?
    I do not see any of it upon you to-day — or perhaps
        I am deceived,
    I will run a furrow with my plough — I will press
        my spade through the sod, and turn it up un-
        derneath,
    I am sure I shall expose some of the foul meat.

4. Behold!
    This is the compost of billions of premature corpses,
    Perhaps every mite has once formed part of a sick
        person — Yet behold!
    The grass covers the prairies,
    The bean bursts noiselessly through the mould in the
        garden,
    The delicate spear of the onion pierces upward,
    The apple-buds cluster together on the apple-branches,
    The resurrection of the wheat appears with pale visage
        out of its graves,
    The tinge awakes over the willow-tree and the mul-
        berry-tree,

18 *

The he-birds carol mornings and evenings, while the
    she-birds sit on their nests,

The young of poultry break through the hatched eggs,

The new-born of animals appear — the calf is dropt
    from the cow, the colt from the mare,

Out of its little hill faithfully rise the potato's dark
    green leaves,

Out of its hill rises the yellow maize-stalk ;

The summer growth is innocent and disdainful above
    all those strata of sour dead.


5. What chemistry !

That the winds are really not infectious,

That this is no cheat, this transparent green-wash of
    the sea, which is so amorous after me,

That it is safe to allow it to lick my naked body all
    over with its tongues,

That it will not endanger me with the fevers that
    have deposited themselves in it,

That all is clean, forever and forever,

That the cool drink from the well tastes so good,

That blackberries are so flavorous and juicy,

That the fruits of the apple-orchard, and of the
    orange-orchard — that melons, grapes, peaches,
    plums, will none of them poison me,

That when I recline on the grass I do not catch any
    disease,

Though probably every spear of grass rises out of
    what was once a catching disease.


6. Now I am terrified at the Earth ! it is that calm and
    patient,

It grows such sweet things out of such corruptions,

It turns harmless and stainless on its axis, with such
    endless successions of diseased corpses,
It distils such exquisite winds out of such infused
    fetor,
It renews, with such unwitting looks, its prodigal,
    annual, sumptuous crops,
It gives such divine materials to men, and accepts
    such leavings from them at last.

# 5.

1. ALL day I have walked the city, and talked with my
    friends, and thought of prudence,
  Of time, space, reality — of such as these, and abreast
    with them, prudence.

2. After all, the last explanation remains to be made
    about prudence,
  Little and large alike drop quietly aside from the
    prudence that suits immortality.

3. The Soul is of itself,
  All verges to it — all has reference to what ensues,
  All that a person does, says, thinks, is of conse-
    quence,
  Not a move can a man or woman make, that affects
    him or her in a day, month, any part of the
    direct life-time, or the hour of death, but the
    same affects him or her onward afterward
    through the indirect life-time.

4. The indirect is more than the direct,
   The spirit receives from the body just as much as it
     gives to the body, if not more.

5. Not one word or deed — not venereal sore, discolor-
     ation, privacy of the onanist, putridity of gluttons
     or rum-drinkers, peculation, cunning, betrayal,
     murder, seduction, prostitution, but has results
     beyond death, as really as before death.

6. Charity and personal force are the only investments
     worth anything.

7. No specification is necessary — all that a male or
     female does, that is vigorous, benevolent, clean,
     is so much profit to him or her, in the unshakable
     order of the universe, and through the whole
     scope of it forever.

8. Who has been wise, receives interest,
   Savage, felon, President, judge, farmer, sailor, me-
     chanic, young, old, it is the same,
   The interest will come round — all will come round.

9. Singly, wholly, to affect now, affected their time, will
     forever affect, all of the past, and all of the
     present, and all of the future,
   All the brave actions of war and peace,
   All help given to relatives, strangers, the poor, old,
     sorrowful, young children, widows, the sick, and
     to shunned persons,
   All furtherance of fugitives, and of the escape of
     slaves,

All self-denial that stood steady and aloof on wrecks,
    and saw others fill the seats of the boats,
All offering of substance or life for the good old cause,
    or for a friend's sake, or opinion's sake,
All pains of enthusiasts, scoffed at by their neighbors,
All the limitless sweet love and precious suffering of
    mothers,
All honest men baffled in strifes recorded or unre-
    corded,
All the grandeur and good of ancient nations whose
    fragments we inherit,
All the good of the hundreds of ancient nations un-
    known to us by name, date, location,
All that was ever manfully begun, whether it suc-
    ceeded or no,
All suggestions of the divine mind of man, or the
    divinity of his mouth, or the shaping of his great
    hands;
All that is well thought or said this day on any part
    of the globe — or on any of the wandering stars,
    or on any of the fixed stars, by those there as we
    are here,
All that is henceforth to be thought or done by you,
    whoever you are, or by any one,
These inure, have inured, shall inure, to the identities
    from which they sprang, or shall spring.


10. Did you guess anything lived only its moment?
    The world does not so exist — no parts palpable or
        impalpable so exist,
    No consummation exists without being from some
        long previous consummation — and that from
        some other,

Without the farthest conceivable one coming a bit
nearer the beginning than any.

11. Whatever satisfies Souls is true,
Prudence entirely satisfies the craving and glut of
Souls,
Itself finally satisfies the Soul,
The Soul has that measureless pride which revolts
from every lesson but its own.

12. Now I give you an inkling,
Now I breathe the word of the prudence that walks
abreast with time, space, reality,
That answers the pride which refuses every lesson but
its own.

13. What is prudence, is indivisible,
Declines to separate one part of life from every part,
Divides not the righteous from the unrighteous, or
the living from the dead,
Matches every thought or act by its correlative,
Knows no possible forgiveness or deputed atonement,
Knows that the young man who composedly perilled
his life and lost it, has done exceeding well for
himself, without doubt,
That he who never perilled his life, but retains it to
old age in riches and ease, has probably achieved
nothing for himself worth mentioning ;
Knows that only the person has really learned, who
has learned to prefer results,
Who favors body and Soul the same,
Who perceives the indirect assuredly following the
direct,
Who in his spirit in any emergency whatever neither
hurries or avoids death.

# 6.

1. PERFECT sanity shows the master among philosophs,
   Time, always without flaw, indicates itself in parts,
   What always indicates the poet, is the crowd of the
   pleasant company of singers, and their words,
   The words of the singers are the hours or minutes of
   the light or dark — but the words of the maker
   of poems are the general light and dark,
   The maker of poems settles justice, reality, immor-
   tality,
   His insight and power encircle things and the human
   race,
   He is the glory and extract, thus far, of things, and
   of the human race.

2. The singers do not beget — only THE POET begets,
   The singers are welcomed, understood, appear often
   enough — but rare has the day been, likewise the
   spot, of the birth of the maker of poems,
   Not every century, or every five centuries, has con-
   tained such a day, for all its names.

3. The singers of successive hours of centuries may have
   ostensible names, but the name of each of them
   is one of the singers,
   The name of each is, a heart-singer, eye-singer, hymn-
   singer, law-singer, ear-singer, head-singer, sweet-
   singer, wise-singer, droll-singer, thrift-singer, sea-
   singer, wit-singer, echo-singer, parlor-singer, love-
   singer, passion-singer, mystic-singer, fable-singer,
   item-singer, weeping-singer, or something else.

4. All this time, and at all times, wait the words of
poems ;
The greatness of sons is the exuding of the greatness
of mothers and fathers,
The words of poems are the tuft and final applause of
science.

5. Divine instinct, breadth of vision, the law of reason,
health, rudeness of body, withdrawnness, gayety,
sun-tan, air-sweetness — such are some of the
words of poems.

6. The sailor and traveller underlie the maker of poems,
The builder, geometer, mathematician, astronomer,
melodist, chemist, anatomist, spiritualist, lan-
guage-searcher, geologist, phrenologist, artist —
all these underlie the maker of poems.

7. The words of poems give you more than poems,
They give you to form for yourself poems, religions,
politics, war, peace, behavior, histories, essays,
romances, and everything else,
They balance ranks, colors, races, creeds, and the
sexes,
They do not seek beauty — they are sought,
Forever touching them, or close upon them, follows
beauty, longing, fain, love-sick.

8. They prepare for death — yet are they not the finish,
but rather the outset,
They bring none to his or her terminus, or to be con-
tent and full ;

Whom they take, they take into space, to behold the
    birth of stars, to learn one of the meanings,
To launch off with absolute faith — to sweep through
    the ceaseless rings, and never be quiet again.

# 7.

I NEED no assurances — I am a man who is pre-
    occupied, of his own Soul;
I do not doubt that whatever I know at a given time,
    there waits for me more, which I do not know;
I do not doubt that from under the feet, and beside
    the hands and face I am cognizant of, are now
    looking faces I am not cognizant of — calm and
    actual faces;
I do not doubt but the majesty and beauty of the
    world are latent in any iota of the world;
I do not doubt there are realizations I have no idea of,
    waiting for me through time, and through the
    universes — also upon this earth;
I do not doubt I am limitless, and that the universes
    are limitless — in vain I try to think how
    limitless;
I do not doubt that the orbs, and the systems of orbs,
    play their swift sports through the air on purpose
    — and that I shall one day be eligible to do as
    much as they, and more than they;
I do not doubt there is far more in trivialities, insects,
    vulgar persons, slaves, dwarfs, weeds, rejected
    refuse, than I have supposed;

I do not doubt there is more in myself than I have
supposed — and more in all men and women —
and more in my poems than I have supposed ;

I do not doubt that temporary affairs keep on and on,
millions of years ;

I do not doubt interiors have their interiors, and
exteriors have their exteriors — and that the
eye-sight has another eye-sight, and the hearing
another hearing, and the voice another voice ;

I do not doubt that the passionately-wept deaths of
young men are provided for — and that the
deaths of young women, and the deaths of little
children, are provided for ;

I do not doubt that wrecks at sea, no matter what the
horrors of them — no matter whose wife, child,
husband, father, lover, has gone down — are pro-
vided for, to the minutest point ;

I do not doubt that shallowness, meanness, malig-
nance, are provided for ;

I do not doubt that cities, you, America, the re-
mainder of the earth, politics, freedom, degra-
dations, are carefully provided for ;

I do not doubt that whatever can possibly happen,
any where, at any time, is provided for, in the
inherences of things.

## 8.

1. WHAT shall I give? and which are my miracles?

2. Realism is mine — my miracles — Take freely,
Take without end — I offer them to you wherever
your feet can carry you, or your eyes reach.

3. Why! who makes much of a miracle?
As to me, I know of nothing else but miracles,
Whether I walk the streets of Manhattan,
Or dart my sight over the roofs of houses toward the
sky,
Or wade with naked feet along the beach, just in the
edge of the water,
Or stand under trees in the woods,
Or talk by day with any one I love — or sleep in the
bed at night with any one I love,
Or sit at the table at dinner with my mother,
Or look at strangers opposite me riding in the car,
Or watch honey-bees busy around the hive, of a sum-
mer forenoon,
Or animals feeding in the fields,
Or birds — or the wonderfulness of insects in the air,
Or the wonderfulness of the sun-down — or of stars
shining so quiet and bright,
Or the exquisite, delicate, thin curve of the new-moon
in spring;
Or whether I go among those I like best, and that like
me best — mechanics, boatmen, farmers,

Or among the savans — or to the soiree — or to the
    opera,

Or stand a long while looking at the movements of
    machinery,

Or behold children at their sports,

Or the admirable sight of the perfect old man, or the
    perfect old woman,

Or the sick in hospitals, or the dead carried to burial,

Or my own eyes and figure in the glass,

These, with the rest, one and all, are to me miracles,

The whole referring — yet each distinct and in its
    place.


4. To me, every hour of the light and dark is a miracle,

Every inch of space is a miracle,

Every square yard of the surface of the earth is spread
    with the same,

Every cubic foot of the interior swarms with the same;

Every spear of grass — the frames, limbs, organs, of
    men and women, and all that concerns them,

All these to me are unspeakably perfect miracles.


5. To me the sea is a continual miracle,

The fishes that swim — the rocks — the motion of the
    waves — the ships, with men in them,

What stranger miracles are there?

# 9.

1 THERE was a child went forth every day,
  And the first object he looked upon and received
      with wonder, pity, love, or dread, that object he
      became,
  And that object became part of him for the day, or a
      certain part of the day, or for many years, or
      stretching cycles of years.

2. The early lilacs became part of this child,
  And grass, and white and red morning-glories, and
      white and red clover, and the song of the phœbe-
      bird,
  And the Third Month lambs, and the sow's pink-faint
      litter, and the mare's foal, and the cow's calf,
  And the noisy brood of the barn-yard, or by the mire
      of the pond-side,
  And the fish suspending themselves so curiously below
      there — and the beautiful curious liquid,
  And the water-plants with their graceful flat heads —
      all became part of him.

3. The field-sprouts of Fourth Month and Fifth Month
      became part of him,
  Winter-grain sprouts, and those of the light-yellow
      corn, and the esculent roots of the garden,
  And the apple-trees covered with blossoms, and the
      fruit afterward, and wood-berries, and the com-
      monest weeds by the road;

19*

And the old drunkard staggering home from the out-
house of the tavern, whence he had lately risen,

And the school-mistress that passed on her way to the
school,

And the friendly boys that passed — and the quarrel-
some boys,

And the tidy and fresh-cheeked girls — and the bare-
foot negro boy and girl,

And all the changes of city and country, wherever he
went.

4.  His own parents,

He that had fathered him, and she that conceived him
in her womb, and birthed him,

They gave this child more of themselves than that,

They gave him afterward every day — they and of
them became part of him.

5.  The mother at home, quietly placing the dishes on the
supper-table,

The mother with mild words — clean her cap and
gown, a wholesome odor falling off her person
and clothes as she walks by;

The father, strong, self-sufficient, manly, mean, an-
gered, unjust,

The blow, the quick loud word, the tight bargain, the
crafty lure,

The family usages, the language, the company, the
furniture — the yearning and swelling heart,

Affection that will not be gainsayed — the sense of
what is real — the thought if, after all, it should
prove unreal,

The doubts of day-time and the doubts of night-time —
the curious whether and how,

Whether that which appears so is so, or is it all flashes
and specks ?

Men and women crowding fast in the streets — if they
are not flashes and specks, what are they ?

The streets themselves, and the façades of houses, and
goods in the windows,

Vehicles, teams, the heavy-planked wharves — the
huge crossing at the ferries,

The village on the highland, seen from afar at sunset —
the river between,

Shadows, aureola and mist, light falling on roofs and
gables of white or brown, three miles off,

The schooner near by, sleepily dropping down the
tide — the little boat slack-towed astern,

The hurrying tumbling waves, quick-broken crests,
slapping,

The strata of colored clouds, the long bar of maroon-
tint, away solitary by itself — the spread of purity
it lies motionless in,

The horizon's edge, the flying sea-crow, the fragrance
of salt-marsh and shore-mud ;

These became part of that child who went forth every
day, and who now goes, and will always go forth
every day,

And these become part of him or her that peruses
them here.

# 10.

1. IT is ended — I dally no more,

     After to-day I inure myself to run, leap, swim, wrestle, fight,

     To stand the cold or heat — to take good aim with a gun — to sail a boat — to manage horses — to beget superb children,

     To speak readily and clearly — to feel at home among common people,

     And to hold my own in terrible positions, on land and sea.

2. Not for an embroiderer,

     (There will always be plenty of embroiderers — I welcome them also;)

     But for the fibre of things, and for inherent men and women.

3. Not to chisel ornaments,

     But to chisel with free stroke the heads and limbs of plenteous Supreme Gods, that The States may realize them, walking and talking.

4. Let me have my own way,

     Let others promulge the laws — I will make no account of the laws,

     Let others praise eminent men and hold up peace — I hold up agitation and conflict,

     I praise no eminent man — I rebuke to his face the one that was thought most worthy.

5. (Who are you? you mean devil! And what are you
     secretly guilty of, all your life?
  Will you turn aside all your life? Will you grub
     and chatter all your life?)

6. (And who are you — blabbing by rote, years, pages,
     languages, reminiscences,
  Unwitting to-day that you do not know how to speak
     a single word?)

7. Let others finish specimens — I never finish specimens,
  I shower them by exhaustless laws, as nature does,
     fresh and modern continually.

8. I give nothing as duties,
  What others give as duties, I give as living impulses;
  (Shall I give the heart's action as a duty?)

9. Let others dispose of questions — I dispose of noth-
     ing — I arouse unanswerable questions;
  Who are they I see and touch, and what about them?
  What about these likes of myself, that draw me so
     close by tender directions and indirections?

10. Let others deny the evil their enemies charge against
     them — but how can I the like?
  Nothing ever has been, or ever can be, charged against
     me, half as bad as the evil I really am;
  I call to the world to distrust the accounts of my
     friends, but listen to my enemies — as I my-
     self do;
  I charge you, too, forever, reject those who would
     expound me — for I cannot expound myself,

I charge that there be no theory or school founded out
of me,
I charge you to leave all free, as I have left all free.

11. After me, vista!
O, I see life is not short, but immeasurably long,
I henceforth tread the world, chaste, temperate, an
early riser, a gymnast, a steady grower,
Every hour the semen of centuries — and still of cen-
turies.

12. I will follow up these continual lessons of the air,
water, earth,
I perceive I have no time to lose.

# 11.

1. Who learns my lesson complete?
Boss, journeyman, apprentice — churchman and athe-
ist,
The stupid and the wise thinker — parents and off-
spring — merchant, clerk, porter, and customer,
Editor, author, artist, and schoolboy — Draw nigh and
commence;
It is no lesson — it lets down the bars to a good
lesson,
And that to another, and every one to another still.

2. The great laws take and effuse without argument,
I am of the same style, for I am their friend,

I love them quits and quits — I do not halt and make
salaams.

3. I lie abstracted, and hear beautiful tales of things,
and the reasons of things,
They are so beautiful, I nudge myself to listen.

4. I cannot say to any person what I hear — I cannot
say it to myself — it is very wonderful.

5. It is no small matter, this round and delicious globe,
moving so exactly in its orbit forever and ever,
without one jolt, or the untruth of a single
second,
I do not think it was made in six days, nor in ten
thousand years, nor ten billions of years,
Nor planned and built one thing after another, as an
architect plans and builds a house.

6. I do not think seventy years is the time of a man or
woman,
Nor that seventy millions of years is the time of a
man or woman,
Nor that years will ever stop the existence of me, or
any one else.

7. Is it wonderful that I should be immortal ? as every
one is immortal,
I know it is wonderful — but my eye-sight is equally
wonderful, and how I was conceived in my moth-
er's womb is equally wonderful ;

And how I was not palpable once, but am now — and was born on the last day of Fifth Month, in the Year 43 of America,

And passed from a babe, in the creeping trance of three summers and three winters, to articulate and walk — All this is equally wonderful.

8. And that I grew six feet high, and that I have become a man thirty-six years old in the Year 79 of America — and that I am here anyhow — are all equally wonderful.

9. And that my Soul embraces you this hour, and we affect each other without ever seeing each other, and never perhaps to see each other, is every bit as wonderful.

10. And that I can think such thoughts as these, is just as wonderful,

And that I can remind you, and you think them and know them to be true, is just as wonderful.

11. And that the moon spins round the earth, and on with the earth, is equally wonderful,

And that they balance themselves with the sun and stars, is equally wonderful.

12. Come ! I should like to hear you tell me what there is in yourself that is not just as wonderful,

And I should like to hear the name of anything between First Day morning and Seventh Day night that is not just as wonderful.

# 12.

1. THIS night I am happy ;
   As I walk the beach where the old mother sways to
      and fro, singing her savage and husky song,
   As I watch the stars shining — I think a thought of
      the clef of the universes, and of the future.

2. What can the future bring me more than I have ?
   Do you suppose I wish to enjoy life in other spheres ?

3. I say distinctly I comprehend no better sphere than
      this earth,
   I comprehend no better life than the life of my body.

4. I do not know what follows the death of my body,
   But I know well that whatever it is, it is best for me,
   And I know well that whatever is really Me shall live
      just as much as before.

5. I am not uneasy but I shall have good housing to
      myself,
   But this is my first — how can I like the rest any
      better ?
   Here I grew up — the studs and rafters are grown
      parts of me.

6. I am not uneasy but I am to be beloved by young and
      old men, and to love them the same,

20

I suppose the pink nipples of the breasts of women
    with whom I shall sleep will touch the side of my
    face the same,
But this is the nipple of a breast of my mother, always
    near and always divine to me, her true child and
    son, whatever comes.


7. I suppose I am to be eligible to visit the stars, in my
    time,
  I suppose I shall have myriads of new experiences —
    and that the experience of this earth will prove
    only one out of myriads;
But I believe my body and my Soul already indicate
    those experiences,
And I believe I shall find nothing in the stars more
    majestic and beautiful than I have already found
    on the earth,
And I believe I have this night a clew through the
    universes,
And I believe I have this night thought a thought of
    the clef of eternity.


8. A VAST SIMILITUDE interlocks all,
  All spheres, grown, ungrown, small, large, suns,
    moons, planets, comets, asteroids,
All the substances of the same, and all that is spiritual,
    upon the same,
All distances of place, however wide,
All distances of time — all inanimate forms,
All Souls — all living bodies, though they be ever so
    different, or in different worlds,
All gaseous, watery, vegetable, mineral processes —
    the fishes, the brutes,

All men and women — me also,
All nations, colors, barbarisms, civilizations, languages,
All identities that have existed, or may exist, on this
    globe or any globe,
All lives and deaths — all of past, present, future,
This vast similitude spans them, and always has
    spanned, and shall forever span them, and
    compactly hold them.

# 13.

1. O BITTER sprig! Confession sprig!
In the bouquet I give you place also — I bind you in,
Proceeding no further till, humbled publicly,
I give fair warning, once for all.

2. I own that I have been sly, thievish, mean, a prevari-
    cator, greedy, derelict,
And I own that I remain so yet.

3. What foul thought but I think it — or have in me the
    stuff out of which it is thought?
What in darkness in bed at night, alone or with a
    companion?

4. You felons on trials in courts,
You convicts in prison cells — you sentenced assas-
    sins, chained and handcuffed with iron,

Who am I, that I am not on trial, or in prison?
Me, ruthless and devilish as any, that my wrists are
    not chained with iron, or my ankles with iron?

5. You prostitutes flaunting over the trottoirs, or obscene
    in your rooms,
   Who am I, that I should call you more obscene than
    myself?

6. O culpable! O traitor!
   O I acknowledge — I exposé!
  (O admirers! praise not me! compliment not me! you
    make me wince,
   I see what you do not — I know what you do not;)
   Inside these breast-bones I lie smutch'd and choked,
   Beneath this face that appears so impassive, hell's
    tides continually run,
   Lusts and wickedness are acceptable to me,
   I walk with delinquents with passionate love,
   I feel I am of them — I belong to those convicts and
    prostitutes myself,
   And henceforth I will not deny them — for how can I
    deny myself?

# 14.

UNFOLDED out of the folds of the woman, man comes
    unfolded, as is always to come unfolded,
Unfolded only out of the superbest woman of the
    earth, is to come the superbest man of the earth,
Unfolded out of the friendliest woman, is to come
    the friendliest man,
Unfolded only out of the perfect body of a woman,
    can a man be formed of perfect body,
Unfolded only out of the inimitable poem of the
    woman, can come the poems of man — only
    thence have my poems come,
Unfolded out of the strong and arrogant woman I
    love, only thence can appear the strong and
    arrogant man I love,
Unfolded by brawny embraces from the well-muscled
    woman I love, only thence come the brawny
    embraces of the man,
Unfolded out of the folds of the woman's brain, come
    all the folds of the man's brain, duly obedient,
Unfolded out of the justice of the woman, all justice
    is unfolded,
Unfolded out of the sympathy of the woman is all
    sympathy;
A man is a great thing upon the earth, and through
    eternity — but every jot of the greatness of man
    is unfolded out of woman,
First the man is shaped in the woman, he can then be
    shaped in himself.

# 15.

1. NIGHT on the Prairies;
  I walk by myself — I stand and look at the stars,
    which I think now I never realized before.

2. Now I absorb immortality and peace,
  I admire death and test propositions.

3. How plenteous! How spiritual! How resumé!
  The same Old Man and Soul — the same old aspi-
    rations, and the same content.

4. I was thinking the day most splendid, till I saw what
    the not-day exhibited,
  I was thinking this globe enough, till there tumbled
    upon me myriads of other globes.

5. Now while the great thoughts of space and eternity
    fill me, I will measure myself by them,
  And now, touched with the lives of other globes,
    arrived as far along as those of the earth,
  Or waiting to arrive, or passed on farther than those
    of the earth,
  I henceforth no more ignore them than I ignore my
    own life,
  Or the lives on the earth arrived as far as mine, or
    waiting to arrive.

6. O how plainly I see now that life cannot exhibit all to
    me — as the day cannot,
  O I see that I am to wait for what will be exhibited
    by death.

# 16.

SEA-WATER, and all living below it,
Forests at the bottom of the sea — the branches and
    leaves,
Sea-lettuce, vast lichens, strange flowers and seeds —
    the thick tangle, the openings, and the pink turf,
Different colors, pale gray and green, purple, white,
    and gold — the play of light through the water,
Dumb swimmers there among the rocks — coral,
    gluten, grass, rushes — and the aliment of the
    swimmers,
Sluggish existences grazing there, suspended, or
    slowly crawling close to the bottom,
The sperm-whale at the surface, blowing air and
    spray, or disporting with his flukes,
The leaden-eyed shark, the walrus, the turtle, the
    hairy sea-leopard, and the sting-ray;
Passions there — wars, pursuits, tribes — sight in
    those ocean-depths — breathing that thick-breath-
    ing air, as so many do,
The change thence to the sight here, and to the subtle
    air breathed by beings like us, who walk this
    sphere;
The change onward from ours to that of beings who
    walk other spheres.

# 17.

I SIT and look out upon all the sorrows of the world, and upon all oppression and shame,

I hear secret convulsive sobs from young men, at anguish with themselves, remorseful after deeds done ;

'I see, in low life, the mother misused by her children, dying, neglected, gaunt, desperate,

I see the wife misused by her husband — I see the treacherous seducer of the young woman,

I mark the ranklings of jealousy and unrequited love, attempted to be hid — I see these sights on the earth,

I see the workings of battle, pestilence, tyranny — I see martyrs and prisoners,

I observe a famine at sea — I observe the sailors casting lots who shall be killed, to preserve the lives of the rest,

I observe the slights and degradations cast by arrogant persons upon laborers, the poor, and upon negroes, and the like ;

All these — All the meanness and agony without end, I sitting, look out upon,

See, hear, and am silent.

# 18.

1. O ME, man of slack faith so long!
   Standing aloof — denying portions so long ;
   Me with mole's eyes, unrisen to buoyancy and vision
       — unfree,
   Only aware to-day of compact, all-diffused truth,
   Discovering to-day there is no lie, or form of lie,
       and can be none, but grows just as inevitably
       upon itself as the truth does upon itself,
   Or as any law of the earth, or any natural production
       of the earth does.

2. (This is curious, and may not be realized immedi-
       ately — But it must be realized ;
   I feel in myself that I represent falsehoods equally
       with the rest,
   And that the universe does.)

3. Where has failed a perfect return, indifferent of lies
       or the truth ?
   Is it upon the ground, or in water or fire ? or in the
       spirit of man ? or in the meat and blood ?

4. Meditating among liars, and retreating sternly into
       myself, I see that there are really no liars or
       lies after all,
   And that nothing fails its perfect return — And that
       what are called lies are perfect returns,

And that each thing exactly represents itself, and
what has preceded it,
And that the truth includes all, and is compact, just
as much as space is compact,
And that there is no flaw or vacuum in the amount
of the truth — but that all is truth without ex-
ception,
And henceforth I will go celebrate anything I see
or am,
And sing and laugh, and deny nothing.

# 19.

FORMS, qualities, lives, humanity, language, thoughts,
The ones known, and the ones unknown — the ones
on the stars,
The stars themselves, some shaped, others unshaped,
Wonders as of those countries — the soil, trees, cities,
inhabitants, whatever they may be,
Splendid suns, the moons and rings, the countless
combinations and effects,
Such-like, and as good as such-like, visible here or
anywhere, stand provided for in a handful of
space, which I extend my arm and half enclose
with my hand,
That contains the start of each and all — the virtue,
the germs of all ;
That is the theory as of origins.

# 20.

So far, and so far, and on toward the end,

Singing what is sung in this book, from the irresistible impulses of me ;

But whether I continue beyond this book, to maturity,

Whether I shall dart forth the true rays, the ones that wait unfired,

(Did you think the sun was shining its brightest ?

No — it has not yet fully risen ;)

Whether I shall complete what is here started,

Whether I shall attain my own height, to justify these, yet unfinished,

Whether I shall make THE POEM OF THE NEW WORLD, transcending all others — depends, rich persons, upon you,

Depends, whoever you are now filling the current Presidentiad, upon you,

Upon you, Governor, Mayor, Congressman,

And you, contemporary America.

# 21.

1. Now I make a leaf of Voices — for I have found nothing mightier than they are,
   And I have found that no word spoken, but is beautiful, in its place.

2. O what is it in me that makes me tremble so at voices?

3. Surely, whoever speaks to me in the right voice, him or her I shall follow, as the waters follow the moon, silently, with fluid steps, any where around the globe.

4. Now I believe that all waits for the right voices;
   Where is the practised and perfect organ? Where is the developed Soul?
   For I see every word uttered thence has deeper, sweeter, new sounds, impossible on less terms.

5. I see brains and lips closed — I see tympans and temples unstruck,
   Until that comes which has the quality to strike and to unclose,
   Until that comes which has the quality to bring forth what lies slumbering, forever ready, in all words.

## 22.

1. What am I, after all, but a child, pleased with the sound of my own name? repeating it over and over,

   I cannot tell why it affects me so much, when I hear it from women's voices, and from men's voices, or from my own voice,

   I stand apart to hear — it never tires me.

2. To you, your name also,

   Did you think there was nothing but two or three pronunciations in the sound of your name?

## 23.

Locations and times — what is it in me that meets them all, whenever and wherever, and makes me at home?

Forms, colors, densities, odors — what is it in me that corresponds with them?

What is the relation between me and them?

21

# 24.

LIFT me close to your face till I whisper,

What you are holding is in reality no book, nor part
of a book,

It is a man, flushed and full-blooded — it is I — *So
long!*

We must separate — Here! take from my lips this
kiss,

Whoever you are, I give it especially to you;

*So long* — and I hope we shall meet again.

# Salut au Monde!

———∘o⟨⟩∘o———

1. O TAKE my hand, Walt Whitman!
   Such gliding wonders! Such sights and sounds!
   Such joined unended links, each hooked to the next!
   Each answering all — each sharing the earth with all.

2. What widens within you, Walt Whitman?
   What waves and soils exuding?
   What climes? What persons and lands are here?
   Who are the infants? Some playing, some slum-
       bering?
   Who are the girls? Who are the married women?
   Who are the three old men going slowly with their
       arms about each others' necks?
   What rivers are these? What forests and fruits are
       these?
   What are the mountains called that rise so high in
       the mists?
   What myriads of dwellings are they, filled with
       dwellers?

3. Within me latitude widens, longitude lengthens,
   Asia, Africa, Europe, are to the east — America is
       provided for in the west,

Banding the bulge of the earth winds the hot equator,
Curiously north and south turn the axis-ends;
Within me is the longest day — the sun wheels in
  slanting rings — it does not set for months,
Stretched in due time within me the midnight sun
  just rises above the horizon, and sinks again,
Within me zones, seas, cataracts, plains, volcanoes,
  groups,
Oceanica, Australasia, Polynesia, and the great West
  Indian islands.

4. What do you hear, Walt Whitman?

5. I hear the workman singing, and the farmer's wife
  singing,
I hear in the distance the sounds of children, and of
  animals early in the day,
I hear quick rifle-cracks from the riflemen of East
  Tennessee and Kentucky, hunting on hills,
I hear emulous shouts of Australians, pursuing the
  wild horse,
I hear the Spanish dance, with castanets, in the chest-
  nut shade, to the rebeck and guitar,
I hear continual echoes from the Thames,
I hear fierce French liberty songs,
I hear of the Italian boat-sculler the musical recitative
  of old poems,
I hear the Virginia plantation chorus of negroes, of
  a harvest night, in the glare of pine knots,
I hear the strong baritone of the 'long-shore-men of
  Manhatta,
I hear the stevedores unlading the cargoes, and
  singing,

I hear the screams of the water-fowl of solitary north-
west lakes,

I hear the rustling pattering of locusts, as they strike
the grain and grass with the showers of their
terrible clouds,

I hear the Coptic refrain, toward sundown, pensively
falling on the breast of the black venerable vast
mother, the Nile,

I hear the bugles of raft-tenders on the streams of
Kanada,

I hear the chirp of the Mexican muleteer, and the
bells of the mule,

I hear the Arab muezzin, calling from the top of the
mosque,

I hear Christian priests at the altars of their churches
— I hear the responsive base and soprano,

I hear the wail of utter despair of the white-haired
Irish grand-parents, when they learn the death
of their grand-son,

I hear the cry of the Cossack, and the sailor's voice,
putting to sea at Okotsk,

I hear the wheeze of the slave-coffle, as the slaves
march on — as the husky gangs pass on by twos
and threes, fastened together with wrist-chains
and ankle-chains,

I hear the entreaties of women tied up for punishment
— I hear the sibilant whisk of thongs through
the air;

I hear the Hebrew reading his records and psalms,

I hear the rhythmic myths of the Greeks, and the
strong legends of the Romans,

I hear the tale of the divine life and bloody death
of the beautiful God, the Christ,

21*

I hear the Hindoo teaching his favorite pupil the loves, wars, adages, transmitted safely to this day from poets who wrote three thousand years ago.

6. What do you see, Walt Whitman?
Who are they who salute, and that one after another salute you?

7. I see a great round wonder rolling through the air,
I see diminute farms, hamlets, ruins, grave-yards, jails, factories, palaces, hovels, huts of barbarians, tents of nomads, upon the surface,
I see the shaded part on one side, where the sleepers are sleeping — and the sun-lit part on the other side,
I see the curious silent change of the light and shade,
I see distant lands, as real and near to the inhabitants of them, as my land is to me.

8. I see plenteous waters,
I see mountain peaks — I see the sierras of Andes and Alleghanies, where they range,
I see plainly the Himmalehs, Chian Shahs, Altays, Gauts,
I see the Rocky Mountains, and the Peak of Winds,
I see the Styrian Alps, and the Karnac Alps,
I see the Pyrenees, Balks, Carpathians — and to the north the Dofrafields, and off at sea Mount Hecla,
I see Vesuvius and Etna — I see the Anahuacs,
I see the Mountains of the Moon, and the Snow Mountains, and the Red Mountains of Madagascar,
I see the Vermont hills, and the long string of Cordilleras;

I see the vast deserts of Western America,
I see the Libyan, Arabian, and Asiatic deserts ;
I see huge dreadful Arctic and Antarctic icebergs,
I see the superior oceans and the inferior ones — the
  Atlantic and Pacific, the sea of Mexico, the Bra-
  zilian sea, and the sea of Peru,
The Japan waters, those of Hindostan, the China Sea,
  and the Gulf of Guinea,
The spread of the Baltic, Caspian, Bothnia, the British
  shores, and the Bay of Biscay,
The clear-sunned Mediterranean, and from one to an-
  other of its islands,
The inland fresh-tasted seas·of North America,
The White Sea, and the sea around Greenland.


9. I behold the mariners of the world,
 Some are in storms — some in the night, with the
  watch on the look-out,
 Some drifting helplessly — some with contagious dis-
  eases.


10. I behold the steam-ships of the world,
 Some double the Cape of Storms — some Cape Verde
  — others Cape Guardafui, Bon, or Bajadore,
 Others Dondra Head — others pass the Straits of Sun-
  da — others Cape Lopatka — others Behring's
  Straits,
 Others Cape Horn — others the Gulf of Mexico, or
  along Cuba or Hayti — others Hudson's Bay or
  Baffin's Bay,
 Others pass the Straits of Dover — others enter the
  Wash — others the Firth of Solway — others round
  Cape Clear — others the Land's End,

Others traverse the Zuyder Zee, or the Scheld,

Others add to the exits and entrances at Sandy Hook,

Others to the comers and goers at Gibraltar, or the Dardanelles,

Others sternly push their way through the northern winter-packs,

Others descend or ascend the Obi or the Lena,

Others the Niger or the Congo — others the Indus, the Burampooter and Cambodia,

Others wait at the wharves of Manahatta, steamed up, ready to start,

Wait, swift and swarthy, in the ports of Australia,

Wait at Liverpool, Glasgow, Dublin, Marseilles, Lisbon, Naples, Hamburg, Bremen, Bourdeaux, the Hague, Copenhagen,

Wait at Valparaiso, Rio Janeiro, Panama,

Wait at their moorings at Boston, Philadelphia, Baltimore, Charleston, New Orleans, Galveston, San Francisco.


11. I see the tracks of the rail-roads of the earth,

I see them welding State to State, city to city, through North America ;

I see them in Great Britain, I see them in Europe,

I see them in Asia and in Africa.


12. I see the electric telegraphs of the earth,

I see the filaments of the news of the wars, deaths, losses, gains, passions, of my race.


13. I see the long river-stripes of the earth,

I see where the Mississippi flows — I see where the Columbia flows,

I see the Great River, and the Falls of Niagara,
I see the Amazon and the Paraguay,
I see the four great rivers of China, the Amour, the
    Yellow River, the Yiang-tse, and the Pearl ;
I see where the Seine flows, and where the Loire, the
    Rhone, and the Guadalquiver flow,
I see the windings of the Volga, the Dnieper, the
    Oder,
I see the Tuscan going down the Arno, and the Vene-
    tian along the Po,
I see the Greek seaman sailing out of Egina bay.

14. I see the site of the old empire of Assyria, and that
    of Persia, and that of India,
I see the falling of the Ganges over the high rim of
    Saukara.

15. I see the place of the idea of the Deity incarnated by
    avatars in human forms,
I see the spots of the successions of priests on the earth
    — oracles, sacrificers, brahmins, sabians, lamas,
    monks, muftis, exhorters ;
I see where druids walked the groves of Mona — I see
    the mistletoe and vervain,
I see the temples of the deaths of the bodies of Gods —
    I see the old signifiers.

16. I see Christ once more eating the bread of his last sup-
    per, in the midst of youths and old persons,
I see where the strong divine young man, the Hercules,
    toiled faithfully and long, and then died,
I see the place of the innocent rich life and hapless
    fate of the beautiful nocturnal son, the full-limbed
    Bacchus,

I see Kneph, blooming, dressed in blue, with the crown
of feathers on his head,

I see Hermes, unsuspected, dying, well-beloved, saying
to the people, *Do not weep for me,*

*This is not my true country, I have lived banished from*
*my true country — I now go back there,*

*I return to the celestial sphere, where every one goes*
*in his turn.*

17. I see the battle-fields of the earth — grass grows upon
them, and blossoms and corn,

I see the tracks of ancient and modern expeditions.

18. I see the nameless masonries, venerable messages of
the unknown events, heroes, records of the earth.

19. I see the places of the sagas,

I see pine-trees and fir-trees torn by northern blasts,

I see granite boulders and cliffs—I see green meadows
and lakes,

I see the burial-cairns of Scandinavian warriors,

I see them raised high with stones, by the marge of
restless oceans, that the dead men's spirits, when
they wearied of their quiet graves, might rise up
through the mounds, and gaze on the tossing
billows, and be refreshed by storms, immensity,
liberty, action.

20. I see the steppes of Asia,

I see the tumuli of Mongolia—I see the tents of Kal-
mucks and Baskirs,

I see the nomadic tribes, with herds of oxen and cows,

I see the table-lands notched with ravines—I see the
jungles and deserts,

I see the camel, the wild steed, the bustard, the fat-tailed sheep, the antelope, and the burrowing wolf.

21. I see the high-lands of Abyssinia,
I see flocks of goats feeding, and see the fig-tree, tamarind, date,
And see fields of teff-wheat, and see the places of verdure and gold.

22. I see the Brazilian vaquero,
I see the Bolivian ascending Mount Sorata,
I see the Wacho crossing the plains — I see the incomparable rider of horses with his lasso on his arm,
I see over the pampas the pursuit of wild cattle for their hides.

23. I see little and large sea-dots, some inhabited, some uninhabited ;
I see two boats with nets, lying off the shore of Paumanok, quite still,
I see ten fishermen waiting — they discover now a thick school of mossbonkers — they drop the joined seine-ends in the water,
The boats separate — they diverge and row off, each on its rounding course to the beach, enclosing the mossbonkers,
The net is drawn in by a windlass by those who stop ashore,
Some of the fishermen lounge in the boats — others stand negligently ankle-deep in the water, poised on strong legs,

The boats are partly drawn up — the water slaps
   against them,
On the sand, in heaps and winrows, well out from the
   water, lie the green-backed spotted mossbonkers.

24. I see the despondent red man in the west, lingering
   about the banks of Moingo, and about Lake
   Pepin,
He has heard the quail and beheld the honey-bee, and
   sadly prepared to depart.

25. I see the regions of snow and ice,
   I see the sharp-eyed Samoiede and the Finn,
   I see the seal-seeker in his boat, poising his lance,
   I see the Siberian on his slight-built sledge, drawn by
      dogs,
   I see the porpoise-hunters — I see the whale-crews of
      the South Pacific and the North Atlantic,
   I see the cliffs, glaciers, torrents, valleys, of Switzer-
      land — I mark the long winters, and the
      isolation.

26. I see the cities of the earth, and make myself at ran-
   dom a part of them,
   I am a real Parisian,
   I am a habitan of Vienna, St. Petersburg, Berlin,
      Constantinople,
   I am of Adelaide, Sidney, Melbourne,
   I am of London, Manchester, Bristol, Edinburgh,
      Limerick,
   I am of Madrid, Cadiz, Barcelona, Oporto, Lyons,
      Brussels, Berne, Frankfort, Stuttgart, Turin,
      Florence,

I belong in Moscow, Cracow, Warsaw — or northward
in Christiania or Stockholm — or in Siberian
Irkutsk — or in some street in Iceland;
I descend upon all those cities, and rise from them
again.

27. I see vapors exhaling from unexplored countries,
I see the savage types, the bow and arrow, the
poisoned splint, the fetish, and the obi.

28. I see African and Asiatic towns,
I see Algiers, Tripoli, Derne, Mogadore, Timbuctoo,
Monrovia,
I see the swarms of Pekin, Canton, Benares, Delhi,
Calcutta, Yedo,
I see the Kruman in his hut, and the Dahoman and
Ashantee-man in their huts,
I see the Turk smoking opium in Aleppo,
I see the picturesque crowds at the fairs of Khiva, and
those of Herat,
I see Teheran — I see Muscat and Medina, and the
intervening sands — I see the caravans toiling
onward;
I see Egypt and the Egyptians — I see the pyramids
and obelisks,
I look on chiselled histories, songs, philosophies, cut
in slabs of sand-stone, or on granite blocks,
I see at Memphis mummy-pits, containing mummies,
embalmed, swathed in linen cloth, lying there
many centuries,
I look on the fall'n Theban, the large-ball'd eyes, the
side-drooping neck, the hands folded across the
breast.

22

29. I see the menials of the earth, laboring,
I see the prisoners in the prisons,
I see the defective human bodies of the earth,
I see the blind, the deaf and dumb, idiots, hunch-
backs, lunatics,
I see the pirates, thieves, betrayers, murderers, slave-
makers of the earth,
I see the helpless infants, and the helpless old men
and women.

30. I see male and female everywhere,
I see the serene brotherhood of philosophs,
I see the constructiveness of my race,
I see the results of the perseverance and industry of
my race,
I see ranks, colors, barbarisms, civilizations — I go
among them — I mix indiscriminately,
And I salute all the inhabitants of the earth.

31. You, where you are!
You daughter or son of England!
You of the mighty Slavic tribes and empires! you
Russ in Russia!
You dim-descended, black, divine-souled African,
large, fine-headed, nobly-formed, superbly des-
tined, on equal terms with me!
You Norwegian! Swede! Dane! Icelander! you
Prussian!
You Spaniard of Spain! you Portuguese!
You Frenchwoman and Frenchman of France!
You Belge! you liberty-lover of the Netherlands!
You sturdy Austrian! you Lombard! Hun! Bohe-
mian! farmer of Styria!

You neighbor of the Danube!

You working-man of the Rhine, the Elbe, or the Weser! you working-woman too!

You Sardinian! you Bavarian! you Swabian! Saxon! Wallachian! Bulgarian!

You citizen of Prague! you Roman! Neapolitan! Greek!

You lithe matador in the arena at Seville!

You mountaineer living lawlessly on the Taurus or Caucasus!

You Bokh horse-herd, watching your mares and stallions feeding!

You beautiful-bodied Persian, at full speed in the saddle, shooting arrows to the mark!

You Chinaman and Chinawoman of China! you Tartar of Tartary!

You women of the earth subordinated at your tasks!

You Jew journeying in your old age through every risk, to stand once on Syrian ground!

You other Jews waiting in all lands for your Messiah!

You thoughtful Armenian, pondering by some stream of the Euphrates! you peering amid the ruins of Nineveh! you ascending Mount Ararat!

You foot-worn pilgrim welcoming the far-away sparkle of the minarets of Mecca!

You sheiks along the stretch from Suez to Babelmandel, ruling your families and tribes!

You olive-grower tending your fruit on fields of Nazareth, Damascus, or Lake Tiberias!

You Thibet trader on the wide inland, or bargaining in the shops of Lassa!

You Japanese man or woman! you liver in Madagascar, Ceylon, Sumatra, Borneo!

All you continentals of Asia, Africa, Europe, Aus-
tralia, indifferent of place!
All you on the numberless islands of the archipelagoes
of the sea!
And you of centuries hence, when you listen to me!
And you, each and everywhere, whom I specify not,
but include just the same!
Health to you! Good will to you all — from me and
America sent,
For we acknowledge you all and each.


31. Each of us inevitable,
Each of us limitless — each of us with his or her
right upon the earth,
Each of us allowed the eternal purport of the earth,
Each of us here as divinely as any is here.


32. You Hottentot with clicking palate!
You woolly-haired hordes! you white or black owners
of slaves!
You owned persons, dropping sweat-drops or blood-
drops!
You human forms with the fathomless ever-impressive
countenances of brutes!
You poor koboo whom the meanest of the rest look
down upon, for all your glimmering language
and spirituality!
You low expiring aborigines of the hills of Utah,
Oregon, California!
You dwarfed Kamtschatkan, Greenlander, Lapp!
You Austral negro, naked, red, sooty, with protrusive
lip, grovelling, seeking your food!
You Caffre, Berber, Soudanese!

You haggard, uncouth, untutored Bedowee!

You plague-swarms in Madras, Nankin, Kaubul, Cairo!

You bather bathing in the Ganges!

You benighted roamer of Amazonia! you Patagonian! you Fegee-man!

You peon of Mexico! you Russian serf! you slave of Carolina, Texas, Tennessee!

I do not prefer others so very much before you either,

I do not say one word against you, away back there, where you stand,

(You will come forward in due time to my side.)

33. My spirit has passed in compassion and determination around the whole earth,

I have looked for equals and lovers, and found them ready for me in all lands;

I think some divine rapport has equalized me with them.

34. O vapors! I think I have risen with you, and moved away to distant continents, and fallen down there, for reasons,

I think I have blown with you, O winds,

O waters, I have fingered every shore with you.

35. I have run through what any river or strait of the globe has run through,

I have taken my stand on the bases of peninsulas, and on the highest embedded rocks, to cry thence.

36. *Salut au Monde!*

What cities the light or warmth penetrates, I penetrate those cities myself,

All islands to which birds wing their way, I wing my
    way myself.

37. Toward all,
    I raise high the perpendicular hand — I make the
        signal,
    To remain after me in sight forever,
    For all the haunts and homes of men.

# Poem of Joys.

1. O TO make a most jubilant poem!
   O full of music! Full of manhood, womanhood,
     infancy!
   O full of common employments! Full of grain and
     trees. ·

2. O for the voices of animals! O for the swiftness and
     balance of fishes!
   O for the dropping of rain-drops in a poem!
   O for the sunshine and motion of waves in a poem.

3. O to be on the sea! the wind, the wide waters
     around;
   O to sail in a ship under full sail at sea.

4. O the joy of my spirit! It is uncaged! It darts like
     lightning!
   It is not enough to have this globe, or a certain time
     — I will have thousands of globes, and all time.

5. O the engineer's joys!
   To go with a locomotive!

To hear the hiss of steam — the merry shriek — the
steam-whistle — the laughing locomotive!
To push with resistless way, and speed off in the
distance.

6. O the horseman's and horsewoman's joys!
The saddle — the gallop — the pressure upon the seat
— the cool gurgling by the ears and hair.

7. O the fireman's joys!
I hear the alarm at dead of night,
I hear bells — shouts! — I pass the crowd — I run!
The sight of the flames maddens me with pleasure.

8. O the joy of the strong-brawned fighter, towering
in the arena, in perfect condition, conscious of
power, thirsting to meet his opponent.

9. O the joy of that vast elemental sympathy which only
the human Soul is capable of generating and
emitting in steady and limitless floods.

10. O the mother's joys!
The watching — the endurance — the precious love —
the anguish — the patiently yielded life.

11. O the joy of increase, growth, recuperation,
The joy of soothing and pacifying — the joy of
concord and harmony.

12. O to go back to the place where I was born!
O to hear the birds sing once more!
To ramble about the house and barn, and over the
fields, once more,

And through the orchard and along the old lanes
    once more.

13. O male and female!
    O the presence of women! (I swear, nothing is more
        exquisite to me than the presence of women;)
    O for the girl, my mate! O for happiness with my
        mate!
    O the young man as I pass! O I am sick after the
        friendship of him who, I fear, is indifferent
        to me.

14. O the streets of cities!
    The flitting faces — the expressions, eyes, feet, cos-
        tumes! O I cannot tell how welcome they are
        to me;
    O of men — of women toward me as I pass — The
        memory of only one look — the boy lingering
        and waiting.

15. O to have been brought up on bays, lagoons, creeks,
        or along the coast!
    O to continue and be employed there all my life!
    O the briny and damp smell — the shore — the salt
        weeds exposed at low water,
    The work of fishermen — the work of the eel-fisher
        and clam-fisher.

16. O it is I!
    I come with my clam-rake and spade! I come with
        my eel-spear;
    Is the tide out? I join the group of clam-diggers on
        the flats,

I laugh and work with them — I joke at my work, like a mettlesome young man.

17. In winter I take my eel-basket and eel-spear and travel out on foot on the ice — I have a small axe to cut holes in the ice;

Behold me, well-clothed, going gayly, or returning in the afternoon — my brood of tough boys accompanying me,

My brood of grown and part-grown boys, who love to be with none else so well as they love to be with me,

By day to work with me, and by night to sleep with me.

18. Or, another time, in warm weather, out in a boat, to lift the lobster-pots, where they are sunk with heavy stones, (I know the buoys;)

O the sweetness of the Fifth Month morning upon the water, as I row, just before sunrise, toward the buoys;

I pull the wicker pots up slantingly — the dark green lobsters are desperate with their claws, as I take them out — I insert wooden pegs in the joints of their pincers,

I go to all the places, one after another, and then row back to the shore,

There, in a huge kettle of boiling water, the lobsters shall be boiled till their color becomes scarlet.

19. Or, another time, mackerel-taking,

Voracious, mad for the hook, near the surface, they seem to fill the water for miles;

Or, another time, fishing for rock-fish in Chesapeake
    Bay — I one of the brown-faced crew ;

Or, another time, trailing for blue-fish off Paumanok,
    I stand with braced body,

My left foot is on the gunwale — my right arm throws
    the coils of slender rope,

In sight around me the quick veering and darting of
    fifty skiffs, my companions.

20. O boating on the rivers !

The voyage down the Niagara, (the St. Lawrence,) —
    the superb scenery — the steamers,

The ships sailing — the Thousand Islands — the occa-
    sional timber-raft, and the raftsmen with long-
    reaching sweep-oars,

The little huts on the rafts, and the stream of smoke
    when they cook supper at evening.

21. O something pernicious and dread !

Something far away from a puny and pious life !

Something unproved ! Something in a trance !

Something escaped from the anchorage, and driving
    free.

22. O to work in mines, or forging iron !

Foundry casting — the foundry itself — the rude high
    roof — the ample and shadowed space,

The furnace — the hot liquid poured out and running.

23. O the joys of the soldier !

To feel the presence of a brave general ! to feel his
    sympathy !

To behold his calmness ! to be warmed in the rays of
    his smile !

To go to battle! to hear the bugles play, and the drums
beat!

To hear the artillery! to see the glittering of the bay-
onets and musket-barrels in the sun!

To see men fall and die and not complain!

To taste the savage taste of blood! to be so devilish!

To gloat so over the wounds and deaths of the enemy.


24. O the whaleman's joys! O I cruise my old cruise
again!

I feel the ship's motion under me — I feel the Atlantic
breezes fanning me,

I hear the cry again sent down from the mast-head,
*There she blows,*

Again I spring up the rigging, to look with the rest —
We see — we descend, wild with excitement,

I leap in the lowered boat — We row toward our prey,
where he lies,

We approach, stealthy and silent — I see the moun-
tainous mass, lethargic, basking,

I see the harpooner standing up — I see the weapon
dart from his vigorous arm;

O swift, again, now, far out in the ocean, the wounded
whale, settling, running to windward, tows me,

Again I see him rise to breathe — We row close
again,

I see a lance driven through his side, pressed deep,
turned in the wound,

Again we back off — I see him settle again — the life
is leaving him fast,

As he rises, he spouts blood — I see him swim in cir-
cles narrower and narrower, swiftly cutting the
water — I see him die,

He gives one convulsive leap in the centre of the cir-
cle, and then falls flat and still in the bloody
foam.

25. O the old manhood of me, my joy!
My children and grand-children — my white hair and
beard,
My largeness, calmness, majesty, out of the long
stretch of my life.

26. O the ripened joy of womanhood!
O perfect happiness at last!
I am more than eighty years of age — my hair, too, is
pure white — I am the most venerable mother;
How clear is my mind! how all people draw nigh to
me!
What attractions are these, beyond any before? what
bloom, more than the bloom of youth?
What beauty is this that descends upon me, and rises
out of me?

27. O the joy of my Soul leaning poised on itself — receiv-
ing identity through materials, and loving them
— observing characters, and absorbing them;
O my Soul, vibrated back to me, from them — from
facts, sight, hearing, touch, my phrenology,
reason, articulation, comparison, memory, and
the like;
O the real life of my senses and flesh, transcending
my senses and flesh;
O my body, done with materials — my sight, done
with my material eyes;
O what is proved to me this day, beyond cavil, that it
is not my material eyes which finally see,

23

Nor my material body which finally loves, walks, laughs, shouts, embraces, procreates.

28. O the farmer's joys!
Ohioan's, Illinoisian's, Wisconsinese', Kanadian's, Iowan's, Kansian's, Missourian's, Oregonese' joys,
To rise at peep of day, and pass forth nimbly to work,
To plough land in the fall for winter-sown crops,
To plough land in the spring for maize,
To train orchards — to graft the trees — to gather apples in the fall.

29. O the pleasure with trees!
The orchard — the forest — the oak, cedar, pine, pekan-tree,
The honey-locust, black-walnut, cottonwood, and magnolia.

30. O Death!
O the beautiful touch of Death, soothing and benumbing a few moments, for reasons;
O that of myself, discharging my excrementitious body, to be burned, or rendered to powder, or buried,
My real body doubtless left to me for other spheres,
My voided body, nothing more to me, returning to the purifications, further offices, eternal uses of the earth.

31. O to bathe in the swimming-bath, or in a good place along shore!
To splash the water! to walk ankle-deep; to race naked along the shore.

32. O to realize space!
    The plenteousness of all — that there are no bounds;
    To emerge, and be of the sky — of the sun and moon,
      and the flying clouds, as one with them.

33. O, while I live, to be the ruler of life — not a slave,
    To meet life as a powerful conqueror,
    No fumes — no ennui — no more complaints or scorn-
      ful criticisms.

34. O me repellent and ugly!
    O to these proud laws of the air, the water, and
      the ground, proving my interior Soul impreg-
      nable,
    And nothing exterior shall ever take command of me.

35. O to attract by more than attraction!
    How it is I know not — yet behold! the something
      which obeys none of the rest,
    It is offensive, never defensive — yet how magnetic
      it draws.

36. O the joy of suffering!
    To struggle against great odds! to meet enemies un-
      daunted!
    To be entirely alone with them! to find how much I
      can stand!
    To look strife, torture, prison, popular odium, death,
      face to face!
    To mount the scaffold! to advance to the muzzles of
      guns with perfect nonchalance!
    To be indeed a God!

37. O the gleesome saunter over fields and hill-sides!
    The leaves and flowers of the commonest weeds — the
        moist fresh stillness of the woods,
    The exquisite smell of the earth at day-break, and all
        through the forenoon.

38. O love-branches! love-root! love-apples!
    O chaste and electric torrents! O mad-sweet drops.

39. O the orator's joys!
    To inflate the chest — to roll the thunder of the voice
        out from the ribs and throat,
    To make the people rage, weep, hate, desire, with
        yourself,
    To lead America — to quell America with a great
        tongue.

40. O the joy of a manly self-hood!
    Personality — to be servile to none — to defer to none
        — not to any tyrant, known or unknown,
    To walk with erect carriage, a step springy and
        elastic,
    To look with calm gaze, or with a flashing eye,
    To speak with a full and sonorous voice, out of a
        broad chest,
    To confront with your personality all the other per-
        sonalities of the earth.

41. O to have my life henceforth my poem of joys!
    To dance, clap hands, exult, shout, skip, leap, roll on,
        float on,
    An athlete — full of rich words — full of joys.

# A WORD OUT OF THE SEA.

Out of the rocked cradle,

Out of the mocking-bird's throat, the musical shuttle,

Out of the boy's mother's womb, and from the nipples
of her breasts,

Out of the Ninth Month midnight,

Over the sterile sands, and the fields beyond, where
the child, leaving his bed, wandered alone, bare-
headed, barefoot,

Down from the showered halo,

Up from the mystic play of shadows, twining and
twisting as if they were alive,

Out from the patches of briers and blackberries,

From the memories of the bird that chanted to me,

From your memories, sad brother — from the fitful
risings and fallings I heard,

From under that yellow half-moon, late-risen, and
swollen as if with tears,

From those beginning notes of sickness and love,
there in the transparent mist,

From the thousand responses of my heart, never to
cease,

From the myriad thence-aroused words,
From the word stronger and more delicious than any,
From such, as now they start, the scene revisiting,
As a flock, twittering, rising, or overhead passing,
Borne hither — ere all eludes me, hurriedly,
A man — yet by these tears a little boy again,
Throwing myself on the sand, confronting the waves,
I, chanter of pains and joys, uniter of here and here-
    after,
Taking all hints to use them — but swiftly leaping
    beyond them,
A reminiscence sing.

## REMINISCENCE.

1. ONCE, Paumanok,
    When the snows had melted, and the Fifth Month
        grass was growing,
    Up this sea-shore, in some briers,
    Two guests from Alabama — two together,
    And their nest, and four light-green eggs, spotted with
        .brown,
    And every day the he-bird, to and fro, near at hand,
    And every day the she-bird, crouched on her nest,
        silent, with bright eyes,
    And every day I, a curious boy, never too close, never
        disturbing them,
    Cautiously peering, absorbing, translating.

2. *Shine ! Shine !*
    *Pour down your warmth, great Sun !*
    *While we bask — we two together.*

3. *Two together !*
   *Winds blow South, or winds blow North,*
   *Day come white, or night come black,*
   *Home, or rivers and mountains from home,*
   *Singing all time, minding no time,*
   *If we two but keep together.*

4. Till of a sudden,
   May-be killed, unknown to her mate,
   One forenoon the she-bird crouched not on the nest,
   Nor returned that afternoon, nor the next,
   Nor ever appeared again.

5. And thenceforward, all summer, in the sound of the
      sea,
   And at night, under the full of the moon, in calmer
      weather,
   Over the hoarse surging of the sea,
   Or flitting from brier to brier by day,
   I saw, I heard at intervals, the remaining one, the
      he-bird,
   The solitary guest from Alabama.

6. *Blow ! Blow !*
   *Blow up sea-winds along Paumanok's shore ;*
   *I wait and I wait, till you blow my mate to me.*

7. Yes, when the stars glistened,
   All night long, on the prong of a moss-scallop'd stake,
   Down, almost amid the slapping waves,
   Sat the lone singer, wonderful, causing tears.

8. He called on his mate,
   He poured forth the meanings which I, of all men,
      know.

9. Yes, my brother, I know,
   The rest might not — but I have treasured every note,
   For once, and more than once, dimly, down to the
     beach gliding,
   Silent, avoiding the moonbeams, blending myself with
     the shadows,
   Recalling now the obscure shapes, the echoes, the
     sounds and sights after their sorts,
   The white arms out in the breakers tirelessly tossing,
   I, with bare feet, a child, the wind wafting my hair,
   Listened long and long.

10. Listened, to keep, to sing — now translating the
      notes,
    Following you, my brother.

11. *Soothe ! Soothe !*
    *Close on its wave soothes the wave behind,*
    *And again another behind, embracing and lapping,*
      *every one close,*
    *But my love soothes not me.*

12. *Low hangs the moon — it rose late,*
    *O it is lagging — O I think it is heavy with love.*

13. *O madly the sea pushes upon the land,*
    *With love — with love.*

14. *O night !*
    *O do I not see my love fluttering out there among the*
      *breakers ?*
    *What is that little black thing I see there in the*
      *white ?*

15. *Loud! Loud!*
   *Loud I call to you my love!*
   *High and clear I shoot my voice over the waves,*
   *Surely you must know who is here,*
   *You must know who I am, my love.*

16. *Low-hanging moon!*
   *What is that dusky spot in your brown yellow?*
   *O it is the shape of my mate!*
   *O moon, do not keep her from me any longer.*

17. *Land! O land!*
   *Whichever way I turn, O I think you could give me*
   *   my mate back again, if you would,*
   *For I am almost sure I see her dimly whichever way*
   *   I look.*

18. *O rising stars!*
   *Perhaps the one I want so much will rise with some*
   *   of you.*

19. *O throat!*
   *Sound clearer through the atmosphere!*
   *Pierce the woods, the earth,*
   *Somewhere listening to catch you must be the one I*
   *   want.*

20. *Shake out, carols!*
   *Solitary here — the night's carols!*
   *Carols of lonesome love! Death's carols!*
   *Carols under that lagging, yellow, waning moon!*
   *O, under that moon, where she droops almost down*
   *   into the sea!*
   *O reckless, despairing carols.*

21. *But soft!*
*Sink low — soft!*
*Soft! Let me just murmur,*
*And do you wait a moment, you husky-noised sea,*
*For somewhere I believe I heard my mate responding*
*to me,*
*So faint — I must be still to listen,*
*But not altogether still, for then she might not come*
*immediately to me.*

22. *Hither, my love!*
*Here I am! Here!*
*With this just-sustained note I announce myself to*
*you,*
*This gentle call is for you, my love.*

23. *Do not be decoyed elsewhere!*
*That is the whistle of the wind — it is not my voice,*
*That is the fluttering of the spray,*
*Those are the shadows of leaves.*

24. *O darkness! O in vain!*
*O I am very sick and sorrowful.*

25. *O brown halo in the sky, near the moon, drooping*
*upon the sea!*
*O troubled reflection in the sea!*
*O throat! O throbbing heart!*
*O all — and I singing uselessly all the night.*

26. *Murmur! Murmur on!*
*O murmurs — you yourselves make me continue to*
*sing, I know not why.*

27. *O past ! O joy !*
*In the air — in the woods — over fields,*
*Loved ! Loved ! Loved ! Loved ! Loved !*
*Loved — but no more with me,*
*We two together no more.*

28. The aria sinking,
All else continuing — the stars shining,
The winds blowing — the notes of the wondrous bird echoing,
With angry moans the fierce old mother yet, as ever, incessantly moaning,
On the sands of Paumanok's shore gray and rustling,
The yellow half-moon, enlarged, sagging down, drooping, the face of the sea almost touching,
The boy extatic — with his bare feet the waves, with his hair the atmosphere dallying,
The love in the heart pent, now loose, now at last tumultuously bursting,
The aria's meaning, the ears, the Soul, swiftly depositing,
The strange tears down the cheeks coursing,
The colloquy there — the trio — each uttering,
The undertone — the savage old mother, incessantly crying,
To the boy's Soul's questions sullenly timing — some drowned secret hissing,
To the outsetting bard of love.

29. Bird ! (then said the boy's Soul,)
Is it indeed toward your mate you sing ? or is it mostly to me ?
For I that was a child, my tongue's use sleeping,
Now that I have heard you,

Now in a moment I know what I am for — I awake,
And already a thousand singers — a thousand songs,
    clearer, louder, more sorrowful than yours,
A thousand warbling echoes have started to life
    within me,
Never to die.

30. O throes!
O you demon, singing by yourself — projecting me,
O solitary me, listening — never more shall I cease
    imitating, perpetuating you,
Never more shall I escape,
Never more shall the reverberations,
Never more the cries of unsatisfied love be absent
    from me,
Never again leave me to be the peaceful child I was
    before what there, in the night,
By the sea, under the yellow and sagging moon,
The dusky demon aroused — the fire, the sweet hell
    within,
The unknown want, the destiny of me.

31. O give me some clew!
O if I am to have so much, let me have more!
O a word! O what is my destination?
O I fear it is henceforth chaos!
O how joys, dreads, convolutions, human shapes, and
    all shapes, spring as from graves around me!
O phantoms! you cover all the land, and all the sea!
O I cannot see in the dimness whether you smile or
    frown upon me;
O vapor, a look, a word! O well-beloved!
O you dear women's and men's phantoms!

32. A word then, (for I will conquer it,)
   The word final, superior to all,
   Subtle, sent up — what is it ? — I listen ;
   Are you whispering it, and have been all the time,
      you sea-waves ?
   Is that it from your liquid rims and wet sands ?


33. Answering, the sea,
   Delaying not, hurrying not,
   Whispered me through the night, and very plainly
      before daybreak,
   Lisped to me constantly the low and delicious word
      DEATH,
   And again Death — ever Death, Death, Death,
   Hissing melodious, neither like the bird, nor like my
      aroused child's heart,
   But edging near, as privately for me, rustling at
      my feet,
   And creeping thence steadily up to my ears,
   Death, Death, Death, Death, Death.


34. Which I do not forget,
   But fuse the song of two together,
   That was sung to me in the moonlight on Paumanok's
      gray beach,
   With the thousand responsive songs, at random,
   My own songs, awaked from that hour,
   And with them the key, the word up from the waves,
   The word of the sweetest song, and all songs,
   That strong and delicious word which, creeping to
      my feet,
   The sea whispered me.

24

# LEAF OF FACES.

1. SAUNTERING the pavement, or riding the country by-road, here then are faces!
Faces of friendship, precision, caution, suavity, ideality,
The spiritual prescient face — the always welcome, common, benevolent face,
The face of the singing of music — the grand faces of natural lawyers and judges, broad at the back-top,
The faces of hunters and fishers, bulged at the brows — the shaved blanched faces of orthodox citizens,
The pure, extravagant, yearning, questioning artist's face,
The ugly face of some beautiful Soul, the handsome detested or despised face,
The sacred faces of infants, the illuminated face of the mother of many children,
The face of an amour, the face of veneration,
The face as of a dream, the face of an immobile rock,
The face withdrawn of its good and bad, a castrated face,
A wild hawk, his wings clipped by the clipper,
A stallion that yielded at last to the thongs and knife of the gelder.

2. Sauntering the pavement, or crossing the ceaseless ferry, here then are faces,
I see them and complain not, and am content with all.

3. Do you suppose I could be content with all, if I thought them their own finale?

4. This now is too lamentable a face for a man,
Some abject louse, asking leave to be — cringing for it,
Some milk-nosed maggot, blessing what lets it wrig to its hole.

5. This face is a dog's snout sniffling for garbage;
Snakes nest in that mouth—I hear the sibilant threat.

6. This face is a haze more chill than the arctic sea,
Its sleepy and wobbling icebergs crunch as they go.

7. This is a face of bitter herbs — this an emetic — they need no label,
And more of the drug-shelf, laudanum, caoutchouc, or hog's-lard.

8. This face is an epilepsy, its wordless tongue gives out the unearthly cry,
Its veins down the neck distend, its eyes roll till they show nothing but their whites,
Its teeth grit, the palms of the hands are cut by the turned-in nails,
The man falls struggling and foaming to the ground while he speculates well.

9. This face is bitten by vermin and worms,
And this is some murderer's knife with a half-pulled scabbard.

10. This face owes to the sexton his dismalest fee,
    An unceasing death-bell tolls there.

11. Those then are really men — the bosses and tufts of
    the great round globe!

12. Features of my equals, would you trick me with your
    creased and cadaverous march?
    Well, you cannot trick me.

13. I see your rounded never-erased flow,
    I see neath the rims of your haggard and mean dis-
    guises.

14. Splay and twist as you like — poke with the tangling
    fores of fishes or rats,
    You'll be unmuzzled, you certainly will.

15. I saw the face of the most smeared and slobbering
    idiot they had at the asylum,
    And I knew for my consolation what they knew not,
    And I knew of the agents that emptied and broke my
    brother,
    The same wait to clear the rubbish from the fallen
    tenement,
    And I shall look again in a score or two of ages,
    And I shall meet the real landlord, perfect and un-
    harmed, every inch as good as myself.

16. The Lord advances, and yet advances,
    Always the shadow in front — always the reached
    hand bringing up the laggards.

17. Out of this face emerge banners and horses — O
    superb! I see what is coming,

I see the high pioneer-caps — I see the staves of
    runners clearing the way,
I hear victorious drums.

18. This face is a life-boat,
    This is the face commanding and bearded, it asks no
      odds of the rest,
    This face is flavored fruit, ready for eating,
    This face of a healthy honest boy is the programme of
      all good.

19. These faces bear testimony slumbering or awake,
    They show their descent from the Master himself.

20. Off the word I have spoken I except not one — red,
      white, black, are all deific,
    In each house is the ovum — it comes forth after a
      thousand years.

21. Spots or cracks at the windows do not disturb me,
    Tall and sufficient stand behind, and make signs to
      me,
    I read the promise, and patiently wait.

22. This is a full-grown lily's face,
    She speaks to the limber-hipp'd man near the garden
      pickets,
    *Come here*, she blushingly cries — *Come nigh to me,*
      *limber-hipp'd man, and give me your finger and*
      *thumb,*
    *Stand at my side till I lean as high as I can upon you,*
    *Fill me with albescent honey, bend down to me,*
    *Rub to me with your chafing beard, rub to my breast*
      *and shoulders.*

23. The old face of the mother of many children!
    Whist! I am fully content.

24. Lulled and late is the smoke of the First Day
      morning,
    It hangs low over the rows of trees by the fences,
    It hangs thin by the sassafras, the wild-cherry, and
      the cat-brier under them.

25. I saw the rich ladies in full dress at the soiree,
    I heard what the singers were singing so long,
    Heard who sprang in crimson youth from the white
      froth and the water-blue.

26. Behold a woman!
    She looks out from her quaker cap — her face is
      clearer and more beautiful than the sky.

27. She sits in an arm-chair, under the shaded porch of
      the farm-house,
    The sun just shines on her old white head.

28. Her ample gown is of cream-hued linen,
    Her grand-sons raised the flax, and her grand-
      daughters spun it with the distaff and the
      wheel.

29. The melodious character of the earth,
    The finish beyond which philosophy cannot go, and
      does not wish to go,
    The justified mother of men.

# EUROPE,

## The 72d and 73d Years of Thefe States.

1. SUDDENLY out of its stale and drowsy lair, the lair of
    slaves,
   Like lightning it le'pt forth, half startled at itself,
   Its feet upon the ashes and the rags — its hands tight
    to the throats of kings.

2. O hope and faith!
   O aching close of exiled patriots' lives!
   O many a sickened heart!
   Turn back unto this day, and make yourselves
    afresh.

3. And you, paid to defile the People! you liars, mark!
   Not for numberless agonies, murders, lusts,
   For court thieving in its manifold mean forms, worm-
    ing from his simplicity the poor man's wages,
   For many a promise sworn by royal lips, and broken,
    and laughed at in the breaking,
   Then in their power, not for all these did the blows
    strike revenge, or the heads of the nobles fall;
   The People scorned the ferocity of kings.

4. But the sweetness of mercy brewed bitter destruction,
    and the frightened rulers come back,

Each comes in state with his train — hangman, priest,
tax-gatherer,
Soldier, lawyer, lords, jailers, and sycophants.

5. Yet behind all, hovering, stealing — lo, a Shape,
Vague as the night, draped interminably, head front
and form, in scarlet folds,
Whose face and eyes none may see,
Out of its robes only this — the red robes, lifted by
the arm,
One finger crook'd, pointed high over the top, like
the head of a snake appears.

6. Meanwhile, corpses lie in new-made graves — bloody
corpses of young men ;
The rope of the gibbet hangs heavily, the bullets of
princes are flying, the creatures of power laugh
aloud,
And all these things bear fruits — and they are good.

7. Those corpses of young men,
Those martyrs that hang from the gibbets — those
hearts pierced by the gray lead,
Cold and motionless as they seem, live elsewhere with
unslaughter'd vitality.

8. They live in other young men, O kings !
They live in brothers, again ready to defy you !
They were purified by death — they were taught and
exalted.

9. Not a grave of the murdered for freedom, but grows
seed for freedom, in its turn to bear seed,
Which the winds carry afar and re-sow, and the rains
and the snows nourish.

10. Not a disembodied spirit can the weapons of tyrants
   let loose,
   But it stalks invisibly over the earth, whispering,
   counselling, cautioning.

11. Liberty! let others despair of you! I never despair
   of you.

12. Is the house shut? Is the master away?
   Nevertheless be ready — be not weary of watching,
   He will soon return — his messengers come anon.

# THOUGHT.

Of Public Opinion,

Of a calm and cool fiat, sooner or later, (How impassive! How certain and final!)

Of the President with pale face asking secretly to himself, *What will the people say at last?*

Of the frivolous Judge — Of the corrupt Congressman, Governor, Mayor — Of such as these, standing helpless and exposed;

Of the mumbling and screaming priest — (soon, soon deserted;)

Of the lessening, year by year, of venerableness, and of the dicta of officers, statutes, pulpits, schools,

Of the rising forever taller and stronger and broader, of the intuitions of men and women, and of self-esteem, and of personality;

Of the New World — Of the Democracies, resplendent, en-masse,

Of the conformity of politics, armies, navies, to them and to me,

Of the shining sun by them — Of the inherent light, greater than the rest,

Of the envelopment of all by them, and of the effusion of all from them.

# Enfans d'Adam.

## 1.

To the garden, the world, anew ascending,
Potent mates, daughters, sons, preluding,
The love, the life of their bodies, meaning and being,
Curious, here behold my resurrection, after slumber,
The revolving cycles, in their wide sweep, having
brought me again,
Amorous, mature — all beautiful to me — all won-
drous,
My limbs, and the quivering fire that ever plays
through them, for reasons, most wondrous;
Existing, I peer and penetrate still,
Content with the present — content with the past,
By my side, or back of me, Eve following,
Or in front, and I following her just the same.

## 2.

FROM that of myself, without which I were nothing,
From what I am determined to make illustrious, even
     if I stand sole among men,
From my own voice resonant — singing the phallus,
Singing the song of procreation,
Singing the need of superb children, and therein
     superb grown people,
Singing the muscular urge and the blending,
Singing the bedfellow's song, (O resistless yearning !
O for any and each, the body correlative attracting !
O for you, whoever you are, your correlative body !
     O it, more than all else, you delighting !)
From the pent up rivers of myself,
From the hungry gnaw that eats me night and day,
From native moments — from bashful pains — sing-
     ing them,
Singing something yet unfound, though I have dili-
     gently sought it, ten thousand years,
Singing the true song of the Soul, fitful, at random,
Singing what, to the Soul, entirely redeemed her, the
     faithful one, the prostitute, who detained me when
     I went to the city,
Singing the song of prostitutes ;
Renascent with grossest Nature, or among animals,
Of that — of them, and what goes with them, my
     poems informing,
Of the smell of apples and lemons — of the pairing
     of birds,
Of the wet of woods — of the lapping of waves,

Of the mad pushes of waves upon the land — I them
    chanting,
The overture lightly sounding — the strain antici-
    pating,
The welcome nearness — the sight of the perfect
    body,
The swimmer swimming naked in the bath, or mo-
    tionless on his back lying and floating,
The female form approaching — I, pensive, love-flesh
    tremulous, aching ;
The slave's body for sale — I, sternly, with harsh
    voice, auctioneering,
The divine list, for myself or you, or for any one,
    making,
The face — the limbs — the index from head to foot,
    and what it arouses,
The mystic deliria — the madness amorous — the utter
    abandonment,
(Hark, close and still, what I now whisper to you,
I love you — O you entirely possess me,
O I wish that you and I escape from the rest, and go
    utterly off — O free and lawless,
Two hawks in the air — two fishes swimming in the
    sea not more lawless than we ;)
The furious storm through me careering — I passion-
    ately trembling,
The oath of the inseparableness of two together — of
    the woman that loves me, and whom I love more
    than my life — That oath swearing,
(O I willingly stake all, for you !
O let me be lost, if it must be so !
O you and I — what is it to us what the rest do or
    think ?

25

What is all else to us ? only that we enjoy each other,
     and exhaust each other, if it must be so ;)
From the master — the pilot I yield the vessel to,
The general commanding me, commanding all — from
     him permission taking,
From time the programme hastening, (I have loitered
     too long, as it is ;)
From sex — From the warp and from the woof,
(To talk to the perfect girl who understands me — the
     girl of The States,
To waft to her these from my own lips — to effuse
     them from my own body ;)
·From privacy — From frequent repinings alone,
From plenty of persons near, and yet the right person
     not near,
From the soft sliding of hands over me, and thrusting
     of fingers through my hair and beard,
From the long-sustained kiss upon the mouth or
     bosom,
From the close pressure that makes me or any man
     drunk, fainting with excess,
From what the divine husband knows — from the
     work of fatherhood,
From exultation, victory, and relief — from the bed-
     fellow's embrace in the night,
From the act-poems of eyes, hands, hips, and bosoms,
From the cling of the trembling arm,
From the bending curve and the clinch,
From side by side, the pliant coverlid off throwing,
From the one so unwilling to have me leave — and
     me just as unwilling to leave,
(Yet a moment, O tender waiter, and I return,)
From the hour of shining stars and dropping dews,

From the night, a moment, I, emerging, flitting out,
Celebrate you, enfans prepared for,
And you, stalwart loins.

3.

1. O MY children! O mates!
O the bodies of you, and of all men and women,
engirth me, and I engirth them,
O they will not let me off, nor I them, till I go with
them, respond to them,
And respond to the contact of them, and discorrupt
them, and charge them with the charge of the
Soul.

2. Was it doubted if those who corrupt their own bodies
conceal themselves?
And if those who defile the living are as bad as they
who defile the dead?
And if the body does not do as much as the Soul?
And if the body were not the Soul, what is the Soul?

3. The love of the body of man or woman balks account
— the body itself balks account,
That of the male is perfect, and that of the female is
perfect.

4. The expression of the face balks account,
But the expression of a well made man appears not
only in his face,

It is in his limbs and joints also, it is curiously in the
joints of his hips and wrists,
It is in his walk, the carriage of his neck, the flex
of his waist and knees — dress does not hide
him,
The strong, sweet, supple quality he has, strikes
through the cotton and flannel,
To see him pass conveys as much as the best poem,
perhaps more,
You linger to see his back, and the back of his neck
and shoulder-side.

5. The sprawl and fulness of babes, the bosoms and
heads of women, the folds of their dress, their
style as we pass in the street, the contour of their
shape downwards,
The swimmer naked in the swimming bath, seen as
he swims through the transparent green-shine, or
lies with his face up, and rolls silently to and fro
in the heave of the water,
The bending forward and backward of rowers in row-
boats — the horseman in his saddle,
Girls, mothers, house-keepers, in all their perform-
ances,
The group of laborers seated at noon-time with their
open dinner-kettles, and their wives waiting,
The female soothing a child — the farmer's daughter
in the garden or cow-yard,
The young fellow hoeing corn — the sleigh-driver
guiding his six horses through the crowd,
The wrestle of wrestlers, two apprentice-boys, quite
grown, lusty, good-natured, native-born, out on
the vacant lot at sun-down, after work,

The coats and caps thrown down, the embrace of love
and resistance,

The upper-hold and under-hold, the hair rumpled
over and blinding the eyes;

The march of firemen in their own costumes, the
play of masculine muscle through clean-setting
trousers and waist-straps,

The slow return from the fire, the pause when the
bell strikes suddenly again, and the listening on
the alert,

The natural, perfect, varied attitudes — the bent head,
the curved neck, and the counting,

Such-like I love — I loosen myself, pass freely, am at
the mother's breast with the little child,

Swim with the swimmers, wrestle with wrestlers,
march in line with the firemen, and pause, listen,
and count.


6. I knew a man,

He was a common farmer — he was the father of five
sons,

And in them were the fathers of sons — and in them
were the fathers of sons.


7. This man was of wonderful vigor, calmness, beauty
of person,

The shape of his head, the richness and breadth of
his manners, the pale yellow and white of his
hair and beard, and the immeasurable meaning
of his black eyes,

These I used to go and visit him to see — he was wise
also,

25 *

He was six feet tall, he was over eighty years old —
    his sons were massive, clean, bearded, tan-faced,
    handsome,

They and his daughters loved him — all who saw him
    loved him,

They did not love him by allowance — they loved him
    with personal love;

He drank water only — the blood showed like scarlet
    through the clear-brown skin of his face,

He was a frequent gunner and fisher — he sailed
    his boat himself — he had a fine one presented
    to him by a ship-joiner — he had fowling-
    pieces, presented to him by men that loved
    him;

When he went with his five sons and many grand-
    sons to hunt or fish, you would pick him out
    as the most beautiful and vigorous of the
    gang,

You would wish long and long to be with him — you
    would wish to sit by him in the boat, that you
    and he might touch each other.


8. I have perceived that to be with those I like is
    enough,

To stop in company with the rest at evening is
    enough,

To be surrounded by beautiful, curious, breathing,
    laughing flesh is enough,

To pass among them, or touch any one, or rest my
    arm ever so lightly round his or her neck for a
    moment — what is this, then?

I do not ask any more delight — I swim in it, as in
    a sea.

9. There is something in staying close to men and women, and looking on them, and in the contact and odor of them, that pleases the Soul well,
All things please the Soul — but these please the Soul well.

10. This is the female form,
A divine nimbus exhales from it from head to foot,
It attracts with fierce undeniable attraction,
I am drawn by its breath as if I were no more than a helpless vapor — all falls aside but myself and it,
Books, art, religion, time, the visible and solid earth, the atmosphere and the clouds, and what was expected of heaven or feared of hell, are now consumed,
Mad filaments, ungovernable shoots play out of it, the response likewise ungovernable,
Hair, bosom, hips, bend of legs, negligent falling hands, all diffused — mine too diffused,
Ebb stung by the flow, and flow stung by the ebb — love-flesh swelling and deliciously aching,
Limitless limpid jets of love hot and enormous, quivering jelly of love, white-blow and delirious juice,
Bridegroom-night of love, working surely and softly into the prostrate dawn,
Undulating into the willing and yielding day,
Lost in the cleave of the clasping and sweet-fleshed day.

11. This is the nucleus — after the child is born of woman, the man is born of woman;

This is the bath of birth — this is the merge of small
and large, and the outlet again.

12. Be not ashamed, women — your privilege encloses
the rest, and is the exit of the rest,
You are the gates of the body, and you are the gates
of the Soul.

13. The female contains all qualities, and tempers them
— she is in her place, and moves with perfect
balance,
She is all things duly veiled — she is both passive and
active,
She is to conceive daughters as well as sons, and sons
as well as daughters.

14. As I see my Soul reflected in nature,
As I see through a mist, one with inexpressible com-
pleteness and beauty,
See the bent head and arms folded over the breast —
the female I see.

15. The male is not less the Soul, nor more — he too is in
his place,
He too is all qualities — he is action and power,
The flush of the known universe is in him,
Scorn becomes him well, and appetite and defiance
become him well,
The wildest largest passions, bliss that is utmost,
sorrow that is utmost, become him well — pride
is for him,
The full-spread pride of man is calming and excellent
to the Soul ;

Knowledge becomes him — he likes it always — he
    brings everything to the test of himself,
Whatever the survey, whatever the sea and the sail,
    he strikes soundings at last only here,
Where else does he strike soundings, except here?

16. The man's body is sacred, and the woman's body is
    sacred,
No matter who it is, it is sacred ;.
Is it a slave? Is it one of the dull-faced immigrants
    just landed on the wharf?
Each belongs here or anywhere just as much as the
    well-off — just as much as you,
Each has his or her place in the procession.

17. All is a procession,
The universe is a procession, with measured and
    beautiful motion.

18. Do you know so much yourself, that you call the slave
    or the dull-face ignorant?
Do you suppose you have a right to a good sight, and
    he or she has no right to a sight?
Do you think matter has cohered together from its
    diffused float — and the soil is on the surface,
    and water runs, and vegetation sprouts,
For you only, and not for him and her?

19. A man's body at auction !
I help the auctioneer — the sloven does not half know
    his business.

20. Gentlemen, look on this wonder !
Whatever the bids of the bidders, they cannot be high
    enough for it,

For it the globe lay preparing quintillions of years,
without one animal or plant,
For it the revolving cycles truly and steadily rolled.

21. In this head the all-baffling brain,
In it and below it, the making of the attributes of
heroes.

22. Examine these limbs, red, black, or white — they are
so cunning in tendon and nerve,
They shall be stript, that you may see them.

23. Exquisite senses, life-lit eyes, pluck, volition,
Flakes of breast-muscle, pliant back-bone and neck,
flesh not flabby, good-sized arms and legs,
And wonders within there yet.

24. Within there runs blood,
The same old blood!
The same red-running blood!
There swells and jets a heart — there all passions,
desires, reachings, aspirations,
Do you think they are not there because they are not
expressed in parlors and lecture-rooms?

25. This is not only one man — this is the father of those
who shall be fathers in their turns,
In him the start of populous states and rich republics,
Of him countless immortal lives, with countless em-
bodiments and enjoyments.

26. How do you know who shall come from the offspring
of his offspring through the centuries?

Who might you find you have come from yourself, if
you could trace back through the centuries?

27. A woman's body at auction!
She too is not only herself — she is the teeming
mother of mothers,
She is the bearer of them that shall grow and be
mates to the mothers.

28. Her daughters, or their daughters' daughters — who
knows who shall mate with them?
Who knows through the centuries what heroes may
come from them?

29. In them, and of them, natal love — in them that
divine mystery, the same old beautiful mystery.

30. Have you ever loved the body of a woman?
Have you ever loved the body of a man?
Your father — where is your father?
Your mother — is she living? have you been much
with her? and has she been much with you?
Do you not see that these are exactly the same to all,
in all nations and times, all over the earth?

31. If any thing is sacred, the human body is sacred,
And the glory and sweet of a man, is the token of
manhood untainted,
And in man or woman, a clean, strong, firm-fibred
body, is beautiful as the most beautiful face.

32. Have you seen the fool that corrupted his own live
body? or the fool that corrupted her own live
body?

For they do not conceal themselves, and cannot conceal themselves.

33. O my body! I dare not desert the likes of you in other men and women, nor the likes of the parts of you;

I believe the likes of you are to stand or fall with the likes of the Soul, (and that they are the Soul,)

I believe the likes of you shall stand or fall with my poems — and that they are poems,

Man's, woman's, child's, youth's, wife's, husband's, mother's, father's, young man's, young woman's poems,

Head, neck, hair, ears, drop and tympan of the ears,

Eyes, eye-fringes, iris of the eye, eye-brows, and the waking or sleeping of the lids,

Mouth, tongue, lips, teeth, roof of the mouth, jaws, and the jaw-hinges,

Nose, nostrils of the nose, and the partition,

Cheeks, temples, forehead, chin, throat, back of the neck, neck-slue,

Strong shoulders, manly beard, scapula, hind-shoulders, and the ample side-round of the chest,

Upper-arm, arm-pit, elbow-socket, lower-arm, arm-sinews, arm-bones,

Wrist and wrist-joints, hand, palm, knuckles, thumb, fore-finger, finger-balls, finger-joints, finger-nails,

Broad breast-front, curling hair of the breast, breast-bone, breast-side,

Ribs, belly, back-bone, joints of the back-bone,

Hips, hip-sockets, hip-strength, inward and outward round, man-balls, man-root,

Strong set of thighs, well carrying the trunk above,

Leg-fibres, knee, knee-pan, upper-leg, under-leg,
Ankles, instep, foot-ball, toes, toe-joints, the heel,
All attitudes, all the shapeliness, all the belongings of
    my or your body, or of any one's body, male or
    female,
The lung-sponges, the stomach-sac, the bowels sweet
    and clean,
The brain in its folds inside the skull-frame,
Sympathies, heart-valves, palate-valves, sexuality, ma-
    ternity,
Womanhood, and all that is a woman — and the man
    that comes from woman,
The womb, the teats, nipples, breast-milk, tears, laugh-
    ter, weeping, love-looks, love-perturbations and
    risings,
The voice, articulation, language, whispering, shout-
    ing aloud,
Food, drink, pulse, digestion, sweat, sleep, walking,
    swimming,
Poise on the hips, leaping, reclining, embracing, arm-
    curving, and tightening,
The continual changes of the flex of the mouth, and
    around the eyes,
The skin, the sun-burnt shade, freckles, hair,
The curious sympathy one feels, when feeling with
    the hand the naked meat of his own body, or
    another person's body,
The circling rivers, the breath, and breathing it in
    and out,
The beauty of the waist, and thence of the hips, and
    thence downward toward the knees,
The thin red jellies within you, or within me — the
    bones, and the marrow in the bones,

The exquisite realization of health,
O I say now these are not the parts and poems of the
body only, but of the Soul,
O I say these are the Soul!

4.

1. A WOMAN waits for me — she contains all, nothing is
lacking,
Yet all were lacking, if sex were lacking, or if the
moisture of the right man were lacking.

2. Sex contains all,
Bodies, Souls, meanings, proofs, purities, delicacies,
results, promulgations,
Songs, commands, health, pride, the maternal mystery,
the semitic milk,
All hopes, benefactions, bestowals,
All the passions, loves, beauties, delights of the
earth,
All the governments, judges, gods, followed persons
of the earth,
These are contained in sex, as parts of itself, and jus-
tifications of itself.

3. Without shame the man I like knows and avows the
deliciousness of his sex,
Without shame the woman I like knows and avows
hers.

4. O I will fetch bully breeds of children yet!
   I will dismiss myself from impassive women,
   I will go stay with her who waits for me, and with
     those women that are warm-blooded and suffi-
     cient for me ;
   I see that they understand me, and do not deny me,
   I see that they are worthy of me — I will be the robust
     husband of those women.

5. They are not one jot less than I am,
   They are tanned in the face by shining suns and blow-
     ing winds,
   Their flesh has the old divine suppleness and strength,
   They know how to swim, row, ride, wrestle, shoot,
     run, strike, retreat, advance, resist, defend them-
     selves,
   They are ultimate in their own right — they are calm,
     clear, well-possessed of themselves.

6. I draw you close to me, you women !
   I cannot let you go, I would do you good,
   I am for you, and you are for me, not only for our
     own sake, but for others' sakes ;
   Enveloped in you sleep greater heroes and bards,
   They refuse to awake at the touch of any man but me.

7. It is I, you women — I make my way,
   I am stern, acrid, large, undissuadable — but I love
     you,
   I do not hurt you any more than is necessary for you,
   I pour the stuff to start sons and daughters fit for These
     States — I press with slow rude muscle,
   I brace myself effectually — I listen to no entreaties,

I dare not withdraw till I deposit what has so long
    accumulated within me.

8. Through you I drain the pent-up rivers of myself,
    In you I wrap a thousand onward years,
    On you I graft the grafts of the best-beloved of me and
        of America,
    The drops I distil upon you shall grow fierce and
        athletic girls, new artists, musicians, and singers,
    The babes I beget upon you are to beget babes in
        their turn,
    I shall demand perfect men and women out of my
        love-spendings,
    I shall expect them to interpenetrate with others, as I
        and you interpenetrate now,
    I shall count on the fruits of the gushing showers of
        them, as I count on the fruits of the gushing
        showers I give now,
    I shall look for loving crops from the birth, life, death,
        immortality, I plant so lovingly now.

## 5.

Spontaneous me, Nature,
The loving day, the friend I am happy with,
The arm of my friend hanging idly over my shoulder,
The hill-side whitened with blossoms of the mountain
    ash,
The same, late in autumn — the gorgeous hues of red,
    yellow, drab, purple, and light and dark green,

The rich coverlid of the grass — animals and birds —
the private untrimmed bank — the primitive apples
— the pebble-stones,

Beautiful dripping fragments — the negligent list of
one after another, as I happen to call them to me,
or think of them,

The real poems, (what we call poems being merely
pictures,)

The poems of the privacy of the night, and of men
like me,

This poem, drooping shy and unseen, that I always
carry, and that all men carry,

(Know, once for all, avowed on purpose, wherever are
men like me, are our lusty, lurking, masculine,
poems,)

Love-thoughts, love-juice, love-odor, love-yielding, love-
climbers, and the climbing sap,

Arms and hands of love — lips of love — phallic thumb
of love — breasts of love — bellies pressed and
glued together with love,

Earth of chaste love — life that is only life after
love,

The body of my love — the body of the woman I
love — the body of the man — the body of the
earth,

Soft forenoon airs that blow from the south-west,

The hairy wild-bee that murmurs and hankers up and
down — that gripes the full-grown lady-flower,
curves upon her with amorous firm legs, takes
his will of her, and holds himself tremulous and
tight upon her till he is satisfied,

The wet of woods through the early hours,

26 *

Two sleepers at night lying close together as they sleep,
one with an arm slanting down across and below
the waist of the other,

The smell of apples, aromas from crushed sage-plant,
mint, birch-bark,

The boy's longings, the glow and pressure as he con-
fides to me what he was dreaming,

The dead leaf whirling its spiral whirl, and falling still
and content to the ground,

The no-formed stings that sights, people, objects, sting
me with,

The hubbed sting of myself, stinging me as much as it
ever can any one,

The sensitive, orbic, underlapped brothers, that only
privileged feelers may be intimate where they
are,

The curious roamer, the hand, roaming all over the
body — the bashful withdrawing of flesh where
the fingers soothingly pause and edge themselves,

The limpid liquid within the young man,

The vexed corrosion, so pensive and so painful,

The torment — the irritable tide that will not be at
rest,

The like of the same I feel — the like of the same in
others,

The young woman that flushes and flushes, and the
young man that flushes and flushes,

The young man that wakes, deep at night, the hot
hand seeking to repress what would master him
— the strange half-welcome pangs, visions, sweats,

The pulse pounding through palms and trembling
encircling fingers — the young man all colored,
red, ashamed, angry ;

The souse upon me of my lover the sea, as I lie willing and naked,

The merriment of the twin-babes that crawl over the grass in the sun, the mother never turning her vigilant eyes from them,

The walnut-trunk, the walnut-husks, and the ripening or ripened long-round walnuts,

The continence of vegetables, birds, animals,

The consequent meanness of me should I skulk or find myself indecent, while birds and animals never once skulk or find themselves indecent,

The great chastity of paternity, to match the great chastity of maternity,

The oath of procreation I have sworn — my Adamic and fresh daughters,

The greed that eats me day and night with hungry gnaw, till I saturate what shall produce boys to fill my place when I am through,

The wholesome relief, repose, content,

And this bunch plucked at random from myself,

It has done its work — I toss it carelessly to fall where it may.

6.

1. O furious ! O confine me not !

(What is this that frees me so in storms ?

What do my shouts amid lightnings and raging winds mean ?)

2. O to drink the mystic deliria deeper than any other man!

O savage and tender achings!

(I bequeath them to you, my children,

  I tell them to you, for reasons, O bridegroom and bride.)

3. O to be yielded to you, whoever you are, and you to be yielded me, in defiance of the world!

(Know, I am a man, attracting, at any time, her I but look upon, or touch with the tips of my fingers,

Or that touches my face, or leans against me.)

4. O to return to Paradise!

O to draw you to me — to plant on you, for the first time, the lips of a determined man!

O rich and feminine! O to show you to realize the blood of life for yourself, whoever you are — and no matter when and where you live.

5. O the puzzle — the thrice-tied knot — the deep and dark pool! O all untied and illumined!

O to speed where there is space enough and air enough at last!

O to be absolved from previous follies and degradations — I from mine, and you from yours!

O to find a new unthought-of nonchalance with the best of nature!

O to have the gag removed from one's mouth!

O to have the feeling, to-day or any day, I am sufficient as I am!

6. O something unproved! something in a trance!

O madness amorous! O trembling!

O to escape utterly from others' anchors and holds!

To drive free! to love free! to dash reckless and dangerous!

To court destruction with taunts — with invitations!

To ascend — to leap to the heavens of the love indicated to me!

To rise thither with my inebriate Soul!

To be lost, if it must be so!

To feed the remainder of life with one hour of fulness and freedom!

With one brief hour of madness and joy.

## 7.

You and I — what the earth is, we are,

We two — how long we were fooled!

Now delicious, transmuted, swiftly we escape, as Nature escapes,

We are Nature — long have we been absent, but now we return,

We become plants, leaves, foliage, roots, bark,

We are bedded in the ground — we are rocks,

We are oaks — we grow in the openings side by side,

We browse — we are two among the wild herds, spontaneous as any,

We are two fishes swimming in the sea together,

We are what the locust blossoms are — we drop scent around the lanes, mornings and evenings,

We are also the coarse smut of beasts, vegetables, minerals,

We are what the flowing wet of the Tennessee is —
we are two peaks of the Blue Mountains, rising
up in Virginia,

We are two predatory hawks — we soar above and
look down,

We are two resplendent suns — we it is who balance
ourselves orbic and stellar — we are as two
comets ;

We prowl fanged and four-footed in the woods — we
spring on prey ;

We are two clouds, forenoons and afternoons, driving
overhead,

We are seas mingling — we are two of those cheerful
waves, rolling over each other, and interwetting
each other,

We are what the atmosphere is, transparent, receptive,
pervious, impervious,

We are snow, rain, cold, darkness — we are each
product and influence of the globe,

We have circled and circled till we have arrived
home again — we two have,

We have voided all but freedom, and all but our
own joy.

## 8.

NATIVE moments ! when you come upon me — Ah
you are here now !

Give me now libidinous joys only !

Give me the drench of my passions !  Give me life
coarse and rank !

To-day, I go consort with nature's darlings — to-night
too,

I am for those who believe in loose delights — I share
    the midnight orgies of young men,
I dance with the dancers, and drink with the drink-
    ers,
The echoes ring with our indecent calls,
I take for my love some prostitute — I pick out some
    low person for my dearest friend,
He shall be lawless, rude, illiterate — he shall be one
    condemned by others for deeds done ;
I will play a part no longer — Why should I exile
    myself from my companions ?
O you shunned persons ! I at least do not shun you,
I come forthwith in your midst — I will be your poet,
I will be more to you than to any of the rest.

9.

ONCE I passed through a populous city, imprinting
    my brain, for future use, with its shows, architec-
    ture, customs, and traditions ;
Yet now, of all that city, I remember only a woman
    I casually met there, who detained me for love
    of me,
Day by day and night by night we were together, —
    All else has long been forgotten by me,
I remember I say only that woman who passionately
    clung to me,
Again we wander — we love — we separate again,
Again she holds me by the hand — I must not go !
I see her close beside me, with silent lips, sad and
    tremulous.

## 10.

INQUIRING, tireless, seeking that yet unfound,

I, a child, very old, over waves, toward the house of
maternity, the land of migrations, look afar,

Look off the shores of my Western Sea — having
arrived at last where I am — the circle almost
circled ;

For coming westward from Hindustan, from the vales
of Kashmere,

From Asia — from the north — from the God, the
sage, and the hero,

From the south — from the flowery peninsulas, and
the spice islands,

Now I face the old home again — looking over to it,
joyous, as after long travel, growth, and sleep ;

But where is what I started for, so long ago ?

And why is it yet unfound ?

## 11.

IN the new garden, in all the parts,

In cities now, modern, I wander,

Though the second or third result, or still further,
primitive yet,

Days, places, indifferent — though various, the same,

Time, Paradise, the Mannahatta, the prairies, finding
me unchanged,

Death indifferent — Is it that I lived long since ?
Was I buried very long ago ?

For all that, I may now be watching you here, this
    moment;
For the future, with determined will, I seek — the
    woman of the future,
You, born years, centuries after me, I seek.

## 12.

AGES and ages, returning at intervals,
Undestroyed, wandering immortal,
Lusty, phallic, with the potent original loins, perfectly
    sweet,
I, chanter of Adamic songs,
Through the new garden, the West, the great cities,
    calling,
Deliriate, thus prelude what is generated, offering
    these, offering myself,
Bathing myself, bathing my songs in sex,
Offspring of my loins.

## 13.

O HYMEN! O hymenee!
Why do you tantalize me thus?
O why sting me for a swift moment only?
Why can you not continue? O why do you now
    cease?
Is it because, if you continued beyond the swift
    moment, you would soon certainly kill me?

## 14.

I am he that aches with love ;
Does the earth gravitate ?   Does not all matter, ach-
    ing, attract all matter ?
So the body of me to all I meet, or that I know.

## 15.

Early in the morning,
Walking forth from the bower, refreshed with sleep,
Behold me where I pass — hear my voice — approach,
Touch me — touch the palm of your hand to my
    body as I pass,
Be not afraid of my body.

# POEM OF THE ROAD.

1. AFOOT and light-hearted I take to the open road,
Healthy, free, the world before me,
The long brown path before me, leading wherever I
choose.

2. Henceforth I ask not good-fortune — I am good-
fortune,
Henceforth I whimper no more, postpone no more,
need nothing,
Strong and content, I travel the open road.

3. The earth — that is sufficient,
I do not want the constellations any nearer,
I know they are very well where they are,
I know they suffice for those who belong to them.

4. Still here I carry my old delicious burdens,
I carry them, men and women — I carry them with
me wherever I go,
I swear it is impossible for me to get rid of them,
I am filled with them, and I will fill them in return.

5. You road I travel and look around! I believe you
are not all that is here,
I believe that much unseen is also here.

6. Here is the profound lesson of reception, neither
    preference or denial,
    The black with his woolly head, the felon, the dis-
    eased, the illiterate person, are not denied;
    The birth, the hasting after the physician, the beg-
    gar's tramp, the drunkard's stagger, the laughing
    party of mechanics,
    The escaped youth, the rich person's carriage, the fop,
    the eloping couple,
    The early market-man, the hearse, the moving of
    furniture into the town, the return back from
    the town,
    They pass, I also pass, any thing passes — none can
    be interdicted,
    None but are accepted, none but are dear to me.


7. You air that serves me with breath to speak!
    You objects that call from diffusion my meanings and
    give them shape!
    You light that wraps me and all things in delicate
    equable showers!
    You animals moving serenely over the earth!
    You birds that wing yourselves through the air! you
    insects!
    You sprouting growths from the farmers' fields! you
    stalks and weeds by the fences!
    You paths worn in the irregular hollows by the road-
    sides!
    I think you are latent with curious existences — you
    are so dear to me.


8. You flagged walks of the cities! you strong curbs at
    the edges!

You ferries! you planks and posts of wharves! you
   timber-lined sides! you distant ships!
You rows of houses! you window-pierced façades!
   you roofs!
You porches and entrances! you copings and iron
   guards!
You windows whose transparent shells might expose
   so much!
You doors and ascending steps! you arches!
You gray stones of interminable pavements! you trod-
   den crossings!
From all that has been near you I believe you have
   imparted to yourselves, and now would impart
   the same secretly to me,
From the living and the dead I think you have peopled
   your impassive surfaces, and the spirits thereof
   would be evident and amicable with me.

9. The earth expanding right hand and left hand,
   The picture alive, every part in its best light,
   The music falling in where it is wanted, and stopping
      where it was not wanted,
   The cheerful voice of the public road — the gay fresh
      sentiment of the road.

10. O highway I travel! O public road! do you say to
      me, Do not leave me?
   Do you say, Venture not? If you leave me, you are
      lost?
   Do you say, I am already prepared — I am well-beaten
      and undenied — adhere to me?

11. O public road! I say back, I am not afraid to leave
      you — yet I love you,

You express me better than I can express myself,
You shall be more to me than my poem.

12. I think heroic deeds were all conceived in the open
    air,
I think I could stop here myself, and do miracles,
I think whatever I meet on the road I shall like, and
    whoever  beholds me shall like me,
I think whoever I see must be happy.

13. From this hour, freedom !
From this hour I ordain myself loosed of limits and
    imaginary lines,
Going where I list — my own master, total and abso-
    lute,
Listening to others, and considering well what they
    say,
Pausing, searching, receiving, contemplating,
Gently, but with undeniable will, divesting myself of
    the holds that would hold me.

14. I inhale great draughts of air,
The east and the west are mine, and the north and
    the south are mine.

15. I am larger than I thought,
I did not know I held so much goodness.

16. All seems beautiful to me,
I can repeat over to men and women, You have done
    such good to me, I would do the same to you.

17. I will recruit for myself and you as I go,
I will scatter myself among men and women as I go,

I will toss the new gladness and roughness among
them;
Whoever denies me, it shall not trouble me,
Whoever accepts me, he or she shall be blessed, and
shall bless me.

18. Now if a thousand perfect men were to appear, it
would not amaze me,
Now if a thousand beautiful forms of women appeared,
it would not astonish me.

19. Now I see the secret of the making of the best
persons,
It is to grow in the open air, and to eat and sleep
with the earth.

20. Here is space — here a great personal deed has room,
A great deed seizes upon the hearts of the whole race
of men,
Its effusion of strength and will overwhelms law, and
mocks all authority and all argument against it.

21. Here is the test of wisdom,
Wisdom is not finally tested in schools,
Wisdom cannot be passed from one having it, to an-
other not having it,
Wisdom is of the Soul, is not susceptible of proof, is
its own proof,
Applies to all stages and objects and qualities, and is
content,
Is the certainty of the reality and immortality of
things, and the excellence of things;
Something there is in the float of the sight of things
that provokes it out of the Soul.

22. Now I reëxamine philosophies and religions,
    They may prove well in lecture-rooms, yet not prove
        at all under the spacious clouds, and along the
        landscape and flowing currents.

23. Here is realization,
    Here is a man tallied — he realizes here what he has
        in him,
    The animals, the past, the future, light, space,
        majesty, love, if they are vacant of you, you
        are vacant of them.

24. Only the kernel of every object nourishes ;
    Where is he who tears off the husks for you and me ?
    Where is he that undoes stratagems and envelopes for
        you and me ?

25. Here is adhesiveness — it is not previously fashioned
        — it is apropos ;
    Do you know what it is, as you pass, to be loved by
        strangers ?
    Do you know the talk of those turning eye-balls ?

26. Here is the efflux of the Soul,
    The efflux of the Soul comes through beautiful gates
        of laws, provoking questions ;
    These yearnings, why are they ? These thoughts in
        the darkness, why are they ?
    Why are there men and women that while they are
        nigh me, the sun-light expands my blood ?
    Why, when they leave me, do my pennants of joy sink
        flat and lank ?
    Why are there trees I never walk under, but large and
        melodious thoughts descend upon me ?

(I think they hang there winter and summer on those
  trees, and always drop fruit as I pass;)
What is it I interchange so suddenly with strangers?
What with some driver, as I ride on the seat by his
  side?
What with some fisherman, drawing his seine by the
  shore, as I walk by and pause?
What gives me to be free to a woman's or man's good-
  will? What gives them to be free to mine?


27. The efflux of the Soul is happiness — here is
  happiness,
I think it pervades the air, waiting at all times,
Now it flows into us — we are rightly charged.


28. Here rises the fluid and attaching character;
  The fluid and attaching character is the freshness and
    sweetness of man and woman,
  The herbs of the morning sprout no fresher and
    sweeter every day out of the roots of them-
    selves, than it sprouts fresh and sweet contin-
    ually out of itself.


29. Toward the fluid and attaching character exudes the
    sweat of the love of young and old,
  From it falls distilled the charm that mocks beauty
    and attainments,
  Toward it heaves the shuddering longing ache of
    contact.


30. Allons! Whoever you are, come travel with me!
  Travelling with me, you find what never tires.

31. The earth never tires,
    The earth is rude, silent, incomprehensible at first —
        Nature is rude and incomprehensible at first;
    Be not discouraged — keep on — there are divine
        things, well enveloped,
    I swear to you there are divine things more beautiful
        than words can tell.

32. Allons! We must not stop here!
    However sweet these laid-up stores — however con-
        venient this dwelling, we cannot remain here,
    However sheltered this port, and however calm these
        waters, we must not anchor here,
    However welcome the hospitality that surrounds us,
        we are permitted to receive it but a little while.

33. Allons! The inducements shall be great to you;
    We will sail pathless and wild seas,
    We will go where winds blow, waves dash, and the
        Yankee clipper speeds by under full sail.

34. Allons! With power, liberty, the earth, the elements!
    Health, defiance, gayety, self-esteem, curiosity;
    Allons! from all formules!
    From your formules, O bat-eyed and materialistic
        priests!

35. The stale cadaver blocks up the passage — the burial
        waits no longer.

36. Allons! Yet take warning!
    He travelling with me needs the best blood, thews,
        endurance,

None may come to the trial, till he or she bring
courage and health.

37. Come not here if you have already spent the best of
yourself;
Only those may come, who come in sweet and deter-
mined bodies,
No diseased person — no rum-drinker or venereal
taint is permitted here.

38. I and mine do not convince by arguments, similes,
rhymes,
We convince by our presence.

39. Listen! I will be honest with you,
I do not offer the old smooth prizes, but offer rough
new prizes,
These are the days that must happen to you:

40. You shall not heap up what is called riches,
You shall scatter with lavish hand all that you earn
or achieve,
You but arrive at the city to which you were des-
tined — you hardly settle yourself to satisfaction,
before you are called by an irresistible call to
depart,
You shall be treated to the ironical smiles and mock-
ings of those who remain behind you,
What beckonings of love you receive, you shall only
answer with passionate kisses of parting,
You shall not allow the hold of those who spread
their reached hands toward you.

41. Allons! After the GREAT COMPANIONS! and to belong
to them!

They too are on the road! they are the swift and
majestic men! they are the greatest women.

42. Over that which hindered them — over that which
retarded — passing impediments large or small,
Committers of crimes, committers of many beautiful
virtues,
Enjoyers of calms of seas, and storms of seas,
Sailors of many a ship, walkers of many a mile of
land,
Habitues of many different countries, habitues of far-
distant dwellings,
Trusters of men and women, observers of cities, soli-
tary toilers,
Pausers and contemplaters of tufts, blossoms, shells of
the shore,
Dancers at wedding-dances, kissers of brides, tender
helpers of children, bearers of children,
Soldiers of revolts, standers by gaping graves, lower-
ers down of coffins,
Journeyers over consecutive seasons, over the years —
the curious years, each emerging from that which
preceded it,
Journeyers as with companions, namely, their own
diverse phases,
Forth-steppers from the latent unrealized baby-days,
Journeyers gayly with their own youth — journeyers
with their bearded and well-grained manhood,
Journeyers with their womanhood, ample, unsur-
passed, content,
Journeyers with their sublime old age of manhood or
womanhood,
Old age, calm, expanded, broad with the haughty
breadth of the universe,

Old age, flowing free with the delicious near-by free-
dom of death.

43. Allons! To that which is endless, as it was beginning-
less,
To undergo much, tramps of days, rests of nights,
To merge all in the travel they tend to, and the days
and nights they tend to,
Again to merge them in the start of superior jour-
neys;
To see nothing anywhere but what you may reach it
and pass it,
To conceive no time, however distant, but what you
may reach it and pass it,
To look up or down no road but it stretches and waits
for you—however long, but it stretches and waits
for you;
To see no being, not God's or any, but you also go
thither,
To see no possession but you may possess it — enjoy-
ing all without labor or purchase — abstracting
the feast, yet not abstracting one particle of it;
To take the best of the farmer's farm and the rich
man's elegant villa, and the chaste blessings of
the well-married couple, and the fruits of or-
chards and flowers of gardens,
To take to your use out of the compact cities as you
pass through,
To carry buildings and streets with you afterward
wherever you go,
To gather the minds of men out of their brains as you
encounter them — to gather the love out of their
hearts,

28

To take your own lovers on the road with you, for all
that you leave them behind you,
To know the universe itself as a road — as many
roads — as roads for travelling Souls.

44. The Soul travels,
The body does not travel as much as the Soul,
The body has just as great a work as the Soul, and
parts away at last for the journeys of the Soul.

45. All parts away for the progress of Souls,
All religion, all solid things, arts, governments — all
that was or is apparent upon this globe or any
globe, falls into niches and corners before the
procession of Souls along the grand roads of the
universe.

46. Of the progress of the Souls of men and women along
the grand roads of the universe, all other prog-
ress is the needed emblem and sustenance.

47. Forever alive, forever forward,
Stately, solemn, sad, withdrawn, baffled, mad, turbu-
lent, feeble, dissatisfied,
Desperate, proud, fond, sick, accepted by men, re-
jected by men,
They go! they go! I know that they go, but I know
not where they go,
But I know that they go toward the best — toward
something great.

48. Allons! Whoever you are! come forth!
You must not stay sleeping and dallying there in the
house, though you built it, or though it has been
built for you.

49. Allons ! out of the dark confinement !
    It is useless to protest — I know all, and expose it.

50. Behold, through you as bad as the rest,
    Through the laughter, dancing, dining, supping, of
        people,
    Inside of dresses and ornaments, inside of those
        washed and trimmed faces,
    Behold a secret silent loathing and despair.

51. No husband, no wife, no friend, no lover, so trusted
        as to hear the confession,
    Another self, a duplicate of every one, skulking
        and hiding it goes, open and above board it
        goes,
    Formless and wordless through the streets of the
        cities, polite and bland in the parlors,
    In the cars of rail-roads, in steam-boats, in the public
        assembly,
    Home to the houses of men and women, among their
        families, at the table, in the bed-room, every-
        where,
    Smartly attired, countenance smiling, form upright,
        death under the breast-bones, hell under the
        skull-bones,
    Under the broadcloth and gloves, under the ribbons
        and artificial flowers,
    Keeping fair with the customs, speaking not a syllable
        of itself,
    Speaking of anything else, but never of itself.

52. Allons ! Through struggles and wars !
    The goal that was named cannot be countermanded.

53. Have the past struggles succeeded?
    What has succeeded? Yourself? Your nation?
        Nature?
    Now understand me well — It is provided in the
        essence of things, that from any fruition of suc-
        cess, no matter what, shall come forth something
        to make a greater struggle necessary.

54. My call is the call of battle — I nourish active re-
        bellion,
    He going with me must go well armed,
    He going with me goes often with spare diet, poverty,
        angry enemies, desertions.

55. Allons! The road is before us!
    It is safe — I have tried it — my own feet have tried
        it well.

56. Allons! Be not detained!
    Let the paper remain on the desk unwritten, and the
        book on the shelf unopened!
    Let the tools remain in the workshop! let the money
        remain unearned!
    Let the school stand! mind not the cry of the teacher!
    Let the preacher preach in his pulpit! let the lawyer
        plead in the court, and the judge expound the
        law.

57. Mon enfant! I give you my hand!
    I give you my love, more precious than money,
    I give you myself, before preaching or law;
    Will you give me yourself? Will you come travel
        with me?
    Shall we stick by each other as long as we live?

# TO THE SAYERS OF WORDS.

1. EARTH, round, rolling, compact — suns, moons, animals — all these are words to be said,
   Watery, vegetable, sauroid advances — beings, premonitions, lispings of the future,
   Behold! these are vast words to be said.

2. Were you thinking that those were the words — those upright lines? those curves, angles, dots?
   No, those are not the words — the substantial words are in the ground and sea,
   They are in the air — they are in you.

3. Were you thinking that those were the words — those delicious sounds out of your friends' mouths?
   No, the real words are more delicious than they.

4. Human bodies are words, myriads of words,
   In the best poems re-appears the body, man's or woman's, well-shaped, natural, gay,
   Every part able, active, receptive, without shame or the need of shame.

28*

(329)

5. Air, soil, water, fire, these are words,
   I myself am a word with them — my qualities inter-
       penetrate with theirs — my name is nothing to
       them,
   Though it were told in the three thousand languages,
       what would air, soil, water, fire, know of my
       name ?


6. A healthy presence, a friendly or commanding ges-
       ture, are words, sayings, meanings,
   The charms that go with the mere looks of some men
       and women, are sayings and meanings also.


7. The workmanship of Souls is by the inaudible words
       of the earth,
   The great masters, the sayers, know the earth's words,
       and use them more than the audible words.


8. Amelioration is one of the earth's words,
   The earth neither lags nor hastens,
   It has all attributes, growths, effects, latent in itself
       from the jump,
   It is not half beautiful only — defects and excres-
       cences show just as much as perfections show.


9. The earth does not withhold, it is generous enough,
   The truths of the earth continually wait, they are
       not so concealed either,
   They are calm, subtle, untransmissible by print,
   They are imbued through all things, conveying them-
       selves willingly,
   Conveying a sentiment and invitation of the earth —
       I utter and utter,

I speak not, yet if you hear me not, of what avail am
    I to you ?
To bear — to better — lacking these, of what avail
    am I ?

10. Accouche ! Accouchez !
    Will you rot your own fruit in yourself there ?
    Will you squat and stifle there ?

11. The earth does not argue,
    Is not pathetic, has no arrangements,
    Does not scream, haste, persuade, threaten, promise,
    Makes no discriminations, has no conceivable fail-
        ures,
    Closes nothing, refuses nothing, shuts none out,
    Of all the powers, objects, states, it notifies, shuts
        none out.

12. The earth does not exhibit itself, nor refuse to exhibit
    itself — possesses still underneath,
    Underneath the ostensible sounds, the august chorus
        of heroes, the wail of slaves,
    Persuasions of lovers, curses, gasps of the dying,
        laughter of young people, accents of bargainers,
    Underneath these, possessing the words that never
        fail.

13. To her children, the words of the eloquent dumb
    great mother never fail,
    The true words do not fail, for motion does not fail,
    and reflection does not fail,
    Also the day and night do not fail, and the voyage
    we pursue does not fail.

14. Of the interminable sisters,
   Of the ceaseless cotillions of sisters,
   Of the centripetal and centrifugal sisters, the elder
      and younger sisters,
   The beautiful sister we know dances on with the rest.

15. With her ample back toward every beholder,
   With the fascinations of youth, and the equal fascina-
      tions of age,
   Sits she whom I too love like the rest — sits undis-
      turbed,
   Holding up in her hand what has the character of a
      mirror, while her eyes glance back from it,
   Glance as she sits, inviting none, denying none,
   Holding a mirror day and night tirelessly before her
      own face.

16. Seen at hand, or seen at a distance,
   Duly the twenty-four appear in public every day,
   Duly approach and pass with their companions, or
      a companion,
   Looking from no countenances of their own, but from
      the countenances of those who are with them,
   From the countenances of children or women, or the
      manly countenance,
   From the open countenances of animals, or from
      inanimate things,
   From the landscape or waters, or from the exquisite
      apparition of the sky,
   From our countenances, mine and yours, faithfully
      returning them,
   Every day in public appearing without fail, but never
      twice with the same companions.

17. Embracing man, embracing all, proceed the three
    hundred and sixty-five resistlessly round the sun,
    Embracing all, soothing, supporting, follow close three
    hundred and sixty-five offsets of the first, sure
    and necessary as they.

18. Tumbling on steadily, nothing dreading,
    Sunshine, storm, cold, heat, forever withstanding,
      passing, carrying,
    The Soul's realization and determination still inherit-
      ing,
    The fluid vacuum around and ahead still entering
      and dividing,
    No balk retarding, no anchor anchoring, on no rock
      striking,
    Swift, glad, content, unbereaved, nothing losing,
    Of all able and ready at any time to give strict
      account,
    The divine ship sails the divine sea.

19. Whoever you are! motion and reflection are espe-
    cially for you,
    The divine ship sails the divine sea for you.

20. Whoever you are! you are he or she for whom the
    earth is solid and liquid,
    You are he or she for whom the sun and moon hang
    in the sky,
    For none more than you are the present and the past,
    For none more than you is immortality.

21. Each man to himself, and each woman to herself, is
    the word of the past and present, and the word
    of immortality,

No one can acquire for another — not one !
Not one can grow for another — not one !

22. The song is to the singer, and comes back most to
    him,
    The teaching is to the teacher, and comes back most
    to him,
    The murder is to the murderer, and comes back most
    to him,
    The theft is to the thief, and comes back most to him,
    The love is to the lover, and comes back most to him,
    The gift is to the giver, and comes back most to him
    — it cannot fail,
    The oration is to the orator, and the acting is to the
    actor and actress, not to the audience,
    And no man understands any greatness or goodness
    but his own, or the indication of his own.

23. I swear the earth shall surely be complete to him or
    her who shall be complete !
    I swear the earth remains broken and jagged only to
    him or her who remains broken and jagged !

24. I swear there is no greatness or power that does not
    emulate those of the earth !
    I swear there can be no theory of any account, unless
    it corroborate the theory of the earth !
    No politics, art, religion, behavior, or what not, is of
    account, unless it compare with the amplitude of
    the earth,
    Unless it face the exactness, vitality, impartiality,
    rectitude of the earth.

25. I swear I begin to see love with sweeter spasms than
    that which responds love !

It is that which contains itself, which never invites
and never refuses.

26. I swear I begin to see little or nothing in audible
words!
I swear I think all merges toward the presentation of
the unspoken meanings of the earth!
Toward him who sings the songs of the body, and of
the truths of the earth,
Toward him who makes the dictionaries of the words
that print cannot touch.

27. I swear I see what is better than to tell the best,
It is always to leave the best untold.

28. When I undertake to tell the best, I find I cannot,
My tongue is ineffectual on its pivots,
My breath will not be obedient to its organs,
I become a dumb man.

29. The best of the earth cannot be told anyhow — all or
any is best,
It is not what you anticipated — it is cheaper, easier,
nearer,
Things are not dismissed from the places they held
before,
The earth is just as positive and direct as it was
before,
Facts, religions, improvements, politics, trades, are as
real as before,
But the Soul is also real, — it too is positive and
direct,
No reasoning, no proof has established it,
Undeniable growth has established it.

30. This is a poem for the sayers of words — these are
      hints of meanings,
    These are they that echo the tones of Souls, and the
      phrases of Souls ;
    If they did not echo the phrases of Souls, what were
      they then ?
    If they had not reference to you in especial, what were
      they then ?

31. I swear I will never henceforth have to do with the
      faith that tells the best !
    I will have to do with that faith only that leaves the
      best untold.

32. Say on, sayers !
    Delve ! mould ! pile the words of the earth !
    Work on — it is materials you bring, not breaths ;
    Work on, age after age ! nothing is to be lost,
    It may have to wait long, but it will certainly come
      in use,
    When the materials are all prepared, the architects
      shall appear.

33. I swear to you the architects shall appear without fail !
      I announce them and lead them,
    I swear to you they will understand you and justify
      you,
    I swear to you the greatest among them shall be he
      who best knows you, and encloses all, and is
      faithful to all,
    I swear to you, he and the rest shall not forget you
      — they shall perceive that you are not an iota
      less than they,
    I swear to you, you shall be glorified in them.

# A BOSTON BALLAD,

## The 78th Year of Thefe States.

1. CLEAR the way there, Jonathan!
   Way for the President's marshal! Way for the government cannon!
   Way for the federal foot and dragoons—and the apparitions copiously tumbling.

2. I rose this morning early, to get betimes in Boston town,
   Here's a good place at the corner, I must stand and see the show.

3. I love to look on the stars and stripes, I hope the fifes will play Yankee Doodle.

4. How bright shine the cutlasses of the foremost troops!
   Every man holds his revolver, marching stiff through Boston town.

5. A fog follows — antiques of the same come limping,
   Some appear wooden-legged, and some appear bandaged and bloodless.

6. Why this is a show ! It has called the dead out of
    the earth !

The old grave-yards of the hills have hurried to
    see !

Uncountable phantoms gather by flank and rear
    of it !

Cocked hats of mothy mould ! crutches made of
    mist !

Arms in slings ! old men leaning on young men's
    shoulders !

7. What troubles you, Yankee phantoms ?   What is all
    this chattering of bare gums ?

Does the ague convulse your limbs ?   Do you mis-
    take your crutches for fire-locks, and level
    them ?

8. If you blind your eyes with tears, you will not see
    the President's marshal,

If you groan such groans you might balk the govern-
    ment cannon.

9. For shame, old maniacs ! Bring down those tossed
    arms, and let your white hair be,

Here gape your smart grand-sons — their wives gaze
    at them from the windows,

See how well-dressed — see how orderly they conduct
    themselves.

10. Worse and worse ! Can't you stand it ? Are you
    retreating ?

Is this hour with the living too dead for you ?

11. Retreat then ! Pell-mell !
    Back to your graves ! Back to the hills, old
        limpers !
    I do not think you belong here, anyhow.


12. But there is one thing that belongs here — shall I tell
    you what it is, gentlemen of Boston ?


13. I will whisper it to the Mayor — he shall send a com-
        mittee to England,
    They shall get a grant from the Parliament, go with a
        cart to the royal vault — haste !
    Dig out King George's coffin, unwrap him quick
        from the grave-clothes, box up his bones for a
        journey,
    Find a swift Yankee clipper — here is freight for you,
        black-bellied clipper,
    Up with your anchor ! shake out your sails ! steer
        straight toward Boston bay.


14. Now call for the President's marshal again, bring out
        the government cannon,
    Fetch home the roarers from Congress, make an-
        other procession, guard it with foot and dra-
        goons.


15. This centre-piece for them :
    Look ! all orderly citizens — look from the windows,
        women !


16. The committee open the box, set up the regal ribs,
        glue those that will not stay,

Clap the skull on top of the ribs, and clap a crown on
top of the skull.

17. You have got your revenge, old buster ! The crown is
come to its own, and more than its own.

18. Stick your hands in your pockets, Jonathan — you
are a made man from this day,
You are mighty cute — and here is one of your
bargains.

# CALAMUS.

## 1.

In paths untrodden,
In the growth by margins of pond-waters,
Escaped from the life that exhibits itself,
From all the standards hitherto published — from
    the pleasures, profits, conformities,
Which too long I was offering to feed to my Soul;
Clear to me now, standards not yet published —
    clear to me that my Soul,
That the Soul of the man I speak for, feeds, rejoices
    only in comrades;
Here, by myself, away from the clank of the world,
Tallying and talked to here by tongues aromatic,
No longer abashed — for in this secluded spot I can
    respond as I would not dare elsewhere,
Strong upon me the life that does not exhibit itself,
    yet contains all the rest,
Resolved to sing no songs to-day but those of manly
    attachment,
Projecting them along that substantial life,
Bequeathing, hence, types of athletic love,

Afternoon, this delicious Ninth Month, in my forty-
first year,
I proceed, for all who are, or have been, young
men,
To tell the secret of my nights and days,
To celebrate the need of comrades.

# 2.

Scented herbage of my breast,
Leaves from you I yield, I write, to be perused best
afterwards,
Tomb-leaves, body-leaves, growing up above me, above
death,
Perennial roots, tall leaves — O the winter shall not
freeze you, delicate leaves,
Every year shall you bloom again — Out from where
you retired, you shall emerge again ;
O I do not know whether many, passing by, will dis-
cover you, or inhale your faint odor — but I
believe a few will ;
O slender leaves ! O blossoms of my blood ! I permit
you to tell, in your own way, of the heart that is
under you,
O burning and throbbing — surely all will one day be
accomplished ;
O I do not know what you mean, there underneath
yourselves — you are not happiness,
You are often more bitter than I can bear — you burn
and sting me,

Yet you are very beautiful to me, you faint-tinged
    roots — you make me think of Death,
Death is beautiful from you — (what indeed is beau-
    tiful, except Death and Love ?)
O I think it is not for life I am chanting here my
    chant of lovers — I think it must be for Death,
For how calm, how solemn it grows, to ascend to the
    atmosphere of lovers,
Death or life I am then indifferent — my Soul de-
    clines to prefer,
I am not sure but the high Soul of lovers welcomes
    death most ;
Indeed, O Death, I think now these leaves mean pre-
    cisely the same as you mean ;
Grow up taller, sweet leaves, that I may see ! Grow
    up out of my breast !
Spring away from the concealed heart there !
Do not fold yourselves so in your pink-tinged roots,
    timid leaves !
Do not remain down there so ashamed, herbage of my
    breast !
Come, I am determined to unbare this broad breast of
    mine — I have long enough stifled and choked ;
Emblematic and capricious blades, I leave you — now
    you serve me not,
Away ! I will say what I have to say, by itself,
I will escape from the sham that was proposed to me,
I will sound myself and comrades only — I will never
    again utter a call, only their call,
I will raise, with it, immortal reverberations through
    The States,
I will give an example to lovers, to take permanent
    shape and will through The States ;

Through me shall the words be said to make death
     exhilarating,
Give me your tone therefore, O Death, that I may
     accord with it,
Give me yourself — for I see that you belong to me
     now above all, and are folded together above all
     — you Love and Death are,
Nor will I allow you to balk me any more with what
     I was calling life,
For now it is conveyed to me that you are the pur-
     ports essential,
That you hide in these shifting forms of life, for
     reasons — and that they are mainly for you,
That you, beyond them, come forth, to remain, the
     real reality,
That behind the mask of materials you patiently
     wait, no matter how long,
That you will one day, perhaps, take control of all,
That you will perhaps dissipate this entire show of
     appearance,
That may be you are what it is all for — but it does
     not last so very long,
But you will last very long.

## 3.

1. WHOEVER you are holding me now in hand,
Without one thing all will be useless,
  I give you fair warning, before you attempt me
     further,
  I am not what you supposed, but far different.

2. Who is he that would become my follower?
Who would sign himself a candidate for my affec-
tions? Are you he?

3. The way is suspicious — the result slow, uncertain,
may-be destructive;
You would have to give up all else — I alone would
expect to be your God, sole and exclusive,
Your novitiate would even then be long and ex-
hausting,
The whole past theory of your life, and all conformity
to the lives around you, would have to be aban-
doned;
Therefore release me now, before troubling yourself
any further — Let go your hand from my
shoulders,
Put me down, and depart on your way.

4. Or else, only by stealth, in some wood, for trial,
Or back of a rock, in the open air,
(For in any roofed room of a house I emerge not —
nor in company,
And in libraries I lie as one dumb, a gawk, or unborn,
or dead,)
But just possibly with you on a high hill — first
watching lest any person, for miles around,
approach unawares,
Or possibly with you sailing at sea, or on the beach of
the sea, or some quiet island,
Here to put your lips upon mine I permit you,
With the comrade's long-dwelling kiss, or the new
husband's kiss,
For I am the new husband, and I am the comrade.

5. Or, if you will, thrusting me beneath your clothing,
   Where I may feel the throbs of your heart, or rest
      upon your hip,
   Carry me when you go forth over land or sea ;
   For thus, merely touching you, is enough — is best,
   And thus, touching you, would I silently sleep and be
      carried eternally.

6. But these leaves conning, you con at peril,
   For these leaves, and me, you will not understand,
   They will elude you at first, and still more after-
      ward — I will certainly elude you,
   Even while you should think you had unquestionably
      caught me, behold !
   Already you see I have escaped from you.

7. For it is not for what I have put into it that I have
      written this book,
   Nor is it by reading it you will acquire it,
   Nor do those know me best who admire me, and
      vauntingly praise me,
   Nor will the candidates for my love, (unless at most a
      very few,) prove victorious,
   Nor will my poems do good only — they will do just
      as much evil, perhaps more,
   For all is useless without that which you may guess
      at many times and not hit — that which I
      hinted at,
   Therefore release me, and depart on your way.

# 4.

THESE I, singing in spring, collect for lovers,
(For who but I should understand lovers, and all their
    sorrow and joy ?
And who but I should be the poet of comrades ?)
Collecting, I traverse the garden, the world — but
    soon I pass the gates,
Now along the pond-side — now wading in a little,
    fearing not the wet,
Now by the post-and-rail fences, where the old stones
    thrown there, picked from the fields, have accu-
    mulated,
Wild-flowers and vines and weeds come up through
    the stones, and partly cover them — Beyond these
    I pass,
Far, far in the forest, before I think where I get,
Solitary, smelling the earthy smell, stopping now and
    then in the silence,
Alone I had thought — yet soon a silent troop gathers
    around me,
Some walk by my side, and some behind, and some
    embrace my arms or neck,
They, the spirits of friends, dead or alive — thicker
    they come, a great crowd, and I in the middle,
Collecting, dispensing, singing in spring, there I wan-
    der with them,
Plucking something for tokens — something for these,
    till I hit upon a name — tossing toward whoever
    is near me,

Here ! lilac, with a branch of pine,

Here, out of my pocket, some moss which I pulled off
     a live-oak in Florida, as it hung trailing down,

Here, some pinks and laurel leaves, and a handful of
     sage,

And here what I now draw from the water, wading in
     the pond-side,

(O here I last saw him that tenderly loves me — and
     returns again, never to separate from me,

And this, O this shall henceforth be the token of
     comrades — this calamus-root shall,

Interchange it, youths, with each other ! Let none
     render it back !)

And twigs of maple, and a bunch of wild orange, and
     chestnut,

And stems of currants, and plum-blows, and the
     aromatic cedar ;

These I, compassed around by a thick cloud of
     spirits,

Wandering, point to, or touch as I pass, or throw them
     loosely from me,

Indicating to each one what he shall have — giving
     something to each,

But what I drew from the water by the pond-side, that
     I reserve,

I will give of it — but only to them that love, as I
     myself am capable of loving.

## 5.

1. STATES!
   Were you looking to be held together by the lawyers?
   By an agreement on a paper? Or by arms?

2. Away!
   I arrive, bringing these, beyond all the forces of
     courts and arms,
   These! to hold you together as firmly as the earth
     itself is held together.

3. The old breath of life, ever new,
   Here! I pass it by contact to you, America.

4. O mother! have you done much for me?
   Behold, there shall from me be much done for you.

5. There shall from me be a new friendship — It shall
     be called after my name,
   It shall circulate through The States, indifferent of
     place,
   It shall twist and intertwist them through and around
     each other — Compact shall they be, showing
     new signs,
   Affection shall solve every one of the problems of
     freedom,
   Those who love each other shall be invincible,
   They shall finally make America completely victo-
     rious, in my name.

6. One from Massachusetts shall be comrade to a Missourian,
   One from Maine or Vermont, and a Carolinian and an Oregonese, shall be friends triune, more precious to each other than all the riches of the earth.

7. To Michigan shall be wafted perfume from Florida,
   To the Mannahatta from Cuba or Mexico,
   Not the perfume of flowers, but sweeter, and wafted beyond death.

8. No danger shall balk Columbia's lovers,
   If need be, a thousand shall sternly immolate themselves for one,
   The Kanuck shall be willing to lay down his life for the Kansian, and the Kansian for the Kanuck, on due need.

9. It shall be customary in all directions, in the houses and streets, to see manly affection,
   The departing brother or friend shall salute the remaining brother or friend with a kiss.

10. There shall be innovations,
    There shall be countless linked hands — namely, the Northeasterner's, and the Northwesterner's, and the Southwesterner's, and those of the interior, and all their brood,
    These shall be masters of the world under a new power,
    They shall laugh to scorn the attacks of all the remainder of the world.

11. The most dauntless and rude shall touch face to face
    lightly,
    The dependence of Liberty shall be lovers,
    The continuance of Equality shall be comrades.

12. These shall tie and band stronger than hoops of iron,
    I, extatic, O partners! O lands! henceforth with the
    love of lovers tie you.

13. I will make the continent indissoluble,
    I will make the most splendid race the sun ever yet
    shone upon,
    I will make divine magnetic lands.

14. I will plant companionship thick as trees along all the
    rivers of America, and along the shores of the
    great lakes, and all over the prairies,
    I will make inseparable cities, with their arms about
    each other's necks.

15. For you these, from me, O Democracy, to serve you,
    ma femme!
    For you! for you, I am trilling these songs.

Not heaving from my ribbed breast only,
Not in sighs at night, in rage, dissatisfied with myself,
Not in those long-drawn, ill-suppressed sighs,
Not in many an oath and promise broken,
Not in my wilful and savage soul's volition,

Not in the subtle nourishment of the air,
Not in this beating and pounding at my temples and
    wrists,
Not in the curious systole and diastole within, which
    will one day cease,
Not in many a hungry wish, told to the skies only,
Not in cries, laughter, defiances, thrown from me
    when alone, far in the wilds,
Not in husky pantings through clenched teeth,
Not in sounded and resounded words — chattering
    words, echoes, dead words,
Not in the murmurs of my dreams while I sleep,
Nor the other murmurs of these incredible dreams of
    every day,
Nor in the limbs and senses of my body, that take you
    and dismiss you continually — Not there,
Not in any or all of them, O adhesiveness! O pulse
    of my life!
Need I that you exist and show yourself, any more
    than in these songs.

# 7.

Of the terrible question of appearances,
Of the doubts, the uncertainties after all,
That may-be reliance and hope are but speculations
    after all,
That may-be identity beyond the grave is a beautiful
    fable only,
May-be the things I perceive — the animals, plants,
    men, hills, shining and flowing waters,

The skies of day and night — colors, densities, forms
— May-be these are, (as doubtless they are,) only
apparitions, and the real something has yet to be
known,
(How often they dart out of themselves, as if to con-
found me and mock me!
How often I think neither I know, nor any man
knows, aught of them;)
May-be they only seem to me what they are, (as
doubtless they indeed but seem,) as from my
present point of view — And might prove, (as of
course they would,) naught of what they appear,
or naught any how, from entirely changed points
of view;
To me, these, and the like of these, are curiously
answered by my lovers, my dear friends;
When he whom I love travels with me, or sits a long
while holding me by the hand,
When the subtle air, the impalpable, the sense that
words and reason hold not, surround us and
pervade us,
Then I am charged with untold and untellable wis-
dom — I am silent — I require nothing further,
I cannot answer the question of appearances, or that
of identity beyond the grave,
But I walk or sit indifferent — I am satisfied,
He ahold of my hand has completely satisfied me.

## 8.

Long I thought that knowledge alone would suffice
me — O if I could but obtain knowledge!
Then my lands engrossed me — Lands of the prairies,
Ohio's land, the southern savannas, engrossed
me — For them I would live — I would be their
orator;
Then I met the examples of old and new heroes — I
heard of warriors, sailors, and all dauntless per-
sons — And it seemed to me that I too had it
in me to be as dauntless as any — and would
be so;
And then, to enclose all, it came to me to strike up
the songs of the New World — And then I be-
lieved my life must be spent in singing;
But now take notice, land of the prairies, land of
the south savannas, Ohio's land,
Take notice, you Kanuck woods — and you Lake
Huron — and all that with you roll toward
Niagara — and you Niagara also,
And you, Californian mountains — That you each
and all find somebody else to be your singer of
songs,
For I can be your singer of songs no longer — One
who loves me is jealous of me, and withdraws me
from all but love,
With the rest I dispense — I sever from what I
thought would suffice me, for it does not — it is
now empty and tasteless to me,
I heed knowledge, and the grandeur of The States,
and the example of heroes, no more,

I am indifferent to my own songs — I will go with
    him I love,
It is to be enough for us that we are together — We
    never separate again.

# 9.

HOURS continuing long, sore and heavy-hearted,
Hours of the dusk, when I withdraw to a lonesome
    and unfrequented spot, seating myself, leaning
    my face in my hands ;
Hours sleepless, deep in the night, when I go forth,
    speeding swiftly the country roads, or through
    the city streets, or pacing miles and miles, sti-
    fling plaintive cries ;
Hours discouraged, distracted — for the one I cannot
    content myself without, soon I saw him content
    himself without me ;
Hours when I am forgotten, (O weeks and months are
    passing, but I believe I am never to forget !)
Sullen and suffering hours ! (I am ashamed — but it
    is useless — I am what I am ;)
Hours of my torment — I wonder if other men ever
    have the like, out of the like feelings ?
Is there even one other like me — distracted — his
    friend, his lover, lost to him ?
Is he too as I am now ? Does he still rise in the morn-
    ing, dejected, thinking who is lost to him ? and
    at night, awaking, think who is lost ?

Does he too harbor his friendship silent and endless ? harbor his anguish and passion ?

Does some stray reminder, or the casual mention of a name, bring the fit back upon him, taciturn and deprest ?

Does he see himself reflected in me ?   In these hours, does he see the face of his hours reflected ?

# 10.

You bards of ages hence ! when you refer to me, mind not so much my poems,

Nor speak of me that I prophesied of The States, and led them the way of their glories ;

But come, I will take you down underneath this impassive exterior — I will tell you what to say of me :

Publish my name and hang up my picture as that of the tenderest lover,

The friend, the lover's portrait, of whom his friend, his lover, was fondest,

Who was not proud of his songs, but of the measure-less ocean of love within him — and freely poured it forth,

Who often walked lonesome walks, thinking of his dear friends, his lovers,

Who pensive, away from one he loved, often lay sleep-less and dissatisfied at night,

Who knew too well the sick, sick dread lest the one he loved might secretly be indifferent to him,

Whose happiest days were far away, through fields, in
    woods, on hills, he and another, wandering hand
    in hand, they twain, apart from other men,
Who oft as he sauntered the streets, curved with his
    arm the shoulder of his friend — while the arm of
    his friend rested upon him also.

## 11.

When I heard at the close of the day how my name
    had been received with plaudits in the capitol,
    still it was not a happy night for me that fol-
    lowed;
And else, when I caroused, or when my plans were
    accomplished, still I was not happy;
But the day when I rose at dawn from the bed of
    perfect health, refreshed, singing, inhaling the
    ripe breath of autumn,
When I saw the full moon in the west grow pale and
    disappear in the morning light,
When I wandered alone over the beach, and, undress-
    ing, bathed, laughing with the cool waters, and
    saw the sun rise,
And when I thought how my dear friend, my lover,
    was on his way coming, O then I was happy;
O then each breath tasted sweeter — and all that day
    my food nourished me more — And the beautiful
    day passed well,
And the next came with equal joy — And with the
    next, at evening, came my friend;

And that night, while all was still, I heard the waters roll slowly continually up the shores,

I heard the hissing rustle of the liquid and sands, as directed to me, whispering, to congratulate me,

For the one I love most lay sleeping by me under the same cover in the cool night,

In the stillness, in the autumn moonbeams, his face was inclined toward me,

And his arm lay lightly around my breast — And that night I was happy.

# 12.

ARE you the new person drawn toward me, and asking something significant from me ?

To begin with, take warning — I am probably far different from what you suppose ;

Do you suppose you will find in me your ideal ?

Do you think it so easy to have me become your lover ?

Do you think the friendship of me would be unalloyed satisfaction ?

Do you suppose I am trusty and faithful ?

Do you see no further than this façade — this smooth and tolerant manner of me ?

Do you suppose yourself advancing on real ground toward a real heroic man ?

Have you no thought, O dreamer, that it may be all maya, illusion ?   O the next step may precipitate you !

O let some past deceived one hiss in your ears, how
many have prest on the same as you are pressing
now,

How many have fondly supposed what you are sup-
posing now — only to be disappointed.

# 13.

Calamus taste,

(For I must change the strain — these are not to be
pensive leaves, but leaves of joy,)

Roots and leaves unlike any but themselves,

Scents brought to men and women from the wild
woods, and from the pond-side,

Breast-sorrel and pinks of love — fingers that wind
around tighter than vines,

Gushes from the throats of birds, hid in the foliage
of trees, as the sun is risen,

Breezes of land and love — Breezes set from living
shores out to you on the living sea — to you,
O sailors!

Frost-mellowed berries, and Third Month twigs, of-
fered fresh to young persons wandering out in
the fields when the winter breaks up,

Love-buds, put before you and within you, whoever
you are,

Buds to be unfolded on the old terms,

If you bring the warmth of the sun to them, they will
open, and bring form, color, perfume, to you,

If you become the aliment and the wet, they will
become flowers, fruits, tall branches and trees,

They are comprised in you just as much as in them-
　　selves — perhaps more than in themselves,
They are not comprised in one season or succession,
　　but many successions,
They have come slowly up out of the earth and me,
　　and are to come slowly up out of you.

# 14.

NOT heat flames up and consumes,
Not sea-waves hurry in and out,
Not the air, delicious and dry, the air of the ripe
　　summer, bears lightly along white down-balls of
　　myriads of seeds, wafted, sailing gracefully, to
　　drop where they may,
Not these — O none of these, more than the flames
　　of me, consuming, burning for his love whom I
　　love !
O none, more than I, hurrying in and out;
Does the tide hurry, seeking something, and never
　　give up?　O I the same;
O nor down-balls, nor perfumes, nor the high
　　rain-emitting clouds, are borne through the open
　　air,
Any more than my Soul is borne through the open
　　air,
Wafted in all directions, O love, for friendship, for
　　you.

## 15.

O DROPS of me! trickle, slow drops,
Candid, from me falling — drip, bleeding drops,
From wounds made to free you whence you were
    prisoned,
From my face — from my forehead and lips,
From my breast — from within where I was con-
    cealed — Press forth, red drops — confession
    drops,
Stain every page — stain every song I sing, every
    word I say, bloody drops,
Let them know your scarlet heat — let them glisten,
Saturate them with yourself, all ashamed and wet,
Glow upon all I have written or shall write, bleed-
    ing drops,
Let it all be seen in your light, blushing drops.

## 16.

1. WHO is now reading this?

2. May-be one is now reading this who knows some
    wrong-doing of my past life,
  Or may-be a stranger is reading this who has secretly
    loved me,
  Or may-be one who meets all my grand assumptions
    and egotisms with derision,
  Or may-be one who is puzzled at me.

31

3. As if I were not puzzled at myself!

Or as if I never deride myself! (O conscience-struck!
O self-convicted!)

Or as if I do not secretly love strangers! (O tenderly,
a long time, and never avow it;)

Or as if I did not see, perfectly well, interior in
myself, the stuff of wrong-doing,

Or as if it could cease transpiring from me until it
must cease.

# 17.

Of him I love day and night, I dreamed I heard he
was dead,

And I dreamed I went where they had buried him I
love — but he was not in that place,

And I dreamed I wandered, searching among burial-
places, to find him,

And I found that every place was a burial-place,

The houses full of life were equally full of death,
(This house is now,)

The streets, the shipping, the places of amusement,
the Chicago, Boston, Philadelphia, the Manna-
hatta, were as full of the dead as of the living,

And fuller, O vastly fuller, of the dead than of the
living;

— And what I dreamed I will henceforth tell to every
person and age,

And I stand henceforth bound to what I dreamed;

And now I am willing to disregard burial-places, and
dispense with them,

And if the memorials of the dead were put up indifferently everywhere, even in the room where I eat or sleep, I should be satisfied,

And if the corpse of any one I love, or if my own corpse, be duly rendered to powder, and poured in the sea, I shall be satisfied,

Or if it be distributed to the winds, I shall be satisfied.

# 18.

CITY of my walks and joys!

City whom that I have lived and sung there will one day make you illustrious,

Not the pageants of you — not your shifting tableaux, your spectacles, repay me,

Not the interminable rows of your houses — nor the ships at the wharves,

Nor the processions in the streets, nor the bright windows, with goods in them,

Nor to converse with learned persons, or bear my share in the soiree or feast;

Not those — but, as I pass, O Manhattan! your frequent and swift flash of eyes offering me love,

Offering me the response of my own — these repay me,

Lovers, continual lovers, only repay me.

# 19.

1. Mind you the the timid models of the rest, the majority ?
   Long I minded them, but hence I will not — for I have adopted models for myself, and now offer them to The Lands.

2. Behold this swarthy and unrefined face — these gray eyes,
   This beard — the white wool, unclipt upon my neck,
   My brown hands, and the silent manner of me, without charm ;
   Yet comes one, a Manhattanese, and ever at parting, kisses me lightly on the lips with robust love,
   And I, in the public room, or on the crossing of the street, or on the ship's deck, kiss him in return ;
   We observe that salute of American comrades, land and sea,
   We are those two natural and nonchalant persons.

# 20.

I saw in Louisiana a live-oak growing,
All alone stood it, and the moss hung down from the branches,
Without any companion it grew there, uttering joyous leaves of dark green,
And its look, rude, unbending, lusty, made me think of myself,

But I wondered how it could utter joyous leaves,
    standing alone there, without its friend, its
    lover near — for I knew I could not,
And I broke off a twig with a certain number of
    leaves upon it, and twined around it a little
    moss,
And brought it away — and I have placed it in sight
    in my room,
It is not needed to remind me as of my own dear
    friends,
(For I believe lately I think of little else than of
    them,)
Yet it remains to me a curious token — it makes me
    think of manly love ;
For all that, and though the live-oak glistens there in
    Louisiana, solitary, in a wide flat space,
Uttering joyous leaves all its life, without a friend, a
    lover, near,
I know very well I could not.

## 21.

MUSIC always round me, unceasing, unbeginning —
    yet long untaught I did not hear,
But now the chorus I hear, and am elated,
A tenor, strong, ascending, with power and health,
    with glad notes of day-break I hear,
A soprano, at intervals, sailing buoyantly over the
    tops of immense waves,
A transparent base, shuddering lusciously under and
    through the universe,

The triumphant tutti — the funeral wailings, with
    sweet flutes and violins — All these I fill myself
    with;
I hear not the volumes of sound merely — I am
    moved by the exquisite meanings,
I listen to the different voices winding in and out,
    striving, contending with fiery vehemence to
    excel each other in emotion,
I do not think the performers know themselves — But
    now I think I begin to know them.

# 22.

Passing stranger! you do not know how longingly I
    look upon you,
You must be he I was seeking, or she I was seeking,
    (It comes to me, as of a dream,)
I have somewhere surely lived a life of joy with
    you,
All is recalled as we flit by each other, fluid, affec-
    tionate, chaste, matured,
You grew up with me, were a boy with me, or a girl
    with me,
I ate with you, and slept with you — your body has
    become not yours only, nor left my body mine
    only,
You give me the pleasure of your eyes, face, flesh, as
    we pass — you take of my beard, breast, hands,
    in return,
I am not to speak to you — I am to think of you
    when I sit alone, or wake at night alone,

I am to wait — I do not doubt I am to meet you
    again,
I am to see to it that I do not lose you.

# 23.

THIS moment as I sit alone, yearning and thoughtful,
    it seems to me there are other men in other
    lands, yearning and thoughtful;
It seems to me I can look over and behold them,
    in Germany, Italy, France, Spain — Or far, far
    away; in China, or in Russia or India — talking
    other dialects;
And it seems to me if I could know those men better,
    I should become attached to them, as I do to men
    in my own lands,
It seems to me they are as wise, beautiful, benevolent,
    as any in my own lands;
O I know we should be brethren and lovers,
I know I should be happy with them.

# 24.

I HEAR it is charged against me that I seek to destroy
    institutions;
But really I am neither for nor against institutions,
(What indeed have I in common with them ? — Or
    what with the destruction of them ?)

Only I will establish in the Mannahatta, and in every
     city of These States, inland and seaboard,
And in the fields and woods, and above every keel
     little or large, that dents the water,
Without edifices, or rules, or trustees, or any ar-
     gument,
The institution of the dear love of comrades.

## 25.

The prairie-grass dividing — its own odor breathing,
I demand of it the spiritual corresponding,
Demand the most copious and close companionship
     of men,
Demand the blades to rise of words, acts, beings,
Those of the open atmosphere, coarse, sunlit, fresh,
     nutritious,
Those that go their own gait, erect, stepping with
     freedom and command — leading, not following,
Those with a never-quell'd audacity — those with
     sweet and lusty flesh, clear of taint, choice and
     chary of its love-power,
Those that look carelessly in the faces of Presidents
     and Governors, as to say, *Who are you?*
Those of earth-born passion, simple, never constrained,
     never obedient,
Those of inland America.

## 26.

WE two boys together clinging,
One the other never leaving,
Up and down the roads going — North and South
excursions making,
Power enjoying — elbows stretching — fingers clutch-
ing,
Armed and fearless — eating, drinking, sleeping, lov-
ing,
No law less than ourselves owning — sailing, soldier-
ing, thieving, threatening,
Misers, menials, priests alarming — air breathing,
water drinking, on the turf or the sea-beach
dancing,
With birds singing — With fishes swimming — With
trees branching and leafing,
Cities wrenching, ease scorning, statutes mocking,
feebleness chasing,
Fulfilling our foray.

## 27.

O LOVE!
O dying — always dying!
O the burials of me, past and present!
O me, while I stride ahead, material, visible, imperi-
ous as ever!

O me, what I was for years, now dead, (I lament not
   — I am content;)
O to disengage myself from those corpses of me,
   which I turn and look at, where I cast them!
To pass on, (O living! always living!) and leave the
   corpses behind!

## 28.

When I peruse the conquered fame of heroes, and the
   victories of mighty generals, I do not envy the
   generals,
Nor the President in his Presidency, nor the rich in
   his great house;
But when I read of the brotherhood of lovers, how it
   was with them,
How through life, through dangers, odium, un-
   changing, long and long,
Through youth, and through middle and old age, how
   unfaltering, how affectionate and faithful they
   were,
Then I am pensive — I hastily put down the book,
   and walk away, filled with the bitterest envy.

## 29.

ONE flitting glimpse, caught through an interstice,
Of a crowd of workmen and drivers in a bar-room,
    around the stove, late of a winter night — And
    I unremarked, seated in a corner ;
Of a youth who loves me, and whom I love, silently
    approaching, and seating himself near, that he
    may hold me by the hand ;
A long while, amid the noises of coming and going
    — of drinking and oath and smutty jest,
There we two, content, happy in being together,
    speaking little, perhaps not a word.

## 30.

A PROMISE and gift to California,
Also to the great Pastoral Plains, and for Oregon:
Sojourning east a while longer, soon I travel to you,
    to remain, to teach robust American love ;
For I know very well that I and robust love belong
    among you, inland, and along the Western
    Sea,
For These States tend inland, and toward the Western
    Sea — and I will also.

# 31.

1. WHAT ship, puzzled at sea, cons for the true reck-
oning ?
Or, coming in, to avoid the bars, and follow the chan-
nel, a perfect pilot needs ?
Here, sailor ! Here, ship ! take aboard the most per-
fect pilot,
Whom, in a little boat, putting off, and rowing, I,
hailing you, offer.

2. What place is besieged, and vainly tries to raise the
siege ?
Lo ! I send to that place a commander, swift, brave,
immortal,
And with him horse and foot — and parks of artillery,
And artillerymen, the deadliest that ever fired gun.

# 32.

WHAT think you I take my pen in hand to record ?
The battle-ship, perfect-model'd, majestic, that I saw
pass the offing to-day under full sail ?
The splendors of the past day ? Or the splendor of the
night that envelops me ?
Or the vaunted glory and growth of the great city
spread around me ? — No ;
But I record of two simple men I saw to-day, on the
pier, in the midst of the crowd, parting the part-
ing of dear friends,

The one to remain hung on the other's neck, and pas-
    sionately kissed him,
While the one to depart, tightly prest the one to
    remain in his arms.

## 33.

No labor-saving machine,
Nor discovery have I made,
Nor will I be able to leave behind me any wealthy
    bequest to found a hospital or library,
Nor reminiscence of any deed of courage, for America,
Nor literary success, nor intellect — nor book for the
    book-shelf;
Only these carols, vibrating through the air, I leave,
For comrades and lovers.

## 34.

I DREAMED in a dream, I saw a city invincible to the
    attacks of the whole of the rest of the earth,
I dreamed that was the new City of Friends,
Nothing was greater there than the quality of robust
    love — it led the rest,
It was seen every hour in the actions of the men of
    that city,
And in all their looks and words.

## 35.

To you of New England,
To the man of the Seaside State, and of Pennsylvania,
To the Kanadian of the north — to the Southerner I
    love,
These, with perfect trust, to depict you as myself —
    the germs are in all men ;
I believe the main purport of These States is to found
    a superb friendship, exalté, previously unknown,
Because I perceive it waits, and has been always wait-
    ing, latent in all men.

## 36.

EARTH ! my likeness !
Though you look so impassive, ample and spheric
    there,
I now suspect that is not all ;
I now suspect there is something fierce in you, eligible
    to burst forth ;
For an athlete is enamoured of me — and I of him,
But toward him there is something fierce and terrible
    in me, eligible to burst forth,
I dare not tell it in words — not even in these songs.

## 37.

A LEAF for hand in hand!

You natural persons old and young! You on the
Eastern Sea, and you on the Western!

You on the Mississippi, and on all the branches and
bayous of the Mississippi!

You friendly boatmen and mechanics! You roughs!

You twain! And all processions moving along the
streets!

I wish to infuse myself among you till I see it com-
mon for you to walk hand in hand.

## 38.

PRIMEVAL my love for the woman I love,

O bride! O wife! more resistless, more enduring
than I can tell, the thought of you!

Then separate, as disembodied, the purest born,

The ethereal, the last athletic reality, my consolation,

I ascend — I float in the regions of your love, O man,

O sharer of my roving life.

## 39.

SOMETIMES with one I love, I fill myself with rage, for
fear I effuse unreturned love ;

But now I think there is no unreturned love — the
pay is certain, one way or another,

Doubtless I could not have perceived the universe,
or written one of my poems, if I had not freely
given myself to comrades, to love.

# 40.

THAT shadow, my likeness, that goes to and fro, seek-
ing a livelihood, chattering, chaffering,
How often I find myself standing and looking at it
where it flits,
How often I question and doubt whether that is really
me ;
But in these, and among my lovers, and carolling my
songs,
O I never doubt whether that is really me.

# 41.

1. AMONG the men and women, the multitude, I per-
ceive one picking me out by secret and divine
signs,
Acknowledging none else — not parent, wife, hus-
band, brother, child, any nearer than I am ;
Some are baffled — But that one is not — that one
knows me.

2. Lover and perfect equal !
I meant that you should discover me so, by my faint
indirections,
And I, when I meet you, mean to discover you by the
like in you.

# 42.

To the young man, many things to absorb, to engraft,
    to develop, I teach, to help him become élève of
    mine,
But if blood like mine circle not in his veins,
If he be not silently selected by lovers, and do not
    silently select lovers,
Of what use is it that he seek to become élève of
    mine ?

# 43.

O you whom I often and silently come where you
    are, that I may be with you,
As I walk by your side, or sit near, or remain in the
    same room with you,
Little you know the subtle electric fire that for your
    sake is playing within me.

# 44.

HERE my last words, and the most baffling,
Here the frailest leaves of me, and yet my strongest-
    lasting,
Here I shade down and hide my thoughts — I do not
    expose them,
And yet they expose me more than all my other
    poems.

# 45.

1. FULL of life, sweet-blooded, compact, visible,
   I, forty years old the Eighty-third Year of The States,
   To one a century hence, or any number of centuries
   hence,
   To you, yet unborn, these, seeking you.

2. When you read these, I, that was visible, am become
   invisible ;
   Now it is you, compact, visible, realizing my poems,
   seeking me,
   Fancying how happy you were, if I could be with
   you, and become your lover ;
   Be it as if I were with you. Be not too certain but I
   am now with you.

# CROSSING BROOKLYN FERRY.

1. FLOOD-TIDE below me! I watch you, face to face;
Clouds of the west! sun there half an hour high! I
see you also face to face.

2. Crowds of men and women attired in the usual cos-
tumes! how curious you are to me!
On the ferry-boats, the hundreds and hundreds that
cross, returning home, are more curious to me
than you suppose,
And you that shall cross from shore to shore years
hence, are more to me, and more in my med-
itations, than you might suppose.

3. The impalpable sustenance of me from all things, at
all hours of the day,
The simple, compact, well-joined scheme — myself
disintegrated, every one disintegrated, yet part
of the scheme,
The similitudes of the past, and those of the future,
The glories strung like beads on my smallest sights
and hearings — on the walk in the street, and
the passage over the river,

(379)

The current rushing so swiftly, and swimming with
me far away,

The others that are to follow me, the ties between me
and them,

The certainty of others — the life, love, sight, hear-
ing of others.

4. Others will enter the gates of the ferry, and cross
from shore to shore,

Others will watch the run of the flood-tide,

Others will see the shipping of Manhattan north and
west, and the heights of Brooklyn to the south
and east,

Others will see the islands large and small,

Fifty years hence, others will see them as they cross,
the sun half an hour high,

A hundred years hence, or ever so many hundred
years hence, others will see them,

Will enjoy the sunset, the pouring in of the flood-
tide, the falling back to the sea of the ebb-tide.

5. It avails not, neither time or place — distance avails
not,

I am with you, you men and women of a generation,
or ever so many generations hence,

I project myself — also I return — I am with you, and
know how it is.

6. Just as you feel when you look on the river and sky,
so I felt,

Just as any of you is one of a living crowd, I was one
of a crowd,

Just as you are refreshed by the gladness of the river,
and the bright flow, I was refreshed,

Just as you stand and lean on the rail, yet hurry with
the swift current, I stood, yet was hurried,
Just as you look on the numberless masts of ships,
and the thick-stemmed pipes of steamboats, I
looked.

7. I too many and many a time crossed the river, the
sun half an hour high,
I watched the Twelfth Month sea-gulls — I saw them
high in the air, floating with motionless wings,
oscillating their bodies,
I saw how the glistening yellow lit up parts of their
bodies, and left the rest in strong shadow,
I saw the slow-wheeling circles, and the gradual
edging toward the south.

8. I too saw the reflection of the summer sky in the
water,
Had my eyes dazzled by the shimmering track of
beams,
Looked at the fine centrifugal spokes of light round
the shape of my head in the sun-lit water,
Looked on the haze on the hills southward and south-
westward,
Looked on the vapor as it flew in fleeces tinged with
violet,
Looked toward the lower bay to notice the arriving
ships,
Saw their approach, saw aboard those that were near
me,
Saw the white sails of schooners and sloops, saw the
ships at anchor,
The sailors at work in the rigging, or out astride the
spars,

The round masts, the swinging motion of the hulls, the slender serpentine pennants,

The large and small steamers in motion, the pilots in their pilot-houses,

The white wake left by the passage, the quick tremulous whirl of the wheels,

The flags of all nations, the falling of them at sun-set,

The scallop-edged waves in the twilight, the ladled cups, the frolicsome crests and glistening,

The stretch afar growing dimmer and dimmer, the gray walls of the granite store-houses by the docks,

On the river the shadowy group, the big steam-tug closely flanked on each side by the barges — the hay-boat, the belated lighter,

On the neighboring shore, the fires from the foundry chimneys burning high and glaringly into the night,

Casting their flicker of black, contrasted with wild red and yellow light, over the tops of houses, and down into the clefts of streets.


9. These, and all else, were to me the same as they are to you,

I project myself a moment to tell you — also I return.


10. I loved well those cities,

I loved well the stately and rapid river,

The men and women I saw were all near to me,

Others the same — others who look back on me, because I looked forward to them,

(The time will come, though I stop here to-day and to-night.)

11. What is it, then, between us ?
   What is the count of the scores or hundreds of years
   between us ?

12. Whatever it is, it avails not — distance avails not, and
   place avails not.

13. I too lived, (I was of old Brooklyn,)
   I too walked the streets of Manhattan Island, and
   bathed in the waters around it,
   I too felt the curious abrupt questionings stir within
   me,
   In the day, among crowds of people, sometimes they
   came upon me,
   In my walks home late at night, or as I lay in my
   bed, they came upon me.

14. I too had been struck from the float forever held in
   solution,
   I too had received identity by my body,
   That I was, I knew was of my body — and what I
   should be, I knew I should be of my body.

15. It is not upon you alone the dark patches fall,
   The dark threw patches down upon me also,
   The best I had done seemed to me blank and sus-
   picious,
   My great thoughts, as I supposed them, were they not
   in reality meagre ? would not people laugh
   at me ?

16. It is not you alone who know what it is to be evil,
   I am he who knew what it was to be evil,

I too knitted the old knot of contrariety,
Blabbed, blushed, resented, lied, stole, grudged,
Had guile, anger, lust, hot wishes I dared not speak,
Was wayward, vain, greedy, shallow, sly, cowardly,
    malignant,
The wolf, the snake, the hog, not wanting in me,
The cheating look, the frivolous word, the adulterous
    wish, not wanting,
Refusals, hates, postponements, meanness, laziness,
    none of these wanting.

17. But I was a Manhattanese, free, friendly, and proud!
I was called by my nighest name by clear loud voices
    of young men as they saw me approaching or
    passing,
Felt their arms on my neck as I stood, or the neg-
    ligent leaning of their flesh against me as I sat,
Saw many I loved in the street, or ferry-boat, or pub-
    lic assembly, yet never told them a word,
Lived the same life with the rest, the same old laugh-
    ing, gnawing, sleeping,
Played the part th    still looks back on the actor or
    actress,
The same old rôle, the rôle that is what we make it,
    as great as we like,
Or as small as we like, or both great and
    small.

18. Closer yet I approach you,
What thought you have of me, I had as much of you
    — I laid in my stores in advance,
I considered long and seriously of you before you
    were born.

19. Who was to know what should come home to me?
    Who knows but I am enjoying this?
    Who knows but I am as good as looking at you now,
    for all you cannot see me?


20. It is not you alone, nor I alone,
    Not a few races, nor a few generations, nor a few
    centuries,
    It is that each came, or comes, or shall come, from its
    due emission, without fail, either now, or then, or
    henceforth.


21. Every thing indicates — the smallest does, and the
    largest does,
    A necessary film envelops all, and envelops the Soul
    for a proper time.


22. Now I am curious what sight can ever be more stately
    and admirable to me than my mast-hemm'd Man-
    hatta,
    My river and sun-set, and my scallop-edged waves of
    flood-tide,
    The sea-gulls oscillating their bodies, the hay-boat in
    the twilight, and the belated lighter;
    Curious what Gods can exceed these that clasp me
    by the hand, and with voices I love call me
    promptly and loudly by my nighest name as I
    approach,
    Curious what is more subtle than this which ties me
    to the woman or man that looks in my face,
    Which fuses me into you now, and pours my meaning
    into you.

33

23. We understand, then, do we not?

What I promised without mentioning it, have you not
accepted?

What the study could not teach — what the preaching
could not accomplish is accomplished, is it not?

What the push of reading could not start is started by
me personally, is it not?


24. Flow on, river! flow with the flood-tide, and ebb with
the ebb-tide!

Frolic on, crested and scallop-edged waves!

Gorgeous clouds of the sunset! drench with your
splendor me, or the men and women generations
after me;

Cross from shore to shore, countless crowds of pas-
sengers!

Stand up, tall masts of Mannahatta! — stand up,
beautiful hills of Brooklyn!

Bully for you! you proud, friendly, free Manhat-
tanese!

Throb, baffled and curious brain! throw out questions
and answers!

Suspend here and everywhere, eternal float of solu-
tion!

Blab, blush, lie, steal, you or I or any one after us!

Gaze, loving and thirsting eyes, in the house, or street,
or public assembly!

Sound out, voices of young men! loudly and musically
call me by my nighest name!

Live, old life! play the part that looks back on the
actor or actress!

Play the old rôle, the rôle that is great or small,
according as one makes it!

Consider, you who peruse me, whether I may not in
    unknown ways be looking upon you ;

Be firm, rail over the river, to support those who lean
    idly, yet haste with the hasting current ;

Fly on, sea-birds ! fly sideways, or wheel in large
    circles high in the air ;

Receive the summer-sky, you water ! and faithfully
    hold it, till all downcast eyes have time to take
    it from you ;

Diverge, fine spokes of light, from the shape of my
    head, or any one's head, in the sun-lit water ;

Come on, ships from the lower bay ! pass up or down,
    white-sailed schooners, sloops, lighters !

Flaunt away, flags of all nations ! be duly lowered at
    sunset ;

Burn high your fires, foundry chimneys ! cast black
    shadows at nightfall ! cast red and yellow light
    over the tops of the houses ;

Appearances, now or henceforth, indicate what you
    are ;

You necessary film, continue to envelop the Soul ;

About my body for me, and your body for you, be
    hung our divinest aromas ;

Thrive, cities ! bring your freight, bring your shows,
    ample and sufficient rivers ;

Expand, being than which none else is perhaps more
    spiritual ;

Keep your places, objects than which none else is
    more lasting.


25. We descend upon you and all things — we arrest you
    all,

We realize the Soul only by you, you faithful solids
    and fluids,

Through you color, form, location, sublimity, ideality,
Through you every proof, comparison, and all the
suggestions and determinations of ourselves.

26. You have waited, you always wait, you dumb, beauti-
ful ministers! you novices!
We receive you with free sense at last, and are
insatiate henceforward,
Not you any more shall be able to foil us, or with-
hold yourselves from us,
We use you, and do not cast you aside — we plant
you permanently within us,
We fathom you not — we love you — there is per-
fection in you also,
You furnish your parts toward eternity,
Great or small, you furnish your parts toward the
Soul.

# LONGINGS FOR HOME.

O MAGNET-SOUTH! O glistening, perfumed South! My
South!
O quick mettle, rich blood, impulse, and love! Good
and evil! O all dear to me!
O dear to me my birth-things — All moving things,
and the trees where I was born — the grains,
plants, rivers;
Dear to me my own slow sluggish rivers where they
flow, distant, over flats of silvery sands, or
through swamps,
Dear to me the Roanoke, the Savannah, the Altama-
haw, the Pedee, the Tombigbee, the Santee, the
Coosa, and the Sabine;
O pensive, far away wandering, I return with my Soul
to haunt their banks again,
Again in Florida I float on transparent lakes — I float
on the Okeechobee — I cross the hummock land,
or through pleasant openings, or dense forests,
I see the parrots in the woods — I see the papaw tree
and the blossoming titi;
Again, sailing in my coaster, on deck, I coast off
Georgia — I coast up the Carolinas,
I see where the live-oak is growing — I see where the
yellow-pine, the scented bay-tree, the lemon and
orange, the cypress, the graceful palmetto;
I pass rude sea-headlands and enter Pamlico Sound
through an inlet, and dart my vision inland,

33 *                                        (389)

O the cotton plant! the growing fields of rice, sugar,
    hemp!

The cactus, guarded with thorns — the laurel-tree,
    with large white flowers,

The range afar — the richness and barrenness — the
    old woods charged with mistletoe and trailing
    moss,

The piney odor and the gloom — the awful natural
    stillness, (Here in these dense swamps the free-
    booter carries his gun, and the fugitive slave has
    his concealed hut;)

O the strange fascination of these half-known, half-
    impassable swamps, infested by reptiles, resound-
    ing with the bellow of the alligator, the sad noises
    of the night-owl and the wild-cat, and the whirr
    of the rattlesnake;

The mocking-bird, the American mimic, singing all
    the forenoon — singing through the moon-lit
    night,

The humming-bird, the wild-turkey, the raccoon, the
    opossum;

A Tennessee corn-field — the tall, graceful, long-leaved
    corn — slender, flapping, bright green, with tas-
    sels — with beautiful ears, each well-sheathed in
    its husk,

An Arkansas prairie — a sleeping lake, or still bayou;

O my heart! O tender and fierce pangs — I can stand
    them not — I will depart;

O to be a Virginian, where I grew up! O to be a
    Carolinian!

O longings irrepressible! O I will go back to old Ten-
    nessee, and never wander more!

# MESSENGER LEAVES.

## To You, Whoever You Are.

WHOEVER you are, I fear you are walking the walks of
    dreams,
I fear those realities are to melt from under your feet
    and hands ;
Even now, your features, joys, speech, house, trade,
    manners, troubles, follies, costume, crimes, dis-
    sipate away from you,
Your true Soul and body appear before me,
They stand forth out of affairs — out of commerce,
    shops, law, science, work, farms, clothes, the
    house, medicine, print, buying, selling, eating,
    drinking, suffering, dying.

2. Whoever you are, now I place my hand upon you,
    that you be my poem,
I whisper with my lips close to your ear,
I have loved many women and men, but I love none
    better than you.

3. O I have been dilatory and dumb,
  I should have made my way straight to you long ago,
I should have blabbed nothing but you, I should have
    chanted nothing but you.

(391)

4. I will leave all, and come and make the hymns of
   you ;
   None have understood you, but I understand you,
   None have done justice to you — you have not done
   justice to yourself,
   None but have found you imperfect — I only find no
   imperfection in you,
   None but would subordinate you — I only am he who
   will never consent to subordinate you,
   I only am he who places over you no master, owner,
   better, God, beyond what waits intrinsically in
   yourself.

5. Painters have painted their swarming groups, and the
   centre figure of all,
   From the head of the centre figure spreading a nim-
   bus of gold-colored light,
   But I paint myriads of heads, but paint no head with-
   out its nimbus of gold-colored light,
   From my hand, from the brain of every man and
   woman it streams, effulgently flowing forever.

6. O I could sing such grandeurs and glories about you !
   You have not known what you are — you have slum-
   bered upon yourself all your life,
   Your eyelids have been the same as closed most of
   the time,
   What you have done returns already in mockeries,
   Your thrift, knowledge, prayers, if they do not return
   in mockeries, what is their return ?

7. The mockeries are not you,
   Underneath them, and within them, I see you lurk,
   I pursue you where none else has pursued you,

Silence, the desk, the flippant expression, the night,
the accustomed routine, if these conceal you from
others, or from yourself, they do not conceal you
from me,

The shaved face, the unsteady eye, the impure com-
plexion, if these balk others, they do not balk
me,

The pert apparel, the deformed attitude, drunken-
ness, greed, premature death, all these I part
aside,

I track through your windings and turnings — I come
upon you where you thought eye should never
come upon you.

8. There is no endowment in man or woman that is not
tallied in you,

There is no virtue, no beauty, in man or woman, but
as good is in you,

No pluck, no endurance in others, but as good is
in you,

No pleasure waiting for others, but an equal pleasure
waits for you.

9. As for me, I give nothing to any one, except I give
the like carefully to you,

I sing the songs of the glory of none, not God, sooner
than I sing the songs of the glory of you.

10. Whoever you are! claim your own at any hazard!

These shows of the east and west are tame compared
to you,

These immense meadows — these interminable rivers
— you are immense and interminable as they,

These furies, elements, storms, motions of Nature,
    throes of apparent dissolution — you are he or
    she who is master or mistress over them,
Master or mistress in your own right over Nature,
    elements, pain, passion, dissolution.


11. The hopples fall from your ankles — you find an un-
    failing sufficiency,
    Old or young, male or female, rude, low, rejected by
      the rest, whatever you are promulges itself,
    Through birth, life, death, burial, the means are pro-
      vided, nothing is scanted,
    Through angers, losses, ambition, ignorance, ennui,
      what you are picks its way.

# To a Foiled Revolter or Revoltress.

1. Courage! my brother or my sister!
    Keep on! Liberty is to be subserved, whatever occurs;
    That is nothing, that is quelled by one or two failures,
      or any number of failures,
    Or by the indifference or ingratitude of the people,
      or by any unfaithfulness,
    Or the show of the tushes of power — soldiers, cannon,
      penal statutes.


2. What we believe in waits latent forever through
    Asia, Africa, Europe, North and South America,
    Australia, Cuba, and all the islands and archi-
    pelagoes of the sea.

3. What we believe in invites no one, promises nothing,
   sits in calmness and light, is positive and com-
   posed, knows no discouragement,
   Waits patiently its time — a year — a century — a
   hundred centuries.

4. The battle rages with many a loud alarm and fre-
   quent advance and retreat,
   The infidel triumphs — or supposes he triumphs,
   The prison, scaffold, garrote, hand-cuffs, iron necklace
   and anklet, lead-balls, do their work,
   The named and unnamed heroes pass to other
   spheres,
   The great speakers and writers are exiled — they lie
   sick in distant lands,
   The cause is asleep — the strongest throats are still,
   choked with their own blood,
   The young men drop their eyelashes toward the
   ground when they meet,
   But for all this, liberty has not gone out of the place,
   nor the infidel entered into possession.

5. When liberty goes out of a place, it is not the first
   to go, nor the second or third to go,
   It waits for all the rest to go — it is the last.

6. When there are no more memories of the superb
   lovers of the nations of the world,
   The superb lovers' names scouted in the public
   gatherings by the lips of the orators,
   Boys not christened after them, but christened after
   traitors and murderers instead,

Tyrants' and priests' successes really acknowledged anywhere, for all the ostensible appearance,

You or I walking abroad upon the earth, elated at the sight of slaves, no matter who they are,

And when all life, and all the Souls of men and women are discharged from any part of the earth,

Then shall the instinct of liberty be discharged from that part of the earth,

Then shall the infidel and the tyrant come into possession.

7. Then courage!
For till all ceases, neither must you cease.

8. I do not know what you are for, (I do not what I am for myself, nor what any thing is for,)
But I will search carefully for it in being foiled,
In defeat, poverty, imprisonment — for they too are great.

9. Did we think victory great?
So it is — But now it seems to me, when it cannot be helped, that defeat is great,
And that death and dismay are great.

# To Him that was Crucified.

My spirit to yours, dear brother,

Do not mind because many, sounding your name, do not understand you,

I do not sound your name, but I understand you, (there are others also;)

I specify you with joy, O my comrade, to salute you, and to salute those who are with you, before and since — and those to come also,

That we all labor together, transmitting the same charge and succession;

We few, equals, indifferent of lands, indifferent of times,

We, enclosers of all continents, all castes — allowers of all theologies,

Compassionaters, perceivers, rapport of men,

We walk silent among disputes and assertions, but reject not the disputers, nor any thing that is asserted,

We hear the bawling and din — we are reached at by divisions, jealousies, recriminations on every side,

They close peremptorily upon us, to surround us, my comrade,

Yet we walk unheld, free, the whole earth over, journeying up and down, till we make our ineffaceable mark upon time and the diverse eras,

Till we saturate time and eras, that the men and women of races, ages to come, may prove brethren and lovers, as we are.

# To One shortly To Die.

1. FROM all the rest I single out you, having a message
   for you :
   You are to die — Let others tell you what they
   please, I cannot prevaricate,
   I am exact and merciless, but I love you — There is
   no escape for you.

2. Softly I lay my right hand upon you — you just
   feel it,
   I do not argue — I bend my head close, and half-
   envelop it,
   I sit quietly by — I remain faithful,
   I am more than nurse, more than parent or neighbor,
   I absolve you from all except yourself, spiritual,
   bodily — that is eternal,
   (The corpse you will leave will be but excremen-
   titious.)

3. The sun bursts through in unlooked-for directions!
   Strong thoughts fill you, and confidence — you smile!
   You forget you are sick, as I forget you are sick,
   You do not see the medicines — you do not mind the
   weeping friends — I am with you,
   I exclude others from you — there is nothing to be
   commiserated,
   I do not commiserate — I congratulate you.

# To a Common Prostitute.

1. Be composed — be at ease with me — I am Walt
   Whitman, liberal and lusty as Nature,
   Not till the sun excludes you, do I exclude you,
   Not till the waters refuse to glisten for you, and the
   leaves to rustle for you, do my words refuse to
   glisten and rustle for you.

2. My girl, I appoint with you an appointment — and I
   charge you that you make preparation to be
   worthy to meet me,
   And I charge you that you be patient and perfect till
   I come.

3. Till then, I salute you with a significant look, that
   you do not forget me.

# To Rich Givers.

What you give me, I cheerfully accept,
A little sustenance, a hut and garden, a little money
— these as I rendezvous with my poems,
A traveller's lodging and breakfast as I journey
through The States — Why should I be ashamed
to own such gifts? Why to advertise for them?
For I myself am not one who bestows nothing upon
man and woman,
For I know that what I bestow upon any man or
woman is no less than the entrance to all the
gifts of the universe.

# To a Pupil.

1. Is reform needed ? Is it through you ?
The greater the reform needed, the greater the PER-
SONALITY you need to accomplish it.

2. You ! do you not see how it would serve to have eyes,
blood, complexion, clean and sweet ?
Do you not see how it would serve to have such a
body and Soul, that when you enter the crowd,
an atmosphere of desire and command enters
with you, and every one is impressed with your
personality ?

3. O the magnet ! the flesh over and over !
Go, mon cher ! if need be, give up all else, and com-
mence to-day to inure yourself to pluck, reality,
self-esteem, definiteness, elevatedness,
Rest not, till you rivet and publish yourself of your
own personality.

# To The States,

## To Identify the 16th, 17th, or 18th Prefidentiad.

WHY reclining, interrogating ? Why myself and all
drowsing ?
What deepening twilight ! Scum floating atop of the
waters !
Who are they, as bats and night-dogs, askant in the
Capitol ?

What a filthy Presidentiad! (O south, your torrid
    suns! O north, your arctic freezings!)
Are those really Congressmen? Are those the great
    Judges? Is that the President?
Then I will sleep a while yet — for I see that These
    States sleep, for reasons;
(With gathering murk — with muttering thunder and
    lambent shoots, we all duly awake,
South, north, east, west, inland and seaboard, we will
    surely awake.)

# To a Cantatrice.

Here, take this gift!
I was reserving it for some hero, orator, or general,
One who should serve the good old cause, the prog-
    ress and freedom of the race, the cause of
    my Soul;
But I see that what I was reserving belongs to you
    just as much as to any.

# Walt Whitman's Caution.

To The States, or any one of them, or any city of
    The States, *Resist much*, *obey little*,
Once unquestioning obedience, once fully enslaved,
Once fully enslaved, no nation, state, city, of this
    earth, ever afterward resumes its liberty.

34*

# To a President.

ALL you are doing and saying is to America dangled
mirages,
You have not learned of Nature — of the politics of
Nature, you have not learned the great ampli-
tude, rectitude, impartiality,
You have not seen that only such as they are for
These States,
And that what is less than they, must sooner or later
lift off from These States.

# To other Lands.

I HEAR you have been asking for something to repre-
sent the new race, our self-poised Democracy,
Therefore I send you my poems, that you behold in
them what you wanted.

# To Old Age.

I SEE in you the estuary that enlarges and spreads
itself grandly as it pours in the great sea.

# To You.

LET us twain walk aside from the rest;
Now we are together privately, do you discard cer-
    emony,
Come! vouchsafe to me what has yet been vouchsafed
    to none — Tell me the whole story,
Tell me what you would not tell your brother, wife,
    husband, or physician.

# To You.

STRANGER! if you, passing, meet me, and desire to
    speak to me, why should you not speak to me?
And why should I not speak to you?

# MANNAHATTA.

I WAS asking for something specific and perfect for
my city, and behold! here is the aboriginal
name!
Now I see what there is in a name, a word, liquid,
sane, unruly, musical, self-sufficient,
I see that the word of my city, is that word up there,
Because I see that word nested in nests of water-bays,
superb, with tall and wonderful spires,
Rich, hemmed thick all around with sailships and
steamships—an island sixteen miles long, solid-
founded,
Numberless crowded streets — high growths of iron,
slender, strong, light, splendidly uprising toward
clear skies;
Tides swift and ample, well-loved by me, toward sun-
down,
The flowing sea-currents, the little islands, the larger
adjoining islands, the heights, the villas,
The countless masts, the white shore-steamers, the
lighters, the ferry-boats, the black sea-steamers,
well-model'd;
The down-town streets, the jobbers' houses of business
— the houses of business of the ship-merchants,
and money-brokers — the river-streets,

Immigrants arriving, fifteen or twenty thousand in a
week,

The carts hauling goods — the manly race of drivers
of horses — the brown-faced sailors,

The summer-air, the bright sun shining, and the sail-
ing clouds aloft,

The winter snows, the sleigh-bells — the broken ice in
the river, passing along, up or down, with the
flood-tide or ebb-tide ;

The mechanics of the city, the masters, well-formed,
beautiful-faced, looking you straight in the eyes ;

Trottoirs thronged — vehicles — Broadway — the wo-
men — the shops and shows,

The parades, processions, bugles playing, flags flying,
drums beating ;

A million people — manners free and superb — open
voices — hospitality — the most courageous and
friendly young men ;

The free city ! no slaves ! no owners of slaves !

The beautiful city ! the city of hurried and sparkling
waters ! the city of spires and masts !

The city nested in bays ! my city !

The city of such women, I am mad to be with them !
I will return after death to be with them !

The city of such young men, I swear I cannot live
happy, without I often go talk, walk, eat, drink,
sleep, with them !

# FRANCE,

## The 18th Year of Thefe States.

1. A GREAT year and place,
A harsh, discordant, natal scream rising, to touch the
mother's heart closer than any yet.

2. I walked the shores of my Eastern Sea,
Heard over the waves the little voice,
Saw the divine infant, where she woke, mournfully
wailing, amid the roar of cannon, curses, shouts,
crash of falling buildings,
Was not so sick from the blood in the gutters running
— nor from the single corpses, nor those in heaps,
nor those borne away in the tumbrils,
Was not so desperate at the battues of death — was
not so shocked at the repeated fusillades of the
guns.

3. Pale, silent, stern, what could I say to that long-
accrued retribution?
Could I wish humanity different?
Could I wish the people made of wood and stone?
Or that there be no justice in destiny or time?

(406)

4. O Liberty ! O mate for me !
   Here too keeps the blaze, the bullet and the axe, in
       reserve, to fetch them out in case of need,
   Here too, though long deprest, still is not destroyed,
   Here too could rise at last, murdering and extatic,
   Here too would demand full arrears of vengeance.

5. Hence I sign this salute over the sea,
   And I do not deny that terrible red birth and baptism,
   But remember the little voice that I heard wailing —
       and wait with perfect trust, no matter how long,
   And from to-day, sad and cogent, I maintain the
       bequeath'd cause, as for all lands,
   And I send these words to Paris, with my love,
   And I guess some chansonniers there will understand
       them,
   For I guess there is latent music yet in France —
       floods of it,
   O I hear already the bustle of instruments — they
       will soon be drowning all that would interrupt
       them,
   O I think the east wind brings a triumphal and free
       march,
   It reaches hither — it swells me to joyful madness,
   I will run transpose it in words, to justify it,
   I will yet sing a song for you, ma femme.

# THOUGHTS.

## 1.

OF the visages of things — And of piercing through
to the accepted hells beneath ;
Of ugliness — To me there is just as much in it as
there is in beauty — And now the ugliness of
human beings is acceptable to me ;
Of detected persons — To me, detected persons are
not, in any respect, worse than undetected per-
sons — and are not in any respect worse than I
am myself ;
Of criminals — To me, any judge, or any juror, is
equally criminal — and any reputable person is
also — and the President is also.

## 2.

OF waters, forests, hills,
Of the earth at large, whispering through medium
of me ;
Of vista — Suppose some sight in arriere, through the
formative chaos, presuming the growth, fulness,
life, now attained on the journey;

(But I see the road continued, and the journey ever
    continued ;)
Of what was once lacking on the earth, and in due
    time has become supplied — And of what will
    yet be supplied,
Because all I see and know, I believe to have purport
    in what will yet be supplied.

## 3.

OF persons arrived at high positions, ceremonies,
    wealth, scholarships, and the like,
To me, all that those persons have arrived at, sinks
    away from them, except as it results to their
    bodies and Souls,
So that often to me they appear gaunt and naked,
And often, to me, each one mocks the others, and
    mocks himself or herself,
And of each one, the core of life, namely happiness,
    is full of the rotten excrement of maggots,
And often, to me, those men and women pass un-
    wittingly the true realities of life, and go toward
    false realities,
And often, to me, they are alive after what custom
    has served them, but nothing more,
And often, to me, they are sad, hasty, unwaked son-
    nambules, walking the dusk.

## 4.

OF ownership — As if one fit to own things could not
at pleasure enter upon all, and incorporate them
into himself or herself ;

Of Equality — As if it harmed me, giving others the
same chances and rights as myself — As if it
were not indispensable to my own rights that
others possess the same ;

Of Justice — As if Justice could be any thing but
the same ample law, expounded by natural
judges and saviours,

As if it might be this thing or that thing, according
to decisions.

## 5.

As I sit with others, at a great feast, suddenly, while
the music is playing,

To my mind, (whence it comes I know not,) spectral,
in mist, of a wreck at sea,

Of the flower of the marine science of fifty genera-
tions, foundered off the Northeast coast, and
going down — Of the steamship Arctic going
down,

Of the veiled tableau — Women gathered together
on deck, pale, heroic, waiting the moment that
draws so close — O the moment !

O the huge sob — A few bubbles — the white foam
    spirting up — And then the women gone,
Sinking there, while the passionless wet flows on —
    And I now pondering, Are those women indeed
    gone ?
Are Souls drowned and destroyed so ?
Is only matter triumphant ?

# 6.

Of what I write from myself — As if that were not
    the resumé ;
Of Histories — As if such, however complete, were
    not less complete than my poems ;
As if the shreds, the records of nations, could possibly
    be as lasting as my poems ;
As if here were not the amount of all nations, and of
    all the lives of heroes.

# 7.

Of obedience, faith, adhesiveness ;
As I stand aloof and look, there is to me something
    profoundly affecting in large masses of men, fol-
    lowing the lead of those who do not believe in
    men.

# UNNAMED LANDS.

———

1. NATIONS ten thousand years before These States, and many times ten thousand years before These States,

   Garnered clusters of ages, that men and women like us grew up and travelled their course, and passed on;

   What vast-built cities — What orderly republics — What pastoral tribes and nomads,

   What histories, rulers, heroes, perhaps transcending all others,

   What laws, customs, wealth, arts, traditions,

   What sort of marriage — What costumes — What physiology and phrenology,

   What of liberty and slavery among them — What they thought of death and the Soul,

   Who were witty and wise — Who beautiful and poetic — Who brutish and undeveloped,

   Not a mark, not a record remains — And yet all remains.

2. O I know that those men and women were not for nothing, any more than we are for nothing,

(412)

I know that they belong to the scheme of the world every bit as much as we now belong to it, and as all will henceforth belong to it.

3. Afar they stand — yet near to me they stand,
Some with oval countenances, learned and calm,
Some naked and savage — Some like huge collections of insects,
Some in tents — herdsmen, patriarchs, tribes, horsemen,
Some prowling through woods — Some living peaceably on farms, laboring, reaping, filling barns,
Some traversing paved avenues, amid temples, palaces, factories, libraries, shows, courts, theatres, wonderful monuments.

4. Are those billions of men really gone ?
Are those women of the old experience of the earth gone ?
Do their lives, cities, arts, rest only with us ?
Did they achieve nothing for good, for themselves ?

5. I believe of all those billions of men and women that filled the unnamed lands, every one exists this hour, here or elsewhere, invisible to us, in exact proportion to what he or she grew from in life, and out of what he or she did, felt, became, loved, sinned, in life.

6. I believe that was not the end of those nations, or any person of them, any more than this shall be the end of my nation, or of me ;

Of their languages, phrenology, government, coins, med-
als, marriage, literature, products, games, juris-
prudence, wars, manners, amativeness, crimes,
prisons, slaves, heroes, poets, I suspect their re-
sults curiously await in the yet unseen world —
counterparts of what accrued to them in the seen
world,
I suspect I shall meet them there,
I suspect I shall there find each old particular of those
unnamed lands.

## KOSMOS.

WHO includes diversity, and is Nature,
Who is the amplitude of the earth, and the coarseness
and sexuality of the earth, and the great charity
of the earth, and the equilibrium also,
Who has not looked forth from the windows, the eyes,
for nothing, or whose brain held audience with
messengers for nothing ;
Who contains believers and disbelievers — Who is the
most majestic lover ;
Who holds duly his or her triune proportion of realism,
spiritualism, and of the æsthetic, or intellectual,
Who, having considered the body, finds all its organs
and parts good ;
Who, out of the theory of the earth, and of his or her
body, understands by subtle analogies, the theory
of a city, a poem, and of the large politics of
These States ;

Who believes not only in our globe, with its sun and
    moon, but in other globes, with their suns and
    moons ;
Who, constructing the house of himself or herself, not
    for a day, but for all time, sees races, eras, dates,
    generations,
The past, the future, dwelling there, like space, insep-
    arable together.

## A HAND–MIRROR.

HOLD it up sternly ! See this it sends back ! (Who is
    it ? Is it you ?)
Outside fair costume — within, ashes and filth,
No more a flashing eye — no more a sonorous voice
    or springy step,
Now some slave's eye, voice, hands, step,
A drunkard's breath, unwholesome eater's face, ve-
    nerealee's flesh,
Lungs rotting away piecemeal, stomach sour and
    cankerous,
Joints rheumatic, bowels clogged with abomination,
Blood circulating dark and poisonous streams,
Words babble, hearing and touch callous,
No brain, no heart left — no magnetism of sex ;
Such, from one look in this looking-glass ere you go
    hence,
Such a result so soon — and from such a beginning !

## BEGINNERS.

How they are provided for upon the earth, (appear-
    ing at intervals,)
How dear and dreadful they are to the earth,
How they inure to themselves as much as to any —
    What a paradox appears, their age,
How people respond to them, yet know them not,
How there is something relentless in their fate, all
    times,
How all times mischoose the objects of their adulation
    and reward,
And how the same inexorable price must still be paid
    for the same great purchase.


## TESTS.

ALL submit to them, where they sit, inner, secure,
    unapproachable to analysis, in the Soul;
Not traditions — not the outer authorities are the
    judges — they are the judges of outer authori-
    ties, and of all traditions,
They corroborate as they go, only whatever corrobo-
    rates themselves, and touches themselves,
For all that, they have it forever in themselves to cor-
    roborate far and near, without one exception.

## SAVANTISM.

THITHER, as I look, I see each result and glory re-
tracing itself and nestling close, always obli-
gated;
Thither hours, months, years — thither trades, com-
pacts, establishments, even the most minute,
Thither every-day life, speech, utensils, politics, per-
sons, estates,
Thither we also, I with my leaves and songs, trustful,
admirant,
As a father, to his father going, takes his children
along with him.

## PERFECTIONS.

ONLY themselves understand themselves, and the like
of themselves,
As Souls only understand Souls.

# SAYS.

### 1.

I say whatever tastes sweet to the most perfect person, that is finally right.

### 2.

I say nourish a great intellect, a great brain;
If I have said anything to the contrary, I hereby retract it.

### 3.

I say man shall not hold property in man;
I say the least developed person on earth is just as important and sacred to himself or herself, as the most developed person is to himself or herself.

### 4.

I say where liberty draws not the blood out of slavery, there slavery draws the blood out of liberty,
I say the word of the good old cause in These States, and resound it hence over the world.

## 5.

I say the human shape or face is so great, it must
never be made ridiculous;
I say for ornaments nothing outre can be allowed,
And that anything is most beautiful without orna-
ment,
And that exaggerations will be sternly revenged in
your own physiology, and in other persons' phys-
iology also;
And I say that clean-shaped children can be jetted
and conceived only where natural forms prevail
in public, and the human face and form are
never caricatured;
And I say that genius need never more be turned to
romances,
(For facts properly told, how mean appear all
romances.)

## 6.

I say the word of lands fearing nothing — I will
have no other land;
I say discuss all and expose all — I am for every
topic openly;
I say there can be no salvation for These States with-
out innovators — without free tongues, and ears
willing to hear the tongues;
And I announce as a glory of These States, that
they respectfully listen to propositions, reforms,
fresh views and doctrines, from successions of
men and women,
Each age with its own growth.

### 7.

I HAVE said many times that materials and the Soul
    are great, and that all depends on physique ;
Now I reverse what I said, and affirm that all depends
    on the æsthetic or intellectual,
And that criticism is great — and that refinement is
    greatest of all ;
And I affirm now that the mind governs — and that
    all depends on the mind.

### 8.

WITH one man or woman — (no matter which one —
    I even pick out the lowest,)
With him or her I now illustrate the whole law ;
I say that every right, in politics or what-not, shall be
    eligible to that one man or woman, on the same
    terms as any.

# DEBRIS.

HE is wisest who has the most caution,
He only wins who goes far enough.

ANY thing is as good as established, when that is
established that will produce it and continue it.

WHAT General has a good army in himself, has a
good army;
He happy in himself, or she happy in herself, is
happy,
But I tell you you cannot be happy by others, any
more than you can beget or conceive a child by
others.

HAVE you learned lessons only of those who admired
you, and were tender with you, and stood aside
for you?
Have you not learned the great lessons of those who
rejected you, and braced themselves against you?
or who treated you with contempt, or disputed
the passage with you?
Have you had no practice to receive opponents when
they come?

DESPAIRING cries float ceaselessly toward me, day and
    night,
The sad voice of Death — the call of my nearest
    lover, putting forth, alarmed, uncertain,
*This sea I am quickly to sail, come tell me,*
*Come tell me where I am speeding — tell me my*
    *destination.*

<hr/>

I UNDERSTAND your anguish, but I cannot help you,
I approach, hear, behold — the sad mouth, the look
    out of the eyes, your mute inquiry,
*Whither I go from the bed I now recline on, come*
    *tell me;*
Old age, alarmed, uncertain — A young woman's
    voice appealing to me, for comfort,
A young man's voice, *Shall I not escape?*

<hr/>

A THOUSAND perfect men and women appear,
Around each gathers a cluster of friends, and gay
    children and youths, with offerings.

<hr/>

A MASK — a perpetual natural disguiser of herself,
Concealing her face, concealing her form,
Changes and transformations every hour, every ·mo-
    ment,
Falling upon her even when she sleeps.

ONE sweeps by, attended by an immense train,
All emblematic of peace — not a soldier or menial
among them.

———◆———

ONE sweeps by, old, with black eyes, and profuse
white hair,
He has the simple magnificence of health and
strength,
His face strikes as with flashes of lightning whoever
it turns toward.

———◆———

THREE old men slowly pass, followed by three others,
and they by three others,
They are beautiful — the one in the middle of each
group holds his companions by the hand,
As they walk, they give out perfume wherever they
walk.

———◆———

WOMEN sit, or move to and fro — some old, some
young,
The young are beautiful — but the old are more
beautiful than the young.

———◆———

WHAT weeping face is that looking from the window?
Why does it stream those sorrowful tears?
Is it for some burial place, vast and dry?
Is it to wet the soil of graves?

I WILL take an egg out of the robin's nest in the
    orchard,
I will take a branch of gooseberries from the old bush
    in the garden, and go and preach to the world ;
You shall see I will not meet a single heretic or
    scorner,
You shall see how I stump clergymen, and confound
    them,
You shall see me showing a scarlet tomato, and a
    white pebble from the beach.

----

BEHAVIOR — fresh, native, copious, each one for him-
    self or herself,
Nature and the Soul expressed — America and free-
    dom expressed — In it the finest art,
In it pride, cleanliness, sympathy, to have their
    chance,
In it physique, intellect, faith — in it just as much as
    to manage an army or a city, or to write a book
    — perhaps more,
The youth, the laboring person, the poor person,
    rivalling all the rest — perhaps outdoing the
    rest,
The effects of the universe no greater than its ;
For there is nothing in the whole universe that can
    be more effective than a man's or woman's daily
    behavior can be,
In any position, in any one of These States.

Not the pilot has charged himself to bring his ship
    into port, though beaten back, and many times
    baffled,
Not the path-finder, penetrating inland, weary and
    long,
By deserts parched, snows chilled, rivers wet, per-
    severes till he reaches his destination,
More than I have charged myself, heeded or un-
    heeded, to compose a free march for These
    States,
To be exhilarating music to them, years, centuries
    hence.

———

I thought I was not alone, walking here by the shore,
But the one I thought was with me, as now I walk by
    the shore,
As I lean and look through the glimmering light —
    that one has utterly disappeared,
And those appear that perplex me.

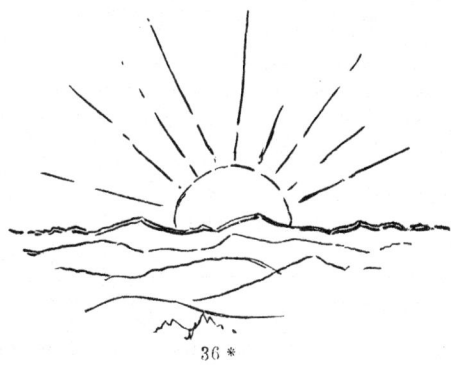

36 *

# SLEEP-CHASINGS.

1. I wander all night in my vision,
   Stepping with light feet, swiftly and noiselessly step-
      ping and stopping,
   Bending with open eyes over the shut eyes of
      sleepers,
   Wandering and confused, lost to myself, ill-assorted,
      contradictory,
   Pausing, gazing, bending, and stopping.

2. How solemn they look there, stretched and still!
   How quiet they breathe, the little children in their
      cradles!

3. The wretched features of ennuyés, the white features
      of corpses, the livid faces of drunkards, the sick-
      gray faces of onanists,
   The gashed bodies on battle-fields, the insane in their
      strong-doored rooms, the sacred idiots, the new-
      born emerging from gates, and the dying emer-
      ging from gates,
   The night pervades them and infolds them.

4. The married couple sleep calmly in their bed — he
      with his palm on the hip of the wife, and she
      with her palm on the hip of the husband,

The sisters sleep lovingly side by side in their bed,
The men sleep lovingly side by side in theirs,
And the mother sleeps, with her little child carefully
wrapped.

5. The blind sleep, and the deaf and dumb sleep,
The prisoner sleeps well in the prison — the run-
away son sleeps,
The murderer that is to be hung next day — how
does he sleep?
And the murdered person — how does he sleep?

6. The female that loves unrequited sleeps,
And the male that loves unrequited sleeps,
The head of the money-maker that plotted all day
sleeps,
And the enraged and treacherous dispositions —
all, all sleep.

7. I stand in the dark with drooping eyes by the worst-
suffering and the most restless,
I pass my hands soothingly to and fro a few inches
from them,
The restless sink in their beds — they fitfully sleep.

8. Now I pierce the darkness — new beings appear,
The earth recedes from me into the night,
I saw that it was beautiful, and I see that what is not
the earth is beautiful.

9. I go from bedside to bedside — I sleep close with
the other sleepers, each in turn,
I dream in my dream all the dreams of the other
dreamers,
And I become the other dreamers.

10. I am a dance — Play up, there! the fit is whirling
me fast!

11. I am the ever-laughing — it is new moon and twilight,
I see the hiding of douceurs — I see nimble ghosts
whichever way I look,
Cache, and cache again, deep in the ground and sea,
and where it is neither ground or sea.

12. Well do they do their jobs, those journeymen divine,
Only from me can they hide nothing, and would not
if they could,
I reckon I am their boss, and they make me a pet
besides,
And surround me and lead me, and run ahead when
I walk,
To lift their cunning covers, to signify me with
stretched arms, and resume the way;
Onward we move! a gay gang of blackguards! with
mirth-shouting music and wild-flapping pennants
of joy!

13. I am the actor, the actress, the voter, the politician,
The emigrant and the exile, the criminal that stood
in the box,
He who has been famous, and he who shall be famous
after to-day,
The stammerer, the well-formed person, the wasted
or feeble person.

14. I am she who adorned herself and folded her hair
expectantly,
My truant lover has come, and it is dark.

15. Double yourself and receive me, darkness!
Receive me and my lover too — he will not let me go
without him.

16. I roll myself upon you, as upon a bed — I resign
myself to the dusk.

17. He whom I call answers me and takes the place of
my lover,
He rises with me silently from the bed.

18. Darkness! you are gentler than my lover — his flesh
was sweaty and panting,
I feel the hot moisture yet that he left me.

19. My hands are spread forth, I pass them in all
directions,
I would sound up the shadowy shore to which you
are journeying.

20. Be careful, darkness! already, what was it touched
me?
I thought my lover had gone, else darkness and he
are one,
I hear the heart-beat — I follow, I fade away.

21. O hot-cheeked and blushing! O foolish hectic!
O for pity's sake, no one must see me now! my
clothes were stolen while I was abed,
Now I am thrust forth, where shall I run?

22. Pier that I saw dimly last night, when I looked from
the windows!

Pier out from the main, let me catch myself with you
and stay — I will not chafe you,
I feel ashamed to go naked about the world.

23. I am curious to know where my feet stand — and
what this is flooding me, childhood or manhood
— and the hunger that crosses the bridge
between.

24. The cloth laps a first sweet eating and drinking,
Laps life-swelling yolks — laps ear of rose-corn, milky
and just ripened ;
The white teeth stay, and the boss-tooth advances in
darkness,
And liquor is spilled on lips and bosoms by touching
glasses, and the best liquor afterward.

25. I descend my western course, my sinews are flaccid,
Perfume and youth course through me, and I am
their wake.

26. It is my face yellow and wrinkled, instead of the
old woman's,
I sit low in a straw-bottom chair, and carefully darn
my grandson's stockings.

27. It is I too, the sleepless widow looking out on the
winter midnight,
I see the sparkles of starshine on the icy and pallid
earth.

28. A shroud I see, and I am the shroud — I wrap a body
and lie in the coffin,

It is dark here under ground — it is not evil or pain here — it is·blank here, for reasons.

29. It seems to me that everything in the light and air ought to be happy,
Whoever is not in his coffin and the dark grave, let him know he has enough.

30. I see a beautiful gigantic swimmer swimming naked through the eddies of the sea,
His brown hair lies close and even to his head — he strikes out with courageous arms — he urges himself with his legs,
I see his white body — I see his undaunted eyes,
I hate the swift-running eddies that would dash him head-foremost on the rocks.

31. What are you doing, you ruffianly red-trickled waves?
Will you kill the courageous giant? Will you kill him in the prime of his middle age?

32. Steady and long he struggles,
He is baffled, banged, bruised — he holds out while his strength holds out,
The slapping eddies are spotted with his blood — they bear him away — they roll him, swing him, turn him,
His beautiful body is borne in the circling eddies, it is continually bruised on rocks,
Swiftly and out of sight is borne the brave corpse.

33. I turn, but do not extricate myself,
Confused, a past-reading, another, but with darkness yet.

34. The beach is cut by the razory ice-wind — the wreck-
     guns sound,
   The tempest lulls — the moon comes floundering
     through the drifts.

35. I look where the ship helplessly heads end on — I
     hear the burst as she strikes — I hear the howls
     of dismay — they grow fainter and fainter.

36. I cannot aid with my wringing fingers,
   I can but rush to the surf, and let it drench me and
     freeze upon me.

37. I search with the crowd — not one of the company is
     washed to us alive ;
   In the morning I help pick up the dead and lay them
     in rows in a barn.

38. Now of the old war-days, the defeat at Brooklyn,
   Washington stands inside the lines — he stands on the
     intrenched hills, amid a crowd of officers,
   His face is cold and damp — he cannot repress the
     weeping drops,
   He lifts the glass perpetually to his eyes — the color
     is blanched from his cheeks,
   He sees the slaughter of the southern braves confided
     to him by their parents.

39. The same, at last and at last, when peace is declared,
   He stands in the room of the old tavern — the well-
     beloved soldiers all pass through,
   The officers speechless and slow draw near in their
     turns,

The chief encircles their necks with his arm, and
kisses them on the cheek,

He kisses lightly the wet cheeks one after another —
he shakes hands, and bids good-by to the army.

40. Now I tell what my mother told me to-day as we sat
at dinner together,

Of when she was a nearly grown girl, living home
with her parents on the old homestead.

41. A red squaw came one breakfast-time to the old
homestead,

On her back she carried a bundle of rushes for
rush-bottoming chairs,

Her hair, straight, shiny, coarse, black, profuse, half-
enveloped her face,

Her step was free and elastic, and her voice sounded
exquisitely as she spoke.

42. My mother looked in delight and amazement at the
stranger,

She looked at the freshness of her tall-borne face, and
full and pliant limbs,

The more she looked upon her she loved her,

Never before had she seen such wonderful beauty and
purity,

She made her sit on a bench by the jamb of the fire-
place — she cooked food for her,

She had no work to give her, but she gave her
remembrance and fondness.

43. The red squaw staid all the forenoon, and toward the
middle of the afternoon she went away,

37

O my mother was loth to have her go away!
All the week she thought of her — she watched for
　　her many a month,
She remembered her many a winter and many a
　　summer,
But the red squaw never came, nor was heard of
　　there again.

44. Now Lucifer was not dead — or if he was, I am his
　　sorrowful terrible heir,
I have been wronged — I am oppressed — I hate him
　　that oppresses me,
I will either destroy him, or he shall release me.

45. Damn him! how he does defile me!
How he informs against my brother and sister, and
　　takes pay for their blood!
How he laughs when I look down the bend, after the
　　steamboat that carries away my woman!

46. Now the vast dusk bulk that is the whale's bulk, it
　　seems mine,
Warily, sportsman! though I lie so sleepy and slug-
　　gish, my tap is death.

47. A show of the summer softness! a contact of some-
　　thing unseen! an amour of the light and air!
I am jealous, and overwhelmed with friendliness,
And will go gallivant with the light and air myself,
And have an unseen something to be in contact with
　　them also.

48. O love and summer! you are in the dreams, and
　　in me!

Autumn and winter are in the dreams — the farmer
goes with his thrift,

The droves and crops increase, and the barns are well-
filled.

49. Elements merge in the night — ships make tacks in
the dreams,

The sailor sails — the exile returns home,

The fugitive returns unharmed — the immigrant is
back beyond months and years,

The poor Irishman lives in the simple house of his
childhood, with the well-known neighbors and
faces,

They warmly welcome him — he is barefoot again, he
forgets he is well off;

The Dutchman voyages home, and the Scotchman
and Welshman voyage home, and the native of
the Mediterranean voyages home,

To every port of England, France, Spain, enter well-
filled ships,

The Swiss foots it toward his hills — the Prussian goes
his way, the Hungarian his way, and the Pole
his way,

The Swede returns, and the Dane and Norwegian
return.

50. The homeward bound, and the outward bound,

The beautiful lost swimmer, the ennuyé, the onanist,
the female that loves unrequited, the money-
maker,

The actor and actress, those through with their parts,
and those waiting to commence,

The affectionate boy, the husband and wife, the voter,
    the nominee that is chosen, and the nominee that
    has failed,
The great already known, and the great any time
    after to-day,
The stammerer, the sick, the perfect-formed, the
    homely,
The criminal that stood in the box, the judge that
    sat and sentenced him, the fluent lawyers, the
    jury, the audience,
The laugher and weeper, the dancer, the midnight
    widow, the red squaw,
The consumptive, the erysipelite, the idiot, he that
    is wronged,
The antipodes, and every one between this and them
    in the dark,
I swear they are averaged now — one is no better
    than the other,
The night and sleep have likened them and restored
    them.

51. I swear they are all beautiful !
Every one that sleeps is beautiful — everything in
    the dim light is beautiful,
The wildest and bloodiest is over, and all is peace.

52. Peace is always beautiful,
The myth of heaven indicates peace and night.

53. The myth of heaven indicates the Soul ;
The Soul is always beautiful — it appears more or it
    appears less — it comes, or it lags behind,

It comes from its embowered garden, and looks
pleasantly on itself, and encloses the world,

Perfect and clean the genitals previously jetting, and
perfect and clean the womb cohering,

The head well-grown, proportioned and plumb, and
the bowels and joints proportioned and plumb.

54. The Soul is always beautiful,

The universe is duly in order, everything is in its
place,

What is arrived is in its place, and what waits is
in its place;

The twisted skull waits, the watery or rotten blood
waits,

The child of the glutton or venerealee waits long, and
the child of the drunkard waits long, and the
drunkard himself waits long,

The sleepers that lived and died wait — the far
advanced are to go on in their turns, and the
far behind are to go on in their turns,

The diverse shall be no less diverse, but they shall
flow and unite — they unite now.

55. The sleepers are very beautiful as they lie unclothed,

They flow hand in hand over the whole earth, from
east to west, as they lie unclothed,

The Asiatic and African are hand in hand — the
European and American are hand in hand,

Learned and unlearned are hand in hand, and male
and female are hand in hand,

The bare arm of the girl crosses the bare breast of
her lover — they press close without lust — his
lips press her neck,

37*

The father holds his grown or ungrown son in his
    arms with measureless love, and the son holds
    the father in his arms with measureless love,

The white hair of the mother shines on the white
    wrist of the daughter,

The breath of the boy goes with the breath of the
    man, friend is inarmed by friend,

The scholar kisses the teacher, and the teacher kisses
    the scholar — the wronged is made right,

The call of the slave is one with the master's call, and
    the master salutes the slave,

The felon steps forth from the prison — the insane
    becomes sane — the suffering of sick persons is
    relieved,

The sweatings and fevers stop — the throat that was
    unsound is sound — the lungs of the consumptive
    are resumed — the poor distressed head is free,

The joints of the rheumatic move as smoothly as ever,
    and smoother than ever,

Stiflings and passages open — the paralyzed become
    supple,

The swelled and convulsed and congested awake to
    themselves in condition,

They pass the invigoration of the night, and the
    chemistry of the night, and awake.

56. I too pass from the night,
    I stay a while away O night, but I return to you
    again, and love you.

57. Why should I be afraid to trust myself to you?
    I am not afraid — I have been well brought forward
    by you,

I love the rich running day, but I do not desert her
in whom I lay so long,
I know not how I came of you, and I know not where
I go with you — but I know I came well, and
shall go well.

58. I will stop only a time with the night, and rise
betimes,
I will duly pass the day, O my mother, and duly
return to you.

# BURIAL.

1. To think of it!
   To think of time — of all that retrospection!
   To think of to-day, and the ages continued hence-forward!

2. Have you guessed you yourself would not continue?
   Have you dreaded those earth-beetles?
   Have you feared the future would be nothing to you?

3. Is to-day nothing? Is the beginningless past nothing?
   If the future is nothing, they are just as surely nothing.

4. To think that the sun rose in the east! that men and women were flexible, real, alive! that everything was alive!
   To think that you and I did not see, feel, think, nor bear our part!
   To think that we are now here, and bear our part!

5. Not a day passes — not a minute or second, without an accouchment!
   Not a day passes — not a minute or second, without a corpse!

6. The dull nights go over, and the dull days also,
   The soreness of lying so much in bed goes over,

(440)

The physician, after long putting off, gives the silent
and terrible look for an answer,

The children come hurried and weeping, and the
brothers and sisters are sent for,

Medicines stand unused on the shelf — (the camphor-
smell has long pervaded the rooms,)

The faithful hand of the living does not desert the
hand of the dying,

The twitching lips press lightly on the forehead of
the dying,

The breath ceases, and the pulse of the heart ceases,

The corpse stretches on the bed, and the living look
upon it,

It is palpable as the living are palpable.

7. The living look upon the corpse with their eye-sight,
But without eye-sight lingers a different living, and
looks curiously on the corpse.

8. To think that the rivers will flow, and the snow fall,
and fruits ripen, and act upon others as upon
us now — yet not act upon us!

To think of all these wonders of city and country,
and others taking great interest in them — and
we taking no interest in them!

9. To think how eager we are in building our houses!
To think others shall be just as eager, and we quite
indifferent!

10. I see one building the house that serves him a few
years, or seventy or eighty years at most,

I see one building the house that serves him longer
than that.

11. Slow-moving and black lines creep over the whole
earth — they never cease — they are the burial
lines,

He that was President was buried, and he that is now
President shall surely be buried.

12. Cold dash of waves at the ferry-wharf — posh and
ice in the river, half-frozen mud in the streets,
a gray discouraged sky overhead, the short last
daylight of Twelfth Month,

A hearse and stages — other vehicles give place —
the funeral of an old Broadway stage-driver, the
cortege mostly drivers.

13. Steady the trot to the cemetery, duly rattles the
death-bell, the gate is passed, the new-dug grave
is halted at, the living alight, the hearse un-
closes,

The coffin is passed out, lowered and settled, the
whip is laid on the coffin, the earth is swiftly
shovelled in,

The mound above is flatted with the spades —
silence,

A minute, no one moves or speaks — it is done,

He is decently put away — is there anything more?

14. He was a good fellow, free-mouthed, quick-tempered,
not bad-looking, able to take his own part, witty,
sensitive to a slight, ready with life or death for
a friend, fond of women, gambled, ate hearty,
drank hearty, had known what it was to be
flush, grew low-spirited toward the last, sickened,
was helped by a contribution, died, aged forty-
one years — and that was his funeral.

15 Thumb extended, finger uplifted, apron, cape, gloves, strap, wet-weather clothes, whip carefully chosen, boss, spotter, starter, hostler, somebody loafing on you, you loafing on somebody, head-way, man before and man behind, good day's work, bad day's work, pet stock, mean stock, first out, last out, turning in at night,

To think that these are so much and so nigh to other drivers — and he there takes no interest in them!

16. The markets, the government, the working-man's wages — to think what account they are through our nights and days!

To think that other working-men will make just as great account of them — yet we make little or no account!

17. The vulgar and the refined — what you call sin and what you call goodness — to think how wide a difference!

To think the difference will still continue to others, yet we lie beyond the difference.

18. To think how much pleasure there is!

Have you pleasure from looking at the sky? have you pleasure from poems?

Do you enjoy yourself in the city? or engaged in business? or planning a nomination and election? or with your wife and family?

Or with your mother and sisters? or in womanly house-work? or the beautiful maternal cares?

These also flow onward to others — you and I flow onward,

But in due time you and I shall take less interest
in them.

19. Your farm, profits, crops, — to think how engrossed
you are!
To think there will still be farms, profits, crops — yet
for you, of what avail?

20. What will be, will be well — for what is, is well,
To take interest is well, and not to take interest shall
be well.

21. The sky continues beautiful,
The pleasure of men with women shall never be sated,
nor the pleasure of women with men, nor the
pleasure from poems,
The domestic joys, the daily house-work or business,
the building of houses — these are not phan-
tasms — they have weight, form, location;
Farms, profits, crops, markets, wages, government,
are none of them phantasms,
The difference between sin and goodness is no
delusion,
The earth is not an echo — man and his life, and all
the things of his life, are well-considered.

22. You are not thrown to the winds — you gather cer-
tainly and safely around yourself,
Yourself! Yourself! Yourself, forever and ever!

23. It is not to diffuse you that you were born of your
mother and father — it is to identify you,
It is not that you should be undecided, but that you
should be decided;

Something long preparing and formless is arrived and
    formed in you,
You are thenceforth secure, whatever comes or goes.

24. The threads that were spun are gathered, the weft
    crosses the warp, the pattern is systematic.

25. The preparations have every one been justified,
    The orchestra have sufficiently tuned their instru-
    ments, the baton has given the signal.

26. The guest that was coming — he waited long, for
    reasons — he is now housed,
    He is one of those who are beautiful and happy —
    he is one of those that to look upon and be
    with is enough.

27. The law of the past cannot be eluded,
    The law of the present and future cannot be eluded,
    The law of the living cannot be eluded — it is eter-
    nal,
    The law of promotion and transformation cannot be
    eluded,
    The law of heroes and good-doers cannot be eluded,
    The law of drunkards, informers, mean persons —
    not one iota of it can be eluded.

28. Slow-moving and black lines go ceaselessly over the
    earth,
    Northerner goes carried, and southerner goes carried,
    and they on the Atlantic side, and they on the
    Pacific, and they between, and all through the
    Mississippi country, and all over the earth.

29. The great masters and kosmos are well as they go —
     the heroes and good-doers are well,
     The known leaders and inventors, and the rich owners
         and pious and distinguished, may be well,
     But there is more account than that — there is strict
         account of all.

30. The interminable hordes of the ignorant and wicked
     are not nothing,
     The barbarians of Africa and Asia are not nothing,
     The common people of Europe are not nothing — the
         American aborigines are not nothing,
     The infected in the immigrant hospital are not
         nothing — the murderer or mean person is not
         nothing,
     The perpetual successions of shallow people are not
         nothing as they go,
     The lowest prostitute is not nothing — the mocker of
         religion is not nothing as he goes.

31. I shall go with the rest — we have satisfaction,
     I have dreamed that we are not to be changed so
         much, nor the law of us changed,
     I have dreamed that heroes and good-doers shall
         be under the present and past law,
     And that murderers, drunkards, liars, shall be under
         the present and past law,
     For I have dreamed that the law they are under now
         is enough.

32. And I have dreamed that the satisfaction is not so
     much changed, and that there is no life with-
     out satisfaction ;
     What is the earth ? what are body and Soul, without
         satisfaction ?

33. I shall go with the rest,
We cannot be stopped at a given point — that is no satisfaction,
To show us a good thing, or a few good things, for a space of time — that is no satisfaction,
We must have the indestructible breed of the best, regardless of time.

34. If otherwise, all these things came but to ashes of dung,
If maggots and rats ended us, then alarm! for we are betrayed!
Then indeed suspicion of death.

35. Do you suspect death? If I were to suspect death, I should die now,
Do you think I could walk pleasantly and well-suited toward annihilation?

36. Pleasantly and well-suited I walk,
Whither I walk I cannot define, but I know it is good,
The whole universe indicates that it is good,
The past and the present indicate that it is good.

37. How beautiful and perfect are the animals! How perfect is my Soul!
How perfect the earth, and the minutest thing upon it!
What is called good is perfect, and what is called bad is just as perfect,
The vegetables and minerals are all perfect, and the imponderable fluids are perfect;
Slowly and surely they have passed on to this, and slowly and surely they yet pass on.

38. My Soul! if I realize you, I have satisfaction,
    Animals and vegetables! if I realize you, I have sat-
        isfaction,
    Laws of the earth and air! if I realize you, I have
        satisfaction.

39. I cannot define my satisfaction, yet it is so,
    I cannot define my life, yet it is so.

40. O it comes to me now!
    I swear I think now that everything without excep-
        tion has an eternal Soul!
    The trees have, rooted in the ground! the weeds of
        the sea have! the animals!

41. I swear I think there is nothing but immortality!
    That the exquisite scheme is for it, and the nebulous
        float is for it, and the cohering is for it!
    And all preparation is for it! and identity is for it!
        and life and death are altogether for it!

# TO MY SOUL.

1. As nearing departure,
   As the time draws nigh, glooming from you,
   A cloud — a dread beyond, of I know not what, dark-
   ens me.

2. I shall go forth,
   I shall traverse The States — but I cannot tell whither
   or how long;
   Perhaps soon, some day or night while I am singing,
   my voice will suddenly cease.

3. O Soul!
   Then all may arrive to but this;
   The glances of my eyes, that swept the daylight,
   The unspeakable love I interchanged with women,
   My joys in the open air — my walks through the Man-
   nahatta,
   The continual good will I have met — the curious
   attachment of young men to me,
   My reflections alone — the absorption into me from
   the landscape, stars, animals, thunder, rain,
   and snow, in my wanderings alone,
   The words of my mouth, rude, ignorant, arrogant —
   my many faults and derelictions,

38*                                          (449)

The light touches, on my lips, of the lips of my com-
   rades, at parting,
The tracks which I leave, upon the side-walks and
   fields,
May but arrive at this beginning of me,
This beginning of me — and yet it is enough, O Soul,
O Soul, we have positively appeared — that is enough.

# *So long!*

1. To conclude — I announce what comes after me,
   The thought must be promulged, that all I know at
   any time suffices for that time only — not subse-
   quent time;
   I announce greater offspring, orators, days, and then
   depart.

2. I remember I said to myself at the winter-close, before
   my leaves sprang at all, that I would become a
   candid and unloosed summer-poet,
   I said I would raise my voice jocund and strong, with
   reference to consummations.

3. When America does what was promised,
   When each part is peopled with free people,
   When there is no city on earth to lead my city, the
   city of young men, the Mannahatta city — But
   when the Mannahatta leads all the cities of the
   earth,
   When there are plentiful athletic bards, inland and
   seaboard,
   When through These States walk a hundred millions
   of superb persons,
   When the rest part away for superb persons, and con-
   tribute to them,

(451)

When fathers, firm, unconstrained, open-eyed — When
breeds of the most perfect mothers denote
America,
Then to me ripeness and conclusion.


4. Yet not me, after all — let none be content with me,
I myself seek a man better than I am, or a woman
better than I am,
I invite defiance, and to make myself superseded,
All I have done, I would cheerfully give to be trod
under foot, if it might only be the soil of supe-
rior poems.


5. I have established nothing for good,
I have but established these things, till things farther
onward shall be prepared to be established,
And I am myself the preparer of things farther
onward.


6. I have pressed through in my own right,
I have offered my style to every one — I have jour-
neyed with confident step,
While my pleasure is yet at the full, I whisper
*So long*,
And take the young woman's hand, and the young
man's hand, for the last time.


7. Once more I enforce you to give play to yourself —
and not depend on me, or on any one but
yourself,
Once more I proclaim the whole of America for each
individual, without exception.

8. As I have announced the true theory of the youth, manhood, womanhood, of The States, I adhere to it;

As I have announced myself on immortality, the body, procreation, hauteur, prudence,

As I joined the stern crowd that still confronts the President with menacing weapons — I adhere to all,

As I have announced each age for itself, this moment I set the example.

9. I demand the choicest edifices to destroy them;

Room! room! for new far-planning draughtsmen and engineers!

Clear that rubbish from the building-spots and the paths!

10. *So long!*

I announce natural persons to arise,

I announce justice triumphant,

I announce uncompromising liberty and equality,

I announce the justification of candor, and the justification of pride.

11. I announce that the identity of These States is a single identity only,

I announce the Union more and more compact,

I announce splendors and majesties to make all the previous politics of the earth insignificant.

12. I announce adhesiveness — I say it shall be limitless, unloosened,

I say you shall yet find the friend you was look-
ing for.

13. *So long!*
I announce a man or woman coming — perhaps you
are the one,
I announce a great individual, fluid as Nature, chaste,
affectionate, compassionate, fully armed.

14. *So long!*
I announce a life that shall be copious, vehement,
spiritual, bold,
And I announce an old age that shall lightly and
joyfully meet its translation.

15. O thicker and faster!
O crowding too close upon me!
I foresee too much — it means more than I thought,
It appears to me I am dying.

16. Now throat, sound your last!
Salute me — salute the future once more. Peal the
old cry once more.

17. Screaming electric, the atmosphere using,
At random glancing, each as I notice absorbing,
Swiftly on, but a little while alighting,
Curious enveloped messages delivering,
Sparkles hot, seed ethereal, down in the dirt dropping,
Myself unknowing, my commission obeying, to ques-
tion it never daring,
To ages, and ages yet, the growth of the seed leaving,

To troops out of me rising — they the tasks I have set
    promulging,
To women certain whispers of myself bequeathing —
    their affection me more clearly explaining,
To young men my problems offering — no dallier I —
    I the muscle of their brains trying,
So I pass — a little time vocal, visible, contrary,
Afterward, a melodious echo, passionately bent for —
    death making me undying,
The best of me then when no longer visible — for
    toward that I have been incessantly preparing.

18. What is there more, that I lag and pause, and crouch
    extended with unshut mouth ?
Is there a single final farewell ?

19. My songs cease — I abandon them,
From behind the screen where I hid, I advance per-
    sonally.

20. This is no book,
Who touches this, touches a man,
(Is it night ? Are we here alone ?)
It is I you hold, and who holds you,
I spring from the pages into your arms — decease
    calls me forth.

21. O how your fingers drowse me !
Your breath falls around me like dew — your pulse
    lulls the tympans of my ears,
I feel immerged from head to foot,
Delicious — enough.

22. Enough, O deed impromptu and secret!
   Enough, O gliding present! Enough, O summed-up
      past!


23. Dear friend, whoever you are, here, take this kiss,
   I give it especially to you — Do not forget me,
   I feel like one who has done his work — I progress on,
   The unknown sphere, more real than I dreamed,
      more direct, darts awakening rays about me —
      *So long!*
   Remember my words — I love you — I depart from
      materials,
   I am as one disembodied, triumphant, dead.

# ANNOTATIONS

There exist a number of ways for readers to examine differences between the various editions of *Leaves of Grass* and between the earlier and later versions of poems that appear in the 1860 edition. These annotations are intended as a tool for the general reader to negotiate Whitman's occasionally obscure or archaic language and references in the 1860 edition. To aid navigation, I have maintained Whitman's novel numbering system from the third edition. Unless otherwise indicated, all definitions (quoted and paraphrased) are from the *Oxford English Dictionary*. Where useful, I have consulted and cited Noah Webster's *An American Dictionary of the English Language* (1846), among other sources contemporary and modern.

PROTO-LEAF

1    "Paumanok" was a Native American name for Long Island, which Whitman already used in the series "Letters from Paumanok" between June and August 1851 in the New York *Evening Post*. Whitman signed these articles "Paumanok," thereby lending the word double meaning in the title and rhetorically investing himself in the Long Island countryside.

"Mannahatta": Manhattan.

"Kanuck": Canadian, from the Iroquois word *canuchsa* or village dweller.[1] Or, from circa 1825–1835, South Sea Islander (*kanaka*) "once identified both French Canadians and such islanders, who . . . were employed in the Pacific Northwest fur trade."[2] The word first appeared in the American press in the 1830s and 1840s.

Whitman's use of "Paumanok," "Mannahatta," and "Kanuck" lent "Proto-Leaf" a Native American and, for his readers, a timeless and autochthonous tone appropriate to "strik[ing] up for a new world." In this regard, Whitman's new world represents a return to an original, unblemished one.

10    "Kanzas": Kansas, named for the Native American tribe (eventually relocated to Oklahoma). In 1860, the struggles over the Lecompton Constitution and the battles between pro- and antislavery forces in the Kansas Territory (1855–1857) were still fresh in readers' memories. John Brown, who was executed in December 1859 for his raid on the Harper's Ferry arsenal, murdered five proslavery men in the Kansas Territory during the height of the violence in 1856.

"Many In One": George Washington Cutter's poem "E Pluribus Unum" (1848) might have inspired Whitman's use of this phrase:

By the bayonet trac'd at the midnight war,
    On the fields where our glory was won;
Oh! perish the heart or the hand that would mar
    Our motto of "MANY IN ONE."[3]

22    "evangel-poem": evangel = gospel.

24    "Omnes!": (Latin) everyone / all, used as a stage direction to cue actors to speak the same lines simultaneously. Whitman frequented the theater throughout the late 1840s and 1850s.

36    "adhesive": from *adhesiveness*, a phrenological term meaning "Friendship; social feeling; love of society; desire to congregate, associate, visit, seek company, entertain friends, form and reciprocate attachments."[4]

60    This list offers a transcontinental survey of Native

American tribes and place names: Okonee, Koosa = Southeast; Ottawa = Upper Midwest; Monongahela = western Pennsylvania, eastern Ohio; Sauk = Upper Midwest; Natchez = Mississippi basin; Chattahoochee = Southeast; Kaqueta (Caquetá?) = South America; Oronoco (Orinoco?) = river in Venezuela and Columbia; Wabash = Midwest; Miami = Midwest; Saginaw, Chippewa = Midwest; Oshkosh (Menominee) = Upper Midwest; Walla Walla = Pacific Northwest.

63    "arriere": "a rear division of an army" or a proprietary sub-holding.

WALT WHITMAN

25    "kelson": or keelson, "A line of timber placed inside a ship along the floor-timbers and parallel with the keel, to which it is bolted, so as to fasten the floor-timbers and the keel together; a similar bar or combination of iron plates in iron vessels." Whitman's use of kelson presented creation as an entity built for motion; love is its essential framework.

"worm-fence": a simple fence constructed by placing wooden beams in an interlocking pattern at slight angles to each other, thus creating a zig-zag pattern.

"elder": *Sambucus*, elderberry.

"mullen": *Verbascum thapsus*, biennial plant common throughout North America.

"pokeweed": *Phytolacca Americana*, common perennial that grows in spring and summer throughout the United States and Canada; thrives in coarse soil.[5]

30    "Tuckahoe": lowlands Virginian. Originally a name for a kind of tuber grown by Native Americans, first cited by John Smith (1612).

"Cuff": African American, abbreviation for *Cuffee* or *Cuffy*, meaning Friday, from the Akan language spoken along the Ivory Coast. Naming a child after the day of the week on which he or she was born remained popular in Gullah English into the twentieth century.[6]

77   "First Day": Whitman uses the traditional Quaker designation of days of the week; First Day is Sunday. He also terms months in this manner; Fifth Month = May.[7]

"loafe"; Probably from the German noun *Landläufer*, tramp;[8] before Whitman, Charles Dickens in *The Life and Adventures of Martin Chuzzlewit* (1844) and Henry David Thoreau in *Walden* (1854) used the term "loafer."

"parturition chamber": birthing room.

"Chattahooche": river that runs from northern Georgia to the Florida panhandle.

"Altamahaw": river that runs from central Georgia to the southeastern coast of the state.[9]

78   "Elkhorn": a creek in central Kentucky.

"Hoosier": resident of Indiana, first used in the *Chicago Tribune* (1826) and *Knickerbocker* (1834), also used to denote an inexperienced or uneducated individual starting in the 1840s. The origin of the word is unknown.

"Badger": popular name for a native of Wisconsin that might originate in the mammal's name (sixteenth century) or in the name for an individual who trades in agriculture products (sixteenth century).

"Buckeye": popular name for a resident of Ohio, another name for the American horse-chestnut (eighteenth century).

"Poke-easy": a lazy, slow, or easygoing person, chiefly a Southern term.[10]

88    "embouchures": the setting of lips and facial muscles for the playing of a wind instrument.[11]

90    "venerealee": an individual who suffers from a venereal disease.

126   "scrofula": a form of tuberculosis that infects the lymphatic glands.

133   "stonecrop": "The common name of *Sedum acre* (N.O. *Crassulaceæ*), an herb with bright yellow flowers and small cylindrical fleshy sessile leaves, growing in masses on rocks, old walls."

147   "colter": "The iron blade fixed in front of the share in a plough; it makes a vertical cut in the soil, which is then sliced horizontally by the share."

179   "red marauder": Lines 179–82 appear to reflect a thinly veiled sexual encounter that began, perhaps, with too much drink; an anagram for "red marauder" is "a dear red rum."[12]

189   "pismire": ant.

222   "I tell not the fall of Alamo": Whitman here refers to the Battle of the Alamo (1836) in San Antonio, Texas, where approximately two hundred Texans were defeated and massacred by the Mexican Army during the Texas Revolution. "Hear now the tale of the murder in cold blood . . ." in 223 probably refers to the Battle of Goliad (1836) in southeastern Texas during the Texas Revolution where Mexican forces captured and executed approximately 350 Texans. Texas independence eventually led to the border dispute that became the Mexican-American War (1846–1848). The United States' victory in this war added approximately one million square miles to the Union, including California and

the territories of New Mexico and Arizona. The acquisition of this territory reopened the slavery debate and necessitated the Compromise of 1850 (see introduction).

229 "Did you read in the sea-books of the old-fashioned frigate-fight?": This scene generally describes the Battle of Flamborough Head on September 23, 1779, between the U.S. *Bonhomme Richard* and the H.M.S. *Serapis*. The battle began just after 7 P.M. and lasted until around midnight. Whitman loosely quotes Jones's famous statement, "I have not yet begun to fight," and broadly recounts the details of the battle.[13]

257 "élèves": (French) students.

276 "Jehovah": God in some translations of the Old Testament.

"Kronos": father of the Greek god Zeus.

"Zeus": king of the Greek gods.

"Hercules": half-human heroic son of Zeus.

"Osiris": Egyptian god of the underworld and the dead; also a bringer of rebirth and growth.

"Isis": Osiris's sister and lover.

"Belus": also Ba'al; meaning "Lord" in ancient Middle Eastern religions.

"Brahma": supreme God of Hinduism.

"Buddha": Siddhārtha Gautama (563 BCE to 483 BCE), originator of Buddhism.

"Manito": the Great Spirit in Algonquian.

"Allah": the name for God in the Koran.

"Odin": chief god of Northern Germanic traditions.

"Mexitli": Aztec god of war.

288   "gymnosophist": "A philosopher of India, so called from his going with bare feet, or with little clothing."[14]

"teokallis": or telkalli, Aztec temple structure.

295   "koboo": Probably from Walter M. Gibson's *Prison of Weltevreden*, "Kubu," which Gibson uses to describe "a wild race of human shaped beings, covered with hair," that lived in what is now modern Malaysia.[15]

310   "sauroids": a term for prehistoric fishes and reptiles in the early nineteenth century, from "saurian, [p]ertaining to lizards; designating an order of reptiles."[16]

348   "accoucheur": a male midwife.

## CHANTS DEMOCRATIC AND NATIVE AMERICAN

"Apostroph": "In rhetoric, a diversion of speech; a digressive address; a changing the course of a speech, and addressing a person, who is dead or absent, as if present."[17]

"mater": (Latin) mother, literally "womb."

"fils": (French) son, usually appended to the son of a father of the same name.

1:17   "phrenology": "the science of the human mind. . . . as connected with the supposed organs of thought and passion in the brain."[18] Phrenology was an early form of psychology that was most popularly promulgated by the German physician Johann Gaspar Spurzheim (1776–1832).[19] Whitman probably learned Spurzheim's theories from Orson S. Fowler's (1809–1887) periodical, *American Phrenological Journal*, and from Fowler's books, *Hereditary Descent* and *Love and Parentage*, both

of which he owned.[20] By the 1850s, phrenology was
already mocked as a pseudoscience.

1:28 "amativeness": phrenological term pertaining to
"conjugal love; attachment to the opposite sex;
desire to love, be loved, and married; adapted to
perpetuate the race."[21]

1:29 "amanuenses": "a person whose employment is to write
what another dictates."[22]

1:34 "I have loved the earth, sun, animals": this section,
like much of "Chants Democratic" 1, was originally
a prose introduction of the first *Leaves of Grass*
(1855). In the first edition, this section began "This
is what you shall do . . . ," and what Whitman
here portrays as his own actions originally were
imperatives to the reader in 1855.

2:1: "Broad-axe": an axe with a broad head used historically
both as a weapon and a tool.

2:4 "The house-builder at work": Walter Whitman, Sr.,
was a carpenter and house builder.

"bigots": In antebellum America this term did not
imply racists, as it generally does today. Instead,
it designated someone who obstinately and
unreasonably held to a particular religious position,
often to the point of hypocrisy.

2:16 "Albic": Albanian.

2:25 "Penobscot": Native American tribe originally living
along the Penobscot River in Maine.

"Kennebec": county in Maine named for Canibas chief
called Kennebis.[23]

"Gila": tributary of the Colorado River, runs through
Arizona.

"Minnesota": had only become a state in 1858.

"the Yellowstone river": a branch of the Missouri River
that runs from North Dakota into Montana and
Wyoming.

2:27 "hackmatack-roots": roots "of the American larch
or tamarack [tree] (*Larix Americana*), found in
northern swamps of the United States."

2:29 "The shape of the slats of the bed of a corrupted body":
Whitman described a similar scene almost fifteen
years before in a newspaper article, "The Last of
Lively Frank."[24]

"The sheriff at hand with his deputies . . . the sickening
dangling of the rope": Whitman had been writing
critically of capital punishment since the 1840s.[25]

2:33 "alimentive": alimentiveness was described in
the Fowlers' *The Illustrated Self-Instructor in
Phrenology and Physiology* (1857) as a trait
that "hugs itself down to the dainty dish with
the greediness of an epicure, better seen than
described."[26] Whitman probably means it here
in a positive epicurean sense, as describing
an individual who derives pleasure from the
immediacy of life.

3:5 "Were I to you as the boss employing and paying
you": Historian David R. Roediger notes that the
word *boss* gradually replaced the word *master* in
the 1830s as the apprentice system broke down in
the midst of the industrial revolution. According
to Roediger, "*boss* was specifically and popularly
embraced by employed artisans amidst the rapidly
developing Jacksonian labor movement. . . . A
*hired hand* could claim and perhaps insist upon
small privileges that a *servant* could not."[27] In this
context, Whitman speaks directly to a member of
the predominately white, urban working class as

evident in the eventual title of this poem, "A Song for Occupations."

3:29 "What is learnt in the public school": Whitman taught school in rural Long Island between 1837 and 1841. He described it this way: "O, damnation, damnation! thy other name is school-teaching. . . ."[28]

"marl": "An earthy deposit, typically loose and unconsolidated and consisting chiefly of clay mixed with calcium carbonate, formed in prehistoric seas and lakes and long used to improve the texture of sandy or light soil."

"loam": "Clay, clayey earth, mud."

"curry-comb": a comb used to brush a horse.

"plumbob": "A ball or piece of lead or other dense substance, attached to a plumb line or quadrant for determining the vertical."

"etui": a case for surgical tools.

"oculist": optician.

"aurist": ear specialist.

"smutch'd": dirty.

"puddling-furnace": "The puddling furnace is a metalmaking technology to create wrought iron from the pig iron produced in a blast furnace."[29]

"loup-lump": "A mass of iron in a pasty condition gathered into a ball for the tilt hammer or rolls."[30]

"Oakum": woody fiber used for caulking the seams of wooden ships.

"frisket": "A thin iron frame hinged to the tympan, having tapes or paper strips stretched across it, for keeping the sheet in position while printing."

"tympan": "the parchment frame or panel of a hand-printing press, on which the blank sheets are put in order to be impressed when laid on the form."[31]

"compositor's stick": used by printers to assemble moveable type into words for placement in a press before printing.

"gutta-percha": "a concrete milky juice, forming a gum-resin, obtained in the Eastern archipelago from *Isonandra Gutta*; of extensive use in the arts, and for various economical purposes, being easily shaped and retaining the form given to it."[32]

"quoits": "A kind of horse-shoe to be pitched or thrown at a fixed object in play."[33] Quoits is an outdoor game similar to horseshoes where contestants attempt to throw small metal rings onto metal pegs. This game was popular in the New York and New England through most of the nineteenth century.[34]

"electro-plating": "The process of coating an article with metal by means of electrolysis."

"electrotyping": Making "a copy or duplicate of an object, especially a printing plate, made by a process involving the electrolytic deposition of copper or other metal; a relief printing plate made in this way."

"stereotyping": "The method or process of printing in which a solid plate or type-metal, cast from a papier-mâché or plaster mould taken from the surface of a form of type, is used for printing from instead of the form itself."

"The wires of the electric telegraph . . . laid at the bottom of the sea": The first attempt to lay a transatlantic cable between the United States and Great Britain took place in 1857.

"The column of wants in the one-cent paper, the news by telegraph": In 1846, the New York newspapers *Tribune, Herald, Journal of Commerce, Courier, Enquirer,* and *Express* agreed to share telegraphed reports from the front during the Mexican-American War. This conglomerate became the Associated Press in 1848.

"trottoirs": paved footpath.

"Seventh Day night": Saturday evening.

3:33 "lath": "a thin cleft strip of wood, used in house-building; a runner nailed to a room to support tiles."[35]

"plast": plaster, "a common name in America and other quarters for gypsum . . . a composition of lime and hair; a substance for casting ornaments and figures."[36]

4 "feuillage": foliage.

"Susquehanna": flows into Chesapeake Bay.

"Potomac": flows through Virginia, Washington D.C., and Maryland into Chesapeake Bay.

"Rappahannock": flows across northern Virginia and into Chesapeake Bay.

"Adirondacks": mountain range in northeastern New York.

"Saginaw": river in central Michigan, flows out of Lake Huron via Saginaw Bay.

"Moosehead Lake": is in northern Maine and flows into the Kennebec River.

"Pedee": probably the Pee Dee River, which runs through the Carolinas.

"sachem": Native American tribal chief. Originally used in colonial Northeast.

"Nueces" and "Brazos": Texas rivers.

"Tombigbee": river in Alabama.

"Red River": borders between Texas and Oklahoma.

"Saskatchawan": the Saskatchewan River runs from Saskatchewan to drain in Lake Winnipeg.

"Osage": river in central Missouri.

7:1 "Phenicia": Phoenicia.

"Alb": Albanian.

"skald": ancient Scandinavian poet, synonymous with bard.

10 "Historian! . . . You have treated man as the creature of politics": In 1857, J. B. Lippincott and Company published histories that upheld Whitman's description of contemporary historiography: *Life of Paul Jones*, *The Life of General Jackson*, and *Life of General Zachary Taylor*.

12 "oratists": orators.

16 "alimentive": see note "Chants Democratic" 2:33.

"amative": see "Chants Democratic" 1:28.

"perceptive": in conjunction with the other phrenological terms in this passage, Whitman probably meant to indicate faculties which "bring man into direct intercourse with the physical world; take cognizance of the physical qualities of material things; give practical judgment, and a practical case of mind."[37] In this light, Whitman means these phrenological traits to be popular and pragmatic.

18 "imperturbe": the opposite of perturbed.

2:11   "Great is the greatest Nation—the nation of clusters
of equal nations": This echoes Whitman's phrase
from the preface of the first (1855) edition, "Here
is not merely a nation but a teeming nation of
nations"[38] and implies that in describing "nations"
within the nation, Whitman is referring to the
precarious balance of state and federal power under
the American constitution rather than celebrating
American ethnic diversity. This is not to say that
Whitman rejected ethnic pluralism; however, the
constitutional tensions between state and federal
power were still largely unsettled in Whitman's era;
the poet, like many of his contemporaries, found
the American experiment in federalism unresolved.

3:12   "Cudge": "common name for an African American field
hand."[39]

6:3   "heart-singer": Whitman had used this type of
terminology in his journalism.

8:2   "Realism": Whitman probably means the term here in
the same fashion as American philosopher, John
Fiske (1842–1901), "Arranging and combining
various experiences received from without,
adjusting new inner relations to outer relations
established from time immemorial, man reacts
upon the environment and calls into being new
aggregations of matter, new channels of motion,
new reservoirs of energy. . . . By subtle realism,
he projects the idea of himself out upon the field
of phenomena, and deals with it henceforth as
objective reality."[40]

11:2   "salaams": "peace," used as salutation and farewell in
Arabic.

SALUT AU MONDE!

"Salut au Monde": (French) salute to the world (and/or to everyone in it).

5    "Coptic": an Egyptian Christian sect.

"muezzin": public crier who announces the time for prayer.

"Cossack": Turkic peoples living north of the Black Sea.

"sea at Okotsk": Sea of Okotsk, "northwest arm of the Pacific Ocean, W[est] of the Kamchatka peninsula and the Kuril Islands."[41]

8    "Mount Hecla": Mount Heckla, Icelandic volcano.

"Cordilleras": string of mountain ranges running along western North America, Central America, and South America.

"Bothnia": gulf between Finland and Sweden.

10   "Cape Guardafui": off the coast of modern Somalia.

"Cape . . . Bon": off the coast of Tunisia.

"Cape . . . Bajadore": off the west coast of Africa.

"Dondra Head": cape off the coast of Sri Lanka.

"Straits of Sunda": between Java and Sumatra, Indonesia.

"Cape Lopatka": off the southernmost coast of Kamchatka Peninsula in Siberia.

"Firth of Solway": western bay that divides Scotland and England.

"Zuyder Zee": Dutch North Sea inlet.

"Scheld": Scheldt River in the Netherlands.

"Sandy Hook": peninsula off of the New Jersey coast.

"Obi": Whitman probably refers to the Ob River in western Siberia.

"Lena": river in eastern Siberia.

"Burampooter": Whitman probably refers to the Brahmaputra River in northeastern India.

13 "Guadalquiver": Whitman probably refers to the Guadalquivir River in southern Spain.

15 "groves of Mona": sacred island of the druids between England and Ireland. Whitman could be drawing from the play "Caractacus" by William Mason (1759)[42] or the description of Caractacus's rebellion in Tacitus.[43]

"vervain": "The common European and British herbaceous plant, *Verbena officinalis*, formerly much valued for its reputed medicinal properties."

16 "Kneph": Egyptian God who existed before the cosmos was formed, "dressed in deep blue, . . . wearing on his head a plume of feathers . . ."[44]

20 "Kalmucks": Mongol tribe of western Siberia.

"Baskirs": Mongol tribe of central Asia.

22 "Wacho": probably refers to the Native American Huachos ethnic group in the Ayacucho region of modern Peru.[45]

"pampas": "extensive treeless plain in South America south of the Amazon."

23 "mossbonkers": "Atlantic menhaden (fish), *Brevoortia tyrannus*."

24 "banks of Moingo": perhaps the Moingona River in Iowa.

"Lake Pepin": a lake between Minnesota and

Wisconsin produced by the widening of the
Mississippi River.

25   "Samoiede": Samoyede or Nenets people of Siberia.

28   "Yedo": or Edo, former name for Japanese capital,
Tokyo.

"Kruman": West African tribesman.

"Dahoman": Sudanese tribesman.

"Ashantee-man": West African tribesman.

"Aleppo": northern Syrian city.

"Khiva": city in modern Uzbekistan.

"Herat": city in western Afghanistan.

"Muscat": city in the modern nation of Oman.

"Theban": a resident of the ancient city of Thebes.
Whitman may have been inspired by the painting
*Death of Epaminondas* by Louis Gallait (1810–
1887), which portrayed the death of the Theban
general, Epaminondas (418–362 BCE), in a fashion
similar to Whitman's description. Epaminondas
defeated the Spartans at the Battle of Leuctra (371
BCE) and freed the Helots from Spartan rule (369
BCE), but died fighting a Spartan coalition at the
Battle of Mantinea (362 BCE).

30   "constructiveness": "Mechanical ingenuity and
talent-ability to make, build, construct, and
manufacture."[46]

31   "Bokh": Mongolian wrestling. However, Whitman here
probably means it to designate ethnic Mongolians.

32   "Hottentot": South African tribesman.

"Kamtschatkan": Kamtschatka is a peninsula in far
eastern Russia.

"Caffre": a term, now considered derogatory, for a
  black South African.

"Soudanese": Sudanese.

"peon": from the Spanish *peón*; denotes a worker,
  usually a temporary day laborer, at the bottom of
  the economic hierarchy.

### POEM OF JOYS

16   "I join the group of clam-diggers on the flats":
     Whitman had used clam digging as a symbolically
     egalitarian activity since the early 1840s.[47]

### LEAF OF FACES

7    "caoutchouc": "India-rubber, or Gum Elastic; the
     milky resinous juice of certain trees in S. America,
     the E. Indies, and elsewhere, which coagulates on
     exposure to the air, and becomes highly elastic, and
     is waterproof; it is now a most important substance
     in arts and manufactures."

### ENFANS D'ADAM

     Enfans d'Adam translates to "Children of Adam" in
     English, which became the title in later editions of
     *Leaves of Grass*.

2    "the faithful one, the prostitute, who detained me
     when I went to the city": In his journalism,
     Whitman sympathized with prostitutes, often
     equating them with womanhood in peril in the
     midst of a rapacious economy. See, for example, his
     series on the "sewing girls strike" of 1846–1847 in
     the *Brooklyn Daily Eagle*.[48] In the first edition of
     *Leaves of Grass*, Whitman turned this sensibility
     into a poetic trope and ethical standard: "The
     prostitute draggles her shawl, her bonnet bobs on
     her tipsy and pimpled neck, / The crowd laugh at
     her blackguard oaths, the men jeer and wink to

each other, / (Miserable! I do not laugh at your oaths nor jeer you)."

"The slave's body for sale—I, sternly, with harsh voice, auctioneering": In the first edition, Whitman also portrayed himself as an ironic slave auctioneer who celebrated African American dignity and physical beauty. In the 1860 edition, see "Enfans d'Adam" 3:19–29, which first appeared in 1855.

3:7 "ship-joiner": "a mechanic who does the neat or fine woodwork in ships and buildings, and is therefore distinguished from the shipwright and carpenter."[49]

"fowling pieces": bird-guns, i.e., shotgun.

3:11 "nucleus": "the kernel of a nut . . . [or] any body about which matter is collected . . . [also] [t]he body of a comet . . . which appears to be surrounded with light."[50]

3:16 "dull-faced immigrants": "Between 1840 and 1859 . . . the total number of immigrants soared to 4,242,000. Forty percent were Irish, 32 percent were German, and 16 percent were English."[51]

3:32 "Have you seen the fool that corrupted his own live body?": Some of Whitman's earliest editorials were diatribes against alcohol, caffeine, and tobacco, as in, for example, "Sun-Down Papers" no. 4, from 1840, "Amidst the universal excitement which appears to have been created of late years, with regards to the evils created by ardent spirits, it seems to have been forgotten that there are other, and almost as injurious kinds of intemperance. The practice of using tobacco, in any shape, is one of these."[52]

12 "Deliriate": to make delirious.

13 "O HYMEN! O hymenee!": According to Webster's Dictionary, "Hymen" is "a fabulous deity supposed

to preside over marriages [also] . . . the virginal membrane."[53] Hymen and hyménée could denote a masculine and feminine form of marriage while explicitly connecting marriage (a public act) to sex (culturally expected to be kept private). Esther Shephard argued that Whitman took this phrase from George Sand's *The Countess of Rudolstadt*, "Then twenty manly and generous voices sang in chorus, to an air of antique grandeur and simplicity, *O hymen! O hymenée!*"[54]

## POEM OF THE ROAD

6    "fop": "[a] vain man, of weak understanding and much ostentation; one whose ambition is to gain admiration by showy dress and pertness; a gay, trifling man; a coxcomb."[55]

8    "flagged walks": brick or flagstone sidewalks.

     "copings": "the upper course of masonry on a wall or parapet . . . which forms a projecting or covering course."[56]

21   "Wisdom is of the Soul, is not susceptible of proof, is its own proof": Here Whitman echoes Emerson, especially *Nature* (1836), *The American Scholar* (1837), and the *Divinity School Address* (1838).

30   "Allons!": (French) Let's go!

34   "formules": formulas.

42   "habitues": "a person who may be regularly found in or at a particular place or kind of place."[57]

57   "Mon enfant!": (French) My children!

## TO THE SAYERS OF WORDS

1    "sauroid": see "Proto-Leaf" 310.

10   "Accouche!": (French) to bear or to deliver; childbirth.

"Accouchez!": (French) second-person plural of
accoucher.

A BOSTON BALLAD, THE 78TH YEAR
OF THESE STATES

1    "Clear the way there, Jonathan! / Way for the
     President's marshal!" This poem refers to the arrest
     in 1854 of the runaway slave, Anthony Burns, in
     Boston under the strengthened Fugitive Slave Law
     of 1850. See introduction. "Jonathan" probably
     refers to the early icon of the United States, Brother
     Jonathan.[58]

7    "fire-locks": muskets.

13   "King George's coffin": King George III (1738–1820)
     was England's monarch during the American War
     of Independence (1775–1783).

CALAMUS

     "In antiquity, a pipe or fistula, a wind instrument,
     made of a reed or oaten stalk. [Also,] [a] rush or
     reed used anciently as a pen to write on parchment
     or papyrus [and] [a] short reed, or sweet-scented
     cane, used by the Jews as a perfume."[59] In Greek
     mythology two youths, Calamus (Kalamos) and
     his lover, Karpos, swam the Meander River. When
     Karpos drowned, Kalamos, in his grief, drowned
     himself and was transformed into a reed, which
     sounded of his lamentations when the wind blew
     through it.

4    "calamus-root": "A genus of palms comprising
     many species, the stems of which grow to an
     extraordinary length, and form canes or rattans."

5:8  "Kanuck": see "Proto-Leaf" 1.

6    "systole and diastole": contraction and dilation of the
     heart.

13      "Calamus taste": "Doctors and pharmacists of the early 1800s were aware of the [medicinal] effects of ingesting calamus root. A fluid extract of the root appeared as an official preparation in the *Pharmacopoeia* of the United States of America as early as 1830." Calamus root was ingested to aid digestion and, in larger doses, produced hallucinogenic effects.[60]

21      "triumphant tutti": a tutti was a section in a musical score in which all performers take part.

35      "the Seaside State": New Jersey.

     "exalt": an individual in a state of elation.

## CROSSING BROOKLYN FERRY
1      "flood-tide": the rising tide.

8      "schooners and sloops": a small, two-mast vessel and a small, single-mast vessel, respectively.

24      "lighters": vessels used to transport materials from one ship to another.

## LONGINGS FOR HOME
"the Roanoke": flows through southern Virginia.

"the Savannah": borders Southern Carolina and Georgia.

"the Altamahaw": the Altamaha River flows from central Georgia to the Atlantic Ocean.

"the Pedee": see "Chants Democratic" 4.

"the Tombigbee": flows through western Alabama.

"the Santee": flows through central South Carolina.

"the Coosa": flows through northeastern Alabama.

"the Sabine": borders Texas and Louisiana.

"the Okeechobee": lake in Florida and the largest in the South.

"Pamlico Sound": bay in North Carolina.

"O to be a Virginian, where I grew up!": Whitman spent most of his youth on Long Island, but perhaps intentionally obscures the meaning here so as to imply both that the speaker grew up in Virginia and wishes he had grown up in Virginia.

TO YOU, WHOEVER YOU ARE

11    "The hopples fall from your ankles": a term usually used to denote straps used to bind horses' feet.[61]

TO A FOILED REVOLTER OR REVOLTRESS

4    "garrote": a device used to strangle.

TO A COMMON PROSTITUTE

1    "I am . . . liberal": "[o]f a free heart; free to give or bestow; not close or contracted; munificent; bountiful; generous; giving largely."[62]

TO A PUPIL

3    "self-esteem": For the Fowlers, this was a technical term: "Self-Esteem has its pole externally from that of Firmness, and between the outer portion of the nose and mouth . . . Firmness is in the upper lip, midway between its edge and the nose. . . . Hence, when we would exhort to determined perseverance, we say, 'Keep a stiff upper lip.'"[63] "Definiteness" and "elevatedness" echo phrenological terminology and theory: "by associating his thoughts and arguments with some visible object, and by thus giving them a distinct identity and individuality, [a person] imparts to them a peculiar clearness and definiteness, and seeming tangibility."[64]

## TO THE STATES, TO IDENTIFY THE 16TH, 17TH, OR 18TH PRESIDENTIAD

"Presidentiad": Whitman's term for the duration of a president's tenure. When he wrote this poem, these presidents had not yet assumed office: sixteenth (Abraham Lincoln, 1861–1865), seventeenth (Andrew Johnson, 1865–1869), and eighteenth (Ulysses Grant, 1869–1877). In using the term "presidentiad" to characterize an era, Whitman echoed the ancient Roman republican model of marking historical events and periods by the executive (consuls) in office.

## TO A CANTATRICE

"Cantatrice": a female singer.

## TO A PRESIDENT

James Buchanan (1791–1868) was the president of the United States (1857–1861) upon the publication of the third edition of *Leaves of Grass* and was the second of two "doughfaced" presidents, so called because of their pursuit of policies that sought to satisfy both antislavery and proslavery Democrats during the breakdown of compromise between 1854 and 1861. Buchanan was criticized, especially in the North, for his support of the Kansas's proslavery Lecompton Constitution (subsequently rejected by the people of Kansas) and his do-nothing actions as Southern states seceded over the winter of 1860–1861.

## MANNAHATTA

"Trottoirs": sidewalks.

## FRANCE, THE 18TH YEAR OF THESE STATES

The year 1794 marked the overthrow of Maximilien Robespierre (1758–1794). By 1795, the Terror he initiated ended, and the French Revolution entered a more conservative phase.

"chansonniers": ballad singers.

THOUGHTS

2    "arriere": see "Proto-Leaf" 63.

3    "sonnambules": sleepwalkers.

5    "Arctic": Whitman refers to the wreck of the steamship *Arctic*, a passenger vessel of the New York and Liverpool United States' Mail Steamship Company, which struck the schooner *Vesta* on September 27, 1857, in a thick fog off the coast of Newfoundland during a transatlantic voyage from Liverpool to New York City. Over three hundred passengers died. The Captain of the *Arctic*, James C. Luce, survived to describe the scene, "As I struggled to the surface of the water, a most awful and heart-rending scene presented itself to my view; over two hundred men, women and children struggling together amidst pieces of wreck of every kind, calling on each other for help, and imploring almighty God to help them."[65]

UNNAMED LANDS

1    "phrenology": see "Chants Democratic" 2:33.

6    "amativeness": see "Chants Democratic" 1:28.

KOSMOS

Whitman may have taken this spelling of cosmos from the title of Alexander von Humboldt's *Kosmos: A General Survey of Physical Phenomena of the Universe* (1848).

SLEEP-CHASINGS

3    "ennuyés": individuals in a state of idleness, mental weariness, from ennui.

11   "douceurs": pleasantries.

"cache": a hidden storage place.

12   "blackguards": uncouth individuals.

24   "boss-tooth advances": According to Noah Webster, *boss* also meant "[a] protuberant part; a prominence . . . [and] [a] water-conduit. . . ."[66] Kerry Larson, among others, reads this as a veiled homosexual scene.[67]

41   "A red squaw came one breakfast-time to the old homestead": As Vivian Pollak notes, it is impossible to verify the truth of this story, but itinerant Native American craftsmen and women still plied their trade along Long Island in Louisa Whitman's youth.[68]

44   "Lucifer": In Webster's 1846 dictionary, *Lucifer* meant "[t]he planet Venus, so called from its brightness . . . [as well as] Satan."[69] Webster's two meanings of Lucifer could be significant here, as the catalyst for the speaker's anger is the sale of his lover. Ed Folsom notes that Whitman gave his poetic "I" over entirely to the persona of an African American slave in this passage (originally in the first edition) and allowed both slaveholder and slave to "hear themselves in the 'I' and the 'you' of the democratic poet."[70] According to Folsom, "In combining them [the angry black slave and the rebellious angel, Lucifer] and in expressing sympathy for the resultant figure of rebellion . . . Whitman creates an incendiary image, one that was particularly volatile in the mid-1850s."

50   "erysipelite": sufferer of erysipelas, "a superficial bacterial skin infection that characteristically . . . has been traced back to the Middle Ages where it was referred to as 'St. Anthony's Fire,' named after an Egyptian healer who was known for successfully

treating the infection. . . . The most common complaints during the acute infection include tenderness of the involved area, fever, chills, and swelling. . . . Predisposed patients often develop local recurrence, and this can lead to disfiguring and disabling healing reactions. . . ."[71]

"antipodes": those who stand in direct opposition to each other.

53 "embowered": enclosed, "[t]o lodge or rest in a bower, a bed-chamber; any room in a house except the hall."[72]

55 "The scholar kisses the teacher, and the teacher kisses the scholar—the wronged is made right": This statement might reflect Whitman's condemnation of corporal punishment in contemporary pedagogy; he more explicitly expressed this sentiment in his editorials and in the story "Death in the School Room (a Fact)" in the *United States Magazine and Democratic Review* (August 1841).

## BURIAL

15 "boss": see "Chants Democratic" 3:5.

"spotter" and "starter" are terms for railroad jobs, as used here in James D. McCabe's *Lights and Shadows of New York Life*, "Why do the conductors allow themselves to be imposed on in this way? . . . Because they can't help it. If they don't pay the driver, the driver will not stop for passengers, and the conductor is short in his returns; if they don't have a 'deal' with the starter, the starter will fix him somehow. You see the driver can stop behind time, or go beyond it if he likes. The latest car in the street, you understand, gets the most passengers. So it is that the drivers who are fed by the conductors stay from two to five minutes behind time, to the inconvenience of passengers, but to the profit of the driver, the conductor, the starter, the spotter, and for all I know, the superintendent and president of the company."[73]

"hostler": stable keeper; "pet stock . . . mean stock": probably refers to different gradations of livestock.

SO LONG!

William Sloane Kennedy, in *The Fight of a Book for the World* (1926) claimed, "Walt wrote to me, defining 'so long' thus: 'A salutation of departure, greatly used among sailors, sports, & prostitutes—the sense of it is 'Till we meet again,'— conveying an inference that somehow they will doubtless so meet, sooner or later.' . . . It is in common use among the working classes of Liverpool and among sailors at Newcastle-upon-Tyne, and in Dorsetshire. . . . The *London Globe* suggests that the expression is derived from the Norwegian 'Saa laenge,' a common form of 'farewell. . . .' If so, the phrase was picked up from the Norwegians in America, where 'So long' first was heard."[74] Another source traces the origins of the phrase to the Malayan word *salang* whose origins lie in the Arabic word *salaam*, which means "peace" and is used as a greeting and farewell. The British subsequently picked up the Malayan word and transformed it into "so long."[75] See "Leaves of Grass" 11:2.

## NOTES TO ANNOTATIONS

1. *The Oxford Companion to the English Language* (Oxford: Oxford University Press, 1992).

2. Also Canuck; Dictionary.com, http://dictionary.reference .com/browse/canuck (accessed September 5, 2008).

3. George Washington Cutter, *Buena Vista and Other Poems* (New York: Morgan & Overend, 1848), 38.

4. O. S. Fowler, L. N. Fowler, *The Illustrated Self-Instructor in Phrenology and Physiology with One Hundred Engravings*

*and a Chart of the Character* (New York: Fowler and Wells Publishers, 1857), 57.

5. United States Department of Agriculture, http://www.usda.gov/wps/portal/usdahome (accessed September 8, 2008).

6. See Lorenzo Dow Turner, *Africanisms in the Gullah Dialect* (New York: Arno Press, 1969).

7. "Now as I went towards Nottingham on a First-day in the morning, with Friends to a meeting there. . . ." George Fox, *Journal of George Fox: Being an Historical Account of the Life, Travels, Sufferings, Christian Experiences, and Labour of Love, in the Work of the Ministry, of that Eminent and Faithful Servant of Jesus Christ* (W. and F. G. Cash, 1852), 75; Fox's journal was originally published in 1694. The use of "First-day," "First Month," etc., by Friends originally signified a rejection of the pagan terms implicit in the names of months and days in English.

8. According to Dictionary.com.

9. From the Georgia River Network, http://www.garivers.org (accessed September 21, 2008).

10. Frederic Gomes Cassidy, Joan Houston Hall, eds., *Dictionary of American Regional English* (Cambridge: Harvard University Press, 1985), 243.

11. "Essentials of Music," glossary, www.essentialsofmusic.com (accessed September 12, 2008).

12. Mike Mesterton-Gibbons (2003), http://www.anagramgenius.com/archive/redmar.html (accessed November 23, 2008).

13. Quote by Commodore Richard Dale in John Henry Sherburne, *The Life and Character of John Paul Jones* (1851), in Joseph F. Callo, *John Paul Jones: America's First Sea Warrior* (Annapolis, Maryland: Naval Institute Press, 2006), 205.

14. Noah Webster, *An American Dictionary of the English Language: Exhibiting the Origin, Orthography, Pronunciation, and Definitions of Words* (New York: Harper and Brothers, 1846).

15. Walter M. Gibson, *Prison of Weltevreden: A Glance at the East Indian Archipelago* (New York: J. C. Riker, 1855), 120;

from Andrew Lawson, *Walt Whitman and the Class Struggle* (Iowa City: University of Iowa Press, 2006), 134.

16. Webster (1846).

17. Webster (1846).

18. Webster (1846).

19. See Aspiz, 227–28. Johann Gaspar Spurzheim, *Phrenology, Or, The Doctrine of the Mind; and of the Relations Between Its Manifestations and the Body* (London: Charles Knight, 1825).

20. Aspiz, 228.

21. O. S. Fowler, L. N. Fowler, 51.

22. Webster (1846).

23. "Town and County Histories of Maine," http://history .rays-place.com/me/index.htm (accessed September 21, 2008).

24. *New York Aurora*, March 21, 1842, Bergman, et al., eds., I, 63–64.

25. *The United States Magazine, and Democratic Review*, November 1845, in Bergman, et al., I, 205.

26. O. S. Fowler, L. N. Fowler, 45.

27. David R. Roediger, *The Wages of Whiteness: Race and the Making of the American Working Class* (New York: Verso, 1991), 54–55.

28. Walt Whitman to Abraham Leech, August 11, 1840, quoted in Arthur Golden, ed., "Nine Early Whitman Letters, 1840–1841," *American Literature* 58 (October 1986), 342–460.

29. "The Language of Physics: Dictionary and Research Guide," http://www.123exp-science.com/physics (accessed September 22, 2008).

30. From Dictionary.com (accessed September 22, 2008).

31. Peter Lund Simmonds, *The Dictionary of Trade Products* (London: G. Routledge, 1858).

32. Simmonds (1858).

33. Webster (1846).

34. "The United States Quoiting Association," http://www .quoits.info (accessed September 22, 2008).

35. Simmonds (1858).

36. Simmonds (1858).

37. O. S. Fowler, L. N. Fowler, 105.

38. *Leaves of Grass* (1855), iii.

39. Walt Whitman, *Selected Poems: 1855–1892*, Gary Schmidgall (New York: Macmillan, 2000), 431.

40. John Fiske, *Outlines of Cosmic Philosophy, Based on the Doctrine of Evolution: with Criticisms on the Positive Philosophy* (J. R. Osgood and Company, 1875), 401.

41. *The Columbia Encyclopedia*, Sixth Edition (New York: Columbia University Press).

42. William Mason, *Caractacus: A Dramatic Poem: Written on the Model of the Ancient Greek Tragedy* (J. Knapton, 1759).

43. "Close by stood the Druids, raising their hands to heaven and screaming dreadful curses.... The groves devoted to Mona's barbarous superstitions he [the general Suetonius] demolished," Publius Cornelius Tacitus, *The Annals of Imperial Rome* (New York: Penguin), 328.

44. Constantin-François Volney, *The Ruins: Or, A Survey of the Revolutions of Empires* (S. Shaw, 1822), 233.

45. Steve J. Stern, *Peru's Indian Peoples and the Challenge of Spanish Conquest: Huamanga to 1640* (Madison: University of Wisconsin Press, 1982), 80.

46. Orson Squire Fowler, Samuel Kirkham, *Phrenology Proved, Illustrated, and Applied: Accompanied by a Chart, Embracing an Analysis of the Primary Mental Powers . . . Together with a View of the Moral and Theological Bearing of the Science* (Fowler and Brevoort, 1839), 160.

47. "Sun-Down Papers no. 6—From the Desk of a Schoolmaster," *The Long-Island Farmer and Queen County Advertiser*, July 20, 1841, in Bergman, et al., 31–32.

48. *Brooklyn Daily Eagle*, November 9, 1846, "Working Women"; December 2, 1846, "[Values]"; January 29, 1847, "The Sewing Women of Brooklyn and New York," Bergman, et al., II, 112, 136, 177–78.

49. Simmonds (1858).

50. Webster (1846).

51. Edwin Burrows, Mike Wallace, *Gotham: A History*

of *New York City to 1898* (Oxford: Oxford University Press, 1999), 736.

52. "Sun-Down Papers—From the Desk of a Schoolmaster," *Long-Island Democrat*, April 28, 1840, Bergman, et al., I, 19.

53. Webster (1846).

54. George Sand, *The Countess of Rudolstadt* (William D. Ticknor and Company, 1847), 203; Esther Shephard, *Walt Whitman's Pose* (Harcourt, Brace and Company, 1938), 140–64.

55. Webster (1846).

56. Simmonds (1858).

57. Merriam-Webster Dictionary Online, www.merriam-webster.com (accessed October 19, 2008).

58. Winifred Morgan, *An American Icon: Brother Jonathan and American Identity* (Newark: University of Delaware Press, 1988).

59. Webster (1846).

60. Tracy Auclair, "The Language of Drug Use in Whitman's 'Calamus' Poems," *Papers on Language and Literature: A Journal for Scholars and Critics of Language and Literature* 40:3 (Summer 2004): 227–59.

61. Horse Wagering Dictionary Online, http://www.horsewagering.net/dictionary.html (accessed October 22, 2008).

62. Webster (1846).

63. O. S. Fowler, L. N. Fowler, 32.

64. Orson Squire Fowler, Samuel Kirkham, 184.

65. William H. Flayhart, *Perils Of The Atlantic: Steamship Disasters, 1850 to the Present* (New York: W. W. Norton, 2003), 19–39.

66. Webster (1846).

67. Kerry Larson, *Whitman's Drama of Consensus* (Chicago: University of Chicago Press, 1988), 62.

68. Vivian Pollak, *The Erotic Whitman* (Berkeley: University of California Press, 2000), 14.

69. Webster (1846).

70. Ed Folsom, "Lucifer and Ethopia: Whitman, Race, and Poetics before the Civil War and After," David S. Reynolds, ed.,

A *Historical Guide to Walt Whitman* (Oxford: Oxford University Press, 2000), 49–51.

71. Loretta Davis, "Erysipelas," http://www.emedicine.com/DERM/topic129.htm (accessed October 27, 2009).

72. Webster (1846).

73. James D. McCabe, *Lights and Shadows of New York Life Or, The Sights and Sensations of the Great City. A Work Descriptive of the City of New York in All Its Various Phases* (New York: National Publishing Company, 1872), 180.

74. William Sloane Kennedy, *The Fight of a Book for the World: A Companion Volume to "Leaves of Grass"* (West Yarmouth, Massachusetts: Stonecraft Press, 1926), 110.

75. Joseph Twadell Shipley, *The Origins of English Words: A Discursive Dictionary of Indo-European Roots* (Baltimore, Maryland: Johns Hopkins University Press, 1984), 451.